ADULT PROTECTION AND THE LAW IN SCOTLAND

ADULT PROTECTION AND THE LAW IN SCOTLAND

Hilary Patrick

Solicitor, Honorary Fellow, School of Law at Edinburgh University

and

Nicola Smith

Solicitor, ENABLE Scotland

Bloomsbury Professional

Bloomsbury Professional Limited, Maxwelton House, 41–43 Boltro Road, Haywards Heath, West Sussex, RH16 1BJ

© Bloomsbury Professional Limited 2009

A CIP Catalogue record for this book is available from the British Library.

ISBN: 978 1 84766 487 7

Typeset by Phoenix Photosetting, Chatham, Kent

Printed and bound in Great Britain by M&A Thomson Litho Ltd, East Kilbride, Glasgow

This book is dedicated to our parents, Pat and Dick and Tom and Sandra, without whom it would not have been written.

FOREWORD

It always seemed fitting to me that the first law to be passed by the new Scottish Parliament was the Adults with Incapacity (Scotland) Act 2000. This served as a statement of intent that the Scottish people could rest assured that the new Parliament would consult, listen and then tackle some of the very complex issues that exist in our society around the protection of adults and their rights and freedoms. It was soon followed by the Mental Health (Care and Treatment) (Scotland) Act 2003, which goes even further in the quest to protect the rights of individuals and safeguard their freedom and liberty and is already internationally renowned. The most recent Adult Support and Protection (Scotland) Act continues on this quest, despite being born into a baptism of fire.

Three transformational pieces of legislation in ten short years; each bringing new responsibilities, new institutions, procedures and protocols. By any standard this is vigorous legislating; in the complex world of adult protection it is expeditious in the extreme. Add into this intricate legislative cocktail a new system of regulation, inspection and control and one could feel to be drowning in an uncontrollable whirlpool of change, spinning around in a complex new world governed by an army of legislators and regulators intent on making sure we protect the adult population of Scotland.

If practitioners feel this way, how does the person at the centre feel? How does the young man diagnosed with schizophrenia understand his rights? How does the older woman diagnosed with dementia stay in control of her life choices? We will only ever really know the answer to that when we ourselves are in need and it is our turn to feel the impact of this legislation. A significant proportion of those reading this book will experience mental ill-health at some point, and far too many of us will develop some form of dementia or cognitive impairment as we grow older; or be in the role of supporting a partner, mother or father. We will all feel the reach of this legislation at some point in our life. We will all be touched by the power, the failings and the strengths of this mass of protective legislation.

So how do we know we will be treated well, be at the centre of decisions, protected and empowered and treated with unfaltering equality and reciprocity? The truth is we don't; but thankfully someone at the start of this epic journey realised that good legislation needs at its core sound principles and values. These provide the essential compass that guides this legislation. Whilst I am sure we could all disagree and argue over the merit of each aspect of the legislation, no one will dispute the relevance, importance and pivotal role of the principles behind each Act. These are at the core of this book. The authors have provided a valuable map that will help any practitioner faced with a decision about capacity, restriction of freedom or compulsory treatment; to reflect, think and connect the legislation to its principles and to the interconnecting principles and procedures of each other Act.

We cannot ask our practitioners to be held to account for decisions they take in very difficult, high pressurised and immensely challenging situations if we do not equip them with the navigational skills to make those decisions. This book will not only help guide practitioners towards balanced and principled decision making; its existence will help reassure those whom we set out to protect that their rights, liberties and freedoms are at the core of every and any intervention. It not only adds to and informs our practice in the field of adult protection, it is a critical investment in your, your family's and our community's future protection.

Henry Simmons
Chief Executive
Alzheimer Scotland
October 2009

PREFACE

The law and policy on adult protection in Scotland has seen significant reform over the last decade. Solutions based on the needs and wishes of individuals have been developed, representing a more human and progressive approach to meeting the needs of people who find themselves at risk, either from another person or from self-harm or neglect.

Despite these improvements, it remains true that, when it comes to relationships and lifestyles, things are rarely simple. It is unrealistic to expect any law to eliminate the very real dilemmas encountered by those attempting to protect adults at risk. Interfering in an individual's life is a serious matter, and will require those involved to balance risk with the sometimes conflicting views of the adult and those caring for her. The law provides the framework within which all these decisions must take place.

The introduction of the Adult Support and Protection (Scotland) Act 2007 inspired us to attempt to write an accessible book putting the new legislation in the context of what already exists. We hope it will be helpful for lawyers, doctors, social workers, mental health officers, independent advocates and other professionals as well as private and voluntary organisations and, of course, individual service users and their families and carers.

The book is short enough to be read from start to finish, but each chapter can be read on its own. The early chapters look at the background to the legislation and the key organisations involved in adult protection, including the new adult protection committees.

We then consider the duties of local authorities and others to investigate where there is cause for concern and their powers to act if an adult appears to be at risk. The new Act should be seen as part of a wider legal framework and we attempt to show how both the Adults with Incapacity Act and the Mental Health (Care and Treatment) Act may be relevant. Human rights underpin the domestic law, and human rights law has important things to say both about the respect to be shown to human autonomy and about the duties of public authorities to protect people at risk. Chapter 12 looks at this in some detail.

Some of the changes in the Adult Support and Protection Act impose new duties of cooperation and information sharing on professionals where an individual is at risk. These have important repercussions on the doctrine of patient/client confidentiality, which is rightly considered a cornerstone of client relations. Chapter 11 looks at these issues.

Throughout the book we underline the importance of having a clear ethical framework for taking these difficult decisions. We are fortunate that the legislation, supplemented by human rights law, provides such an ethical background and we attempt, in the *principles and practice* sections of the book, to explore how the principles may help develop good practice. One example is in chapter 9, where we explore how offering an adult appropriate support or helping him plan for the future may remove or reduce the risk he faces and mean that formal adult protection measures are not necessary. This approach reflects the principle of minimum necessary intervention.

In chapter 10 we look at the court remedies available where action needs to be taken. These are not limited to remedies available under adult support legislation but may include, for example, exclusion orders under family law or antisocial behaviour orders.

In some cases it may be appropriate to involve the criminal justice system and chapter 14 looks at this in some detail. We believe that, wherever an adult is at risk from a third party, professionals should formally consider, and record, whether a criminal offence may have been committed. We are concerned that sometimes seeing a problem in terms of 'abuse' may lead to sidelining the fact that it is also a crime.

Sometimes legal text books fail to explain how the law works in practice. We attempt to avoid this pitfall by discussing in chapter 13 how the legal system supports adult protection practice. In particular, we give a brief introduction to the rules of evidence and suggest ways in which they can be adapted to meet the needs of adults who may be vulnerable witnesses.

We are grateful to Paula O'Connell and Karen Reid of Bloomsbury Professional for their support with the project. We are also much indebted to ENABLE Scotland for their continuing commitment to developing the resources available to professionals and services users. Their generosity in terms of resources, time and encouragement greatly assisted us in completing this book.

We would like to thank Henry Simmons for his generous foreword. We would also like to acknowledge the very many people who provided insight, comments and guidance on various drafts, as well as other support, including: John Armstrong, Kieran Burke, Jan Causon, James Chalmers, Alison Cleland, Joyce and John Collie, Sophie Dobson, Nicola Dodds, Sam Evans, Nicky Fagan, Stuart Fowler, Moira Goldie, Susan Hunter, George Kappler, Michael Keegan, Linda Kerr, Jan Killeen, Rosie McIntosh, Kay Munro, Marcia Ramsay, Sandra and Tom Smith, Andrew

Strong, Ailsa Stuart and Jane Walbank. Any errors in the text are entirely the responsibility of the authors.

We would also like to say a very big and personal thank you to friends and family who have encouraged and supported us through the writing of this book especially Bruce, (nearly) always there dispensing food and drink and words of wisdom, and Andrew, who believed in the project from the beginning and, as always, held steady when it mattered most.

The law is as stated at 31 August 2009.

Hilary Patrick
Nicola Smith
October 2009

CONTENTS

Foreword   *vii*
Preface   *ix*
Table of Cases   *xxi*
Table of Statutes   *xxv*
Table of Statutory Instruments   *xxxi*
Table of Conventions   *xxxiii*
Glossary of commonly used terms   *xxxv*

Chapter 1 – The development of adult protection law in Scotland   **1**
Introduction to adult protection   2
Scope of legislation   2
Balancing risk and protection   3
The wider context   4
Conclusion   4

Chapter 2 – The legal framework   **6**
Adult Support and Protection (Scotland) Act 2007   6
   Adults covered by Act   7
   Scope of Act   8
   Potential use of Act   9
   Information needs of adults, relatives and carers   10
   Information for service providers and advice agencies   10
Mental Health (Care and Treatment) (Scotland) Act 2003   11
   People covered by Act   11
   Scope of Act   12
   Relevance to adult protection   13
   Information needs of adults, relatives and carers   14
   Information for service providers and advice agencies   15
Adults with Incapacity (Scotland) Act 2000   15
   Adults covered by Act   16
   Scope of Act   16
   Relevance for adult protection   18
   Information needs of adults, relatives and carers   19
   Information for service providers and advice agencies   19
Codes of Practice   20
Other relevant legislation   20
   Vulnerable Witnesses (Scotland) Act 2004   20

Contents

Social Work (Scotland) 1968   20
Chronically Sick and Disabled Persons Act 1970   21
Housing (Scotland) Act 1987   21
Conclusion   22

Chapter 3 – Key organisations and individuals   **23**
Local authorities   23
    Council officers   24
Adult protection committee   24
    Membership   26
Health care providers   27
Protective bodies   28
    Care Commission   28
    Public Guardian   29
    Mental Welfare Commission   30
Care providers   31
Individuals supporting an adult   32
    Attorneys, guardians and people authorised under intervention
    orders   33
    Nearest relative and named person   33
    Independent advocacy   34
Criminal justice system   35
    The police   35
    Crown Office Procurator Fiscal Service   35
Conclusion   36

Chapter 4 – Principles in adult protection law   **37**
Background to principles   37
Principles in Adults with Incapacity Act   38
Mental Health (Care and Treatment) Act principles   41
Adult Support and Protection Act   43
Human rights concepts   45
Legal impact of principles   45
    Adults with Incapacity Act indemnity   46
    Promoting the principles   46
Conclusion   46

Chapter 5 – Harm and abuse   **48**
Legal definitions of harm and abuse   48
    Adult Support and Protection Act   48
    Mental Health (Care and Treatment) Act   49
    Adults with Incapacity Act   50

Common categories of harm and abuse   50
  Physical abuse   50
  Sexual abuse   51
  Neglect by a third party   51
  Self harm, neglect or abuse   52
  Domestic abuse   53
  Financial abuse   54
Where harm and abuse happen   54
Recognising harm or abuse   55
Conclusion   57

Chapter 6 – Local authorities' role and responsibilities   **58**
Powers and duties under Adult Support and Protection Act   59
  Duty to investigate   59
  Visits   60
  Warrant for visit   62
  Medical examinations   63
  Access to records   64
  Assessment orders   66
  Removal orders   69
  Banning orders   73
  The adult's consent   73
  Undue pressure   74
  Outcome of inquiries   76
Adults with Incapacity Act powers and duties   76
  Duty to investigate   76
  Emergencies   77
  Medical examinations and treatment   77
Powers and duties under Mental Health (Care and Treatment) Act   78
  Duty to inquire   79
  Cooperation with local authority   80
  Warrants for entry   80
  Medical examinations and access to records   81
  Access to records   81
  Removal orders   82
Choice of procedures   85
Conclusion   87

Chapter 7 – Powers and duties of other organisations   **88**
Care Commission   88
  Investigating risk   88

Investigatory powers	89
Enforcement	90
Contacting the Care Commission	90
Mental Welfare Commission	91
Duty to investigate	91
Formal inquiries	92
Visiting powers	92
Interviews and access to records	93
Access to facilities	93
Overlap with local authorities' role	94
Overlap with other bodies	94
Office of the Public Guardian	94
Duty to investigate	94
Powers to investigate	95
Enforcement	95
Overlap with local authorities' role	96
Overlap with Care Commission	97
The police	97
Role in adult protection	97
People at risk in public	97
People not in public place	99
Professional regulators	99
Duty to investigate	100
Powers	100
Contacting a professional regulator	100
Conclusion	100
Chapter 8 – Emergencies	**101**
Adult Support and Protection Act	101
Application to justice of the peace	101
Involving the adult	102
Temporary banning order	103
Using the emergency measures	103
Adults with Incapacity Act	103
Interim guardianship	104
Mental Health (Care and Treatment) Act	105
Removal to a place of safety	106
Emergency detention	106
Criminal Investigations	108
Antisocial Behaviour Orders	109
Urgent medical treatment	109
Conclusion	110

Chapter 9 – Supporting the adult   **111**
Independent Advocacy   111
   Legal right to advocacy   112
   Adult Support and Protection Act   113
   Advocacy and the principles   113
Community care services   113
   Community care assessments   114
   Carers' assessments   114
   Services under Chronically Sick and Disabled Persons Act 115
   Mental Health (Care and Treatment) Act entitlements   115
   Free personal and nursing care   116
   Provision of suitable housing   116
Financial support and advice   117
   Appointees   117
   Concerns about appointee   118
   Access to funds   118
   Concerns about withdrawer   119
   Management of funds in residential homes and hospitals   119
   Concerns about management of funds   120
Planning for the future   120
   Advance directives   120
   Advance statements in psychiatry   121
   Statement of wishes and feelings   122
   Appointing an attorney   122
   Concerns about attorneys   123
   Named person   124
Counselling and mediation   124
Conclusion   124

Chapter 10 – Court measures of protection   **125**
Guardianship and intervention orders   127
   Intervention order   128
   Guardianship   128
   Complaints about guardian or intervener   129
   Misappropriation of funds   130
Mental Health (Care and Treatment) Act measures   130
Orders against abuser   131
   Interdict   131
   Family orders   132
   Non-harassment order   132
Banning order   133
   Making the application   133

Local authority's duties and adult's rights 134
Criteria for order 134
Perpetrator aged under 16 134
Impact of order 135
Temporary orders 136
Notifications 136
Appeals 136
Variation or recall of order 137
Breach of order 137
Expiry of order 139
Antisocial behaviour orders 139
Bail conditions 141
Conclusion 142

Chapter 11 – Cooperation and confidentiality 143
Impact of Adult Support and Protection Act 143
Duty to cooperate 143
Legal duty to share information 144
General practitioners 145
The right to examine records 146
Mental Health (Care and Treatment) Act and Confidentiality 148
Inquiries by local authorities 148
Disclosure of information 149
Adults with Incapacity Act implications 149
The Independent and Voluntary Sector 150
Parents, Informal Carers, Family and Friends 151
Data protection 152
Freedom of information 153
Conclusion 154

Chapter 12 – Adult protection and human rights 155
Human Rights in Scotland 156
The Human Rights Act 1998 156
The Scotland Act 1998 157
Public authorities 158
Human rights issues in adult protection 158
Protection of those at risk 158
Right to liberty 159
Respect for private and family life 165
Undue pressure and human rights 166
Involuntary treatment and human rights 167

The UN Convention on the Rights of Persons with Disabilities 167
Conclusion 169

Chapter 13 – The courts and the legal system 170
Sheriff court 170
    Adults with Incapacity Act 171
    Adult Support and Protection Act cases 172
Mental health tribunals 175
Rules of evidence 177
    The burden of proof 177
    Hearsay 177
    Corroboration 180
    Competence of witnesses 181
    Reliability and credibility of witnesses 182
Support for witnesses 183
    Ensuring courts are accessible 183
    Appropriate adults 185
    Victim information and advice 186
    Victim Support Scotland 186
    Counselling 187
Special measures for vulnerable witnesses 188
    Evidence on Commission 189
    Supporters 189
    Prior statements 190
    Intermediaries 191
Solicitors and legal aid 191
Conclusion 192

Chapter 14 – The criminal justice system 194
Importance of involving police 194
Answering police inquiries 195
Decision to prosecute 196
Some relevant criminal offences 196
    Assault 197
    Breach of the peace 197
    Fraud/theft 198
    Neglect and ill treatment 198
    Sexual offences 199
    Offences under adult protection legislation 200
Criminal injuries compensation 201
Conclusion 201

Chapter 15 – The future of adult protection   **202**
Partnership working   202
Cross border issues   203
   Allocation between local authorities   203
   Adults outside Scotland   204
Self Directed Support   205
Protecting vulnerable groups   206
'Hate Crimes'   207
Review of Scrutiny Boards   208
Young people and adult protection   209
Conclusion   209

Index   **211**

TABLE OF CASES

A

A v Scottish Ministers 2001 SC 1, 2000 SLT 873, [2000] HRLR 450 . . . .   12.7
AB v CD (1851) 14 D 177 . . . .   11.4
A-G v Guardian Newspapers (No 2) *sub nom* A-G v Observer Ltd [1990]
    AC 109, [1988] 3 WLR 776, [1988] 3 All ER 545 . . . . 11.3, 11.4
Aerts v Belgium (2000) EHRR 50, [1998] ECHR 64, [1998] HRCD 749 . . . .   12.7
Airedale NHS Trust v Bland [1993] AC 789, [1993] 2 WLR 316, [1993] 1 All
    ER 821 . . . .   9.21
Anderson, Reid & Docherty v the UK [2001] UKPC D 5, [2003] 2 AC 602,
    [2002] 3 WLR 1460 . . . .   8.11
Application in respect of Mr DM (Glasgow Sheriff Court AW 36/06) 4.7
Application in respect of Mrs LC (Glasgow Sheriff Court, AW 38/05) 13.5

B

Bank of Scotland v Bennett [1997] 1 FLR 801, [1997] 3 FCR 193, [1997] Fam
    LR 477 . . . .   12.12
Byrne v Ross 1992 SC 498, 1993 SLT 307, 1992 SCLR 898 . . . .   13.21

C

C (adult: refusal of medical treatment), Re [1994] 1 WLR 290, [1994] 1 All
    ER 819, [1994] 1 FLR 31 . . . .   9.21
Cinci v HM Advocate 2004 JC 103, 2004 SLT 748, 2004 SCCR 267 . . . .   13.19
Clingham v Royal Borough of Kensington & Chelsea; R v Crown Court at
    Manchester, ex p R (on the application of McCann) v Manchester
    Crown Court [2002] UKHL 39, [2003] 1 AC 787, [2002] 3 WLR 1313 . . .   10.26
Curlett v McKechnie 1938 JC 176, 1939 SLT 11 . . . .   14.3

D

D v Orr *see* H v Lees
Dalton v HM Advocate 1951 JC 76, 1951 SLT 294 . . . .   14.3
Davidson v Brown 1990 JC 324, 1991 SLT 335, 1990 SCCR 304 . . . .   14.3

E

E & others v UK (33218/96) [2002] ECHR 769 . . . .   12.6

F

F (a parent) v Kennedy (reporter to the children's panel) (No 2) 1993 SLT
    1284, 1992 SCLR 750 . . . .   13.18
F, Re *see* K (enduring powers of attorney), Re

G

Glor v Switzerland (Application No 13444/04) (30 April 2009) 12.14
Guzzardi v Italy (1980) ECHR 5, (1981) 3 EHRR 333 . . . .   12.7

H

H v Lees *sub* nom D v Orr 1993 JC 238, 1994 SLT 908, 1993 SCCR 900 . . . .   14.9
HL v UK (45508/99) [2004] ECHR 471 . . . .   12.7
HMA v Skene Black (1887) 1 White 365 . . . .   13.22
HMA v Stott (1894) 1 Adam 386 . . . .   13.22
HM Advocate v Grimmond 2002 SLT 508, 2001 SCCR 708, 2001 GWD 27-
    1083 . . . .   13.23
Halliday v Nevill (1984) 155 CLR 1, 57 ALR 331 . . . .   7.23
Herczegfalvy v Austria (A/242-B) (1993) 15 EHRR 437 . . . .   12.13

K

K, (enduring powers of attorney), Re *sub nom* Re F [1988] Ch 310, [1988] 2
    WLR 781, [1988] 1 All ER 358 . . . .   9.24
Keenan v United Kingdom (27229/95) (2001) 33 EHRR 38, 10 BHRC
    319 . . . .   12.6
Kerr v HM Advocate 1958 JC 14, 1958 SLT 82 . . . .   13.18
Kerr v Hill 1936 JC 71, 1936 SLT 320 . . . .   14.3
King v King (1841) 4 D 124 . . . .   13.23
Kudla v Poland (30210/96) [2000] ECHR 510, (2002) 35 EHRR 11, 10 BHRC
    269 . . . .   12.13

M

M (Petitioner) 2003 SC 52, 2003 SLT 219, 2002 SCLR 1001 . . . .   12.13
MS v Sweden (1999) 28 EHRR 313, 3 BHRC 248, (1999) 45 BMLR 133 . . . .   12.11
McBrearty v HM Advocate 2004 JC 122, 2004 SLT 917, 2004 SCCR 337 . . .   13.23
McGregor v D 1977 SC 330, 1977 SLT 182 . . . .   13.8
McMichael v United Kingdom [1995] 2 FCR 718, (1995) 20 EHRR 205,
    [1995] Fam Law 478 . . . .   13.8
Moffatt v McFadyen 1999 GWD 22-1038 . . . .   12.11
Moorov v HM Advocate 1930 JC 68, 1930 SLT 596 . . . .   13.21
Muldoon, applicant 2005 SLT (Sh Ct) 52, 2005 SCLR 611, 2005 GWD
    5-57 . . . .   12.9
Murray, applicant (1866) 5 Irv 232 . . . .   13.19

N

N v HM Advocate 2003 JC 140, 2003 SLT 761, 2003 SCCR 378 . . . .   13.18

O

Osman v United Kingdom [1999] 1 FLR 193, (2000) 29 EHRR 245, [1998]
    ECHR 101 . . . .   12.6

Table of Cases

R

R v Bournewood Community and Mental Health Trust, ex p L [1998] 2
WLR 764, [1998] 1 All ER 634, (1997-98) 1 CCL Rep 201 .... 12.7
R v Sheppard & another [1981] AC 394, [1980] 3 WLR 960, [1980] 3 All ER
899 .... 14.9
R (on the application of E) v Bristol City Council (2005) EWHC 74
(Admin), [2005] MHLR 83 .... 4.3
R (on the application of Heather) v Leonard Cheshire Foundation (a
charity) [2002] EWCA Civ 366, [2002] 2 All ER 936, [2002] HRLR 30 ... 12.5
R (on the application of Wilkinson) v Broadmoor Special Hospital
Authority [2001] EWCA Civ 1545, [2002] 1 WLR 419, [2002] UKHRR
390 .... 12.13
RM & JM v The Adult Mrs A 2009 WL 873899 .... 12.9

S

Smith v Donnelly 2002 JC 65, 2001 SLT 1007, 2001 SCCR 800 .... 14.8

T

T (adult: refusal of treatment), Re [1993] Fam 95, [1992] 3 WLR 782, [1992]
4 All ER 649 .... 9.21
Tyrer v United Kingdom (1978) 2 EHRR 1 .... 12.13

W

W (a parent) v Kennedy (reporter to the children's hearing) 1988 SC 82,
1988 SLT 583, 1988 SCLR 236 .... 13.8
Walsh v McFadyen 2002 JC 93, 2002 SLT 351, 2001 SCCR 864 .... 14.3
Winterwerp v The Netherlands (1979-80) 2 EHRR 387 .... 4.6; 12.7
Witold Litwa v Poland (no 26629/95) (2001) 33 EHRR 53, (2002) 63 BMLR
199, [2000] MHLR 226 .... 4.6

X

X & Y v The Netherlands (Application No 8978/80) (1984) 6 EHRR CD
311 .... 12.6; 13.8

Y

YL (by her litigation friend the Official Solicitor) v Birmingham City
Council & others [2007] UKHL 27, [2008] 1 AC 95, [2007] 3 WLR 112 .. 12.5
Young v Heatly 1959 JC 66, 1959 SLT 250, [1959] Crim LR 438 .... 14.8

Z

Z v Finland Application (No 9/1996/627/811) 11.5

TABLE OF STATUTES

para

Access to Health Records Act
1990
s 4(3) 11.4

Adoption and Children
(Scotland) Act 2007 ..... 4.1

Adult Support and Protection
(Scotland) Act 2007 .....1.1, 1.3;
2.2, 2.3, 2.4, 2.10, 2.11,
2.15, 2.16, 2.35, 2.37;
3.2, 3.3, 3.4, 3.6, 3.11,
3.12, 3.14; 4.2, 4.3, 4.5,
4.7; 5.2, 5.3, 5.13; 6.2,
6.4, 6.7, 6.8, 6.9, 6.27,
6.33, 6.34, 6.41, 6.43,
6.45, 6.47, 6.48; 7.14,
7.17; 8.2, 8.6, 8.10,
8.15; 9.4, 9.16, 9.25;
10.1, 10.12, 10.13,
10.14; 11.2, 11.3, 11.5,
11.6, 11.9; 12.9, 12.10,
12.12; 13.1, 13.2, 13.8,
13.16, 13.34; 14.12;
15.2, 15.3, 15.9
Pt 1 (ss 1–53) 2.2
s 1 .... 4.5
2 .... 3.12; 4.5
(b) 9.5
(c)(ii), (iii) 3.13
(f) 4.5
3 .... 8.2
(1) 2.3; 5.13
(2) 2.3; 5.3
(b) 5.11
4 .... 2.5; 3.2; 6.2
5 .... 3.6, 3.17; 11.2
(1) 11.2
(g) 11.2, 11.4
(2) 11.2
(3) 3.17; 7.19; 11.3

para

Adult Support and Protection
(Scotland) Act 2007 –
contd
s 6 .... 4.5; 6.2
(2) 9.4
7 .... 6.5
(1), (2) 2.5; 6.4
8 .... 6.6
(1), (2) 6.6
9 .... 6.7
(2) 6.7
10 .... 3.6; 6.8; 11.5; 14.12
(2) 6.8
(4) 6.8; 11.5
(6) 6.8
11 .... 2.7
(1), (2) 6.9
(3) 6.13
12 .... 6.10
(2) 6.22
13 .... 6.10
14(1) 6.15, 6.19
(a) 6.19
(2) 6.21
15 .... 2.7; 6.18; 8.3
(3) 6.22
16 .... 6.15
17(1) 6.25
(2)–(4) 6.23
18(5) 6.24
19 .... 2.7; 6.13, 6.24,
6.26; 10.17
(1), (2), (4) 10.17
20 .... 8.5; 10.15
21(5) 10.18
22 .... 8.5; 10.13
(2) 10.13
(3) 10.18
23 .... 10.17

para

Adult Support and Protection
(Scotland) Act 2007 –
contd

s 24 . . . . 10.21
25 . . . . 10.17
26 . . . . 10.19, 10.21
(4) 10.19
27 . . . . 10.19, 10.21
28 . . . . 10.23
(2) 10.23
29 . . . . 10.24
(2) 10.24
30 . . . . 10.23
(2), (3) 10.23
31 . . . . 10.23
32–34 . . . . 10.24
35 . . . . 6.18, 6.33
(1), (2) 6.27
(3), (4) 6.28
(6) 6.6, 6.28
36(3), (4) 6.4
37 . . . . 6.5
(1)(a) 6.5
(2) 6.5
38 . . . . 6.5
(1) 6.13
(2) 8.3
39(1) 6.19
40 . . . . 8.2
(1) 6.5
(a) 6.17
(2), (7), (8) 8.3
41 . . . . 13.9
(2) 6.22; 10.17;
13.11
(6) 13.10
42 . . . . 2.8; 3.4; 15.2
(1) 3.4
43 . . . . 3.5
(3) 3.4
44 . . . . 3.4, 3.5
45 . . . . 3.5
46 . . . . 3.5
47 . . . . 3.4

para

Adult Support and Protection
(Scotland) Act 2007 –
contd

s 48 . . . . 2.35
49 . . . . 2.11; 11.5; 14.3,
14.12
(1) 15.4
(2) 6.8
51 . . . . 10.20; 13.13
(4) 10.20
52 . . . . 3.6
(2) 6.7, 6.8
53 . . . . 3.12
(1) 2.3; 5.3; 15.3
Pt 2 (ss 54–61) 2.2
Pt 3 (ss 62–67) 2.2
s 64 . . . . 2.37
Adults with Incapacity
(Scotland) Act 2000 . . . . .1.1; 2.2,
2.23, 2.24, 2.25, 2.26,
2.28, 2.30, 2.32, 2.33,
2.35; 3.2, 3.9, 3.12,
3.13; 4.2, 4.3, 4.5, 4.7,
4.8, 4.10; 5.2, 5.5, 5.11,
5.13, 5.22; 6.7, 6.27,
6.30, 6.32, 6.33, 6.47;
7.7, 7.9, 7.15, 7.16,
7.17; 8.7, 8.8, 8.14,
9.18; 10.1, 10.2, 10.6;
11.8; 12.9; 13.1, 13.2,
13.3, 13.8, 13.9, 13.11,
13.14, 13.16, 13.34;
14.9; 15.3
s 1(1), (3) 4.3
(4) 3.12; 4.3; 11.8
(a) 9.5
(5) 4.3
(6) 2.24; 5.13; 6.30;
8.8
2(3) 13.7
3(3) 9.25; 10.5
(4), (5) 13.6
4 . . . . 3.14
6 . . . . 2.26

para

Adults with Incapacity
 (Scotland) Act 2000 –
 contd
s 6(2) 7.14
 (a) 10.5
 (c) 7.14
 (d) 3.9; 7.14
 (f) 7.14
8 .... 7.7
9(1)(c), (d) 7.7
10 .... 2.26
 (1)(b)–(d) 6.31
11 .... 7.7
 (2)(b) 7.7
12(1) 6.31
 (2) 6.31; 11.8
13 .... 2.35
Pt 2 (ss 15–24) 2.27; 7.14
s 15, 16 .... 2.27; 9.24
17 .... 7.7
20(2) 9.25
22A 9.25
 (2) 9.25
24B, 24C 9.16
24D 2.28
Pt 3 (ss 25–33) 3.9; 7.14; 9.16
s 25 .... 2.28
31A 9.17
33 .... 7.7
Pt 4 (ss 34–46) 2.29; 9.18
s 45 .... 9.19
46 .... 9.18
Pt 5 (ss 47–52) 2.30; 8.14
s 47 .... 2.30; 6.7
 (1) 6.33
 (1A) 6.33
 (7) 8.8
 (a), (b) 6.33
Pt 6 (ss 53–79A) ... 3.9; 5.17; 7.14;
 12.7
s 53 .... 10.2, 10.3
 (3) 5.5; 10.2
57 .... 8.8
 (2) 5.5; 10.2

Adults with Incapacity
 (Scotland) Act 2000 –
 contd
s 57(3) 8.8
 (6) 8.8
58(1)(a) 10.4
 (4) 10.4
64 .... 10.2
71 .... 10.5
73 .... 10.5
 (3) 10.5
74 .... 10.5
81 .... 10.6
81A 7.15
82(1) 4.8
83 .... 14.9
87(1) 3.12; 4.3; 15.3
Antisocial Behaviour etc
 (Scotland) Act 2004 ..... 10.26
s 7 .... 8.13
4 .... 10.26
 (4), (5), (11) 10.26
7, 9, 10, 11, 13, 143 .... 10.26
Children (Scotland) Act
 1995 .... 4.1; 15.9
s 15 .... 15.9
76 .... 10.10
93 .... 15.9
Chronically Sick and
 Disabled Persons Act
 1970 .... 2.38; 9.9
s 2(1) 2.38; 9.9
Chronically Sick and
 Disabled Persons
 (Scotland) Act 1972 .... 2.38; 9.9
Civil Evidence (Scotland) Act
 1988
s 2(1) 13.17
8(3) 13.21
Civil Jurisdiction and
 Judgments Act 1982
Sch 8 .... 10.13
Civil Partnership Act 2004
s 104, 113 .... 10.10

	para
Community Care and Health	
(Scotland) Act 2002	5.9
s 8, 9	9.8
Sch 1	
para 1(d)	9.11
Community Care (Direct	
Payments) Act 1996	15.5
Criminal Procedure	
(Scotland) Act 1995	13.29
s 13	14.3
234AA	10.26
259	13.18
262(1)	13.18
271(1)	13.29
271C(7), (8)	13.29
271H	13.29
271I(3), (8)	13.30
271M	13.32
275C	13.23
288C, 288F	13.23
291	13.32
Criminal Proceedings etc	
(Reform) (Scotland) Act	
2007	13.1, 13.30
Data Protection Act 1998: 11.11, 11.12	
s 30	11.11
Sch 1	
Pt I	11.11
Disability Discrimination Act	
1995	
s 21, 49A	13.24
Disability Discrimination Act	
2005	13.24
Disabled Persons (Services,	
Consultation and	
Representation) Act	
1986	2.38; 9.9
Freedom of Information	
(Scotland) Act 2002	11.12
Health and Social Care Act	
2008	
s 145	12.5
Homelessness etc (Scotland)	
Act 2003	2.39

	para
Housing (Scotland) Act	
1987	2.39; 9.12
s 31, 32	9.12
Human Rights Act 1998 . . 12.3, 12.14	
s 4	12.3
Matrimonial Homes (Family	
Protection) (Scotland)	
Act 1981	
s 1(1)	10.17
4(2)	10.10
14, 15	10.10
Mental Capacity Act 2005	
s 4	4.3
(6)	4.3
24	9.21
Mental Health Act 1983	3.14
Mental Health (Care and	
Treatment) (Scotland)	
Act 2003 . . . . 1.1; 2.12, 2.13, 2.14,	
2.17, 2.18, 2.19, 2.20,	
2.21, 2.26, 2.35; 3.2,	
3.12, 3.14; 4.2, 4.3, 4.4,	
4.5, 4.7, 4.9; 5.4, 5.11,	
5.13, 5.22; 6.7, 6.21,	
6.27, 6.34, 6.35, 6.36,	
6.38, 6.41, 6.43, 6.45,	
6.47; 7.7, 7.9, 7.11; 8.9,	
8.10, 8.14, 8.15; 9.3,	
9.4, 9.10, 9.22, 9.26;	
10.1, 10.7; 11.6, 11.7;	
12.7, 12.10; 13.1, 13.5,	
13.14, 13.16; 14.10.	
14.12; 15.3, 15.9	
s 1	4.4
(3)	3.12; 4.4
(a)	4.4; 9.5
(b)	4.4
(e)–(h)	4.4
(5)	3.12; 4.4; 11.7
(6)–(10)	4.4
2	4.4
(4)	4.4
3	4.4
5	4.9

para

Mental Health (Care and
   Treatment) (Scotland)
   Act 2003 – *contd*

s 12 . . . . 3.10; 7.8
  13 . . . . 7.9
    (5) 7.10
  14(1) 7.10
  15, 16 . . . . 7.10
  17 . . . . 7.11
  21 . . . . 13.14
  24 . . . . 2.16
  25 . . . . 9.10
    (2), (3) 9.10
  26 . . . . 9.10
  33 . . . . 2.15; 6.35; 8.9
    (1) 15.3
  34 . . . . 6.36; 11.6
    (4) 6.36
  35 . . . . 2.15; 6.37, 6.39; 8.9
    (1) 6.40
    (2) 6.37
    (4), (6) 6.38
    (7) 6.39
    (10)–(12) 6.40
Pt 5 (ss 36–43) 10.7
s 36 . . . . 6.34; 10.7
    (3)(b), (c) 8.11
    (4) 10.7
    (8) 8.11
Pt 6 (ss 44–56) 10.7
s 44 . . . . 6.34; 10.7
    (4) 10.7
Pt 7 (ss 57–129) 10.7
s 63 . . . . 6.34
  64(3) 13.14
    (5) 5.4
  250 . . . . 3.14; 9.26
  251(1), (5) 3.14
  254 . . . . 3.14
  259 . . . . 2.12; 4.5
    (1), (4), (5) 9.3
  274 . . . . 2.35
  275 . . . . 2.19; 9.22
  276 . . . . 9.22

para

Mental Health (Care and
   Treatment) (Scotland)
   Act 2003 – *contd*

s 293 . . . . 2.15; 6.41; 8.10
    (1), (2) 6.42
    (3) 6.43
    (c) 8.10
    (4), (7), (8) 6.42
  294 . . . . 8.10
  295 . . . . 6.46; 8.10
    (3)–(6) 6.46
  296 . . . . 6.44, 6.46
  297 . . . . 7.20; 8.10
    (2), (3) 7.21
    (4) 7.20
  298(2) 7.22
    (b) 7.22
    (3), (5) 7.22
  300 . . . . 6.45; 7.20;
                          8.10
  311 . . . . 5.8; 14.10
    (1), (3) 14.10
  312 . . . . 5.8
  313 . . . . 5.8
    (3) 14.11
    (a)(i) 14.11
  315 . . . . 14.9
  316–318 . . . . 14.12
  324(2) 13.14
  328(1) 2.13; 5.13
    (2) 2.13
  329 . . . . 3.12, 3.14
National Health Service
   Reform (Scotland) Act
   2004
s 1, 2 . . . . 3.6
National Health Service
   (Scotland) Act 1978
s 17J 3.6
Offences (Aggravation by
   Prejudice) (Scotland) Act
   2009 . . . . 15.7
Police (Scotland) Act 1967
s 41 . . . . 14.3

	para
Primary Medical Services (Scotland) Act 2004	
s 4	3.6
Protection from Abuse (Scotland) Act 2001	
s 1	10.9
4(1)	10.9
Protection from Harassment Act 1997	
s 8, 11	10.11
Protection of Vulnerable Groups (Scotland) Act 2007	10.1; 15.6
s 94	15.6
Sch 3	15.6
Public Health etc (Scotland) Act 2008	12.7
Public Order Act 1986	
s 17	12.1
Regulation of Care (Scotland) Act 2001	3.8; 5.16; 7.24
s 2	7.2
(3)	6.45
(28)	9.11
6(2)	7.6
10, 12, 13, 18	7.5
25(2)	7.4
44	7.25
59(1)	9.10
(2)	3.8
64	7.3
65(2)	7.5

	para
Scotland Act 1998	12.4
s 29	12.4
57(2)	12.4
Sexual Offences (Scotland) Act 2009	5.8; 14.10, 14.11
s 10, 13	14.10
35	14.11
Smoking, Health and Social Care (Scotland) Act 2005	
s 57A	7.24
Social Work (Scotland) Act 1968	2.37; 9.7; 12.9; 15.5
s 12	2.37; 12.5
(1)	3.2
12A	2.37; 5.9; 9.7, 9.8
12AA(1)	2.37; 5.9; 9.8
13A	12.5
13ZA	2.37; 5.5; 12.9
(3), (4)	12.9
86(1)	15.3
Vulnerable Witnesses (Scotland) Act 2004	2.36; 9.1; 12.14; 13.22, 13.23, 13.29, 13.32, 13.33
Pt 2 (ss 11–23)	13.29
s 12(6)	13.29
20–22	13.29
24	13.22
Youth Justice and Criminal Evidence Act 1999	
s 53(3)	13.22

TABLE OF STATUTORY INSTRUMENTS

para

Act of Adjournal (Criminal Procedure Rules Amendment No 6) (Vulnerable Witnesses (Scotland) Act 2004) (Evidence on Commission) 2005, SSI 2005/574 .... 13.29

Act of Sederunt (Summary Applications, Statutory Applications and Appeals etc Rules) Amendment (Mental Health (Care and Treatment) (Scotland) Act 2003) 2005, SSI 2005/504 .... 6.42

Act of Sederunt (Summary of Applications, Statutory Applications and Appeals etc Rules) Amendment (Adult Support and Protection (Scotland) Act 2007) (No 2) 2008, SSI 2008/335 ... 10.18, 10.19, 10.20, 13.12

Act of Sederunt (Summary of Applications, Statutory Applications and Appeals etc Rules) Amendment (Adult Support and Protection (Scotland) Act 2007) (No 3), SSI 2008/375 .... 13.12

Act of Sederunt (Summary Applications, Statutory Applications and Appeals etc Rules) 1999, SI 1999/929:   10.18, 10.19, 10.20, 13.3, 13.5, 13.9, 13.12

para

Adult Support and Protection (Scotland) Act 2007 (Restriction on the Authorisation of Council Officers) Order 2008, SI 2008/306 .... 3.3
  art 4 .... 3.3

Adults with Incapacity (Management of Residents' Finances) (No 2) (Scotland) Regulations 2003, SSI 2003/266 ...... 9.18

Advice and Assistance (Assistance by Way of Representation) (Scotland) Amendment (No 2) Regulations 2005, SSI 2005/482 .... 13.34

Advice and Assistance (Assistance by Way of Representation) (Scotland) Regulations 2003, SSI 2003/179
  reg 9 .... 13.34

Civil Legal Aid (Scotland) Amendment (No 2) Regulations 2006, SSI 2006/325 .... 13.34

Council Tax Benefit (General) Regulations 1992, SI 1992/1814
  reg 61(3) 9.14

Housing Benefit (General) Regulations 1987, SI 1987/1971
  reg 71(3) 9.14

Mental Health (Advance Statements) (Prescribed Class of Persons) (Scotland) Regulations 2004, SSI 2004/387 ..... 9.23

para

Mental Health (Form of
   Documents) (Scotland)
   Regulations 2006, SI
   2006/12 .... 6.40, 6.42
Mental Health (Recall or
   Variation of Removal
   Order) (Scotland)
   Regulations 2006, SSI
   2006/11 .... 6.46
Mental Health Tribunal for
   Scotland (Practice and
   Procedure) (No 2) Rules
   2005, SSI 2005/519
r 47(1) 13.14
  66(1), (6) 13.14
  70(3) 13.14

para

National Health Service (General
   Medical Services Contracts)
   (Scotland) Regulations 2004,
   SSI 2004/115 .... 3.6
Sch 5
  Pt 5
   para 70 .... 11.4
Regulation of Care (Require-
   ments as to Care Services)
   (Scotland) Regulations
   2002, SSI 2002/114
reg 21, 25 .... 7.3
Social Security (Claims and
   Payments) Regulations
   1987, SI 1987/1968
reg 33 .... 9.14, 9.15

TABLE OF CONVENTIONS

para

Convention for the
    International Protection
    of Adults (Hague, 13
    January 2000) 15.4
art 1, 10 . . . .   15.4
Convention for the Protection
    of Human Rights and
    Fundamental Freedoms
    (Rome, 4 November
    1950) 3.14; 6.13; 12.2,
                        12.3, 12.4; 13.4
art 2 . . . .   12.6
    3 . . . . 12.1, 12.6,
                        12.13
    4 . . . .   12.6
    5 . . . . 12.7, 12.10
    (1)(e) 12.7
    (5) 12.7
    6 . . . .   13.11
    8 . . . . 11.3, 11.5, 11.11;
                        12.11; 13.4

para

Convention for the Protection of
    Human Rights and Funda-
    mental Freedoms (Rome,
    4 November 1950) – *contd*
Protocol 1
    art 1 . . . .   6.13
United Nations Convention
    on the Rights of Persons
    with Disabilities (New
    York, 30 March 2007) . . .   12.14
    preamble 12.14
    art 1 . . . .   12.14
        12, 14, 19, 22, 23 . . . .   12.14
United Nations Convention
    on the Rights of the
    Child (New York, 20
    November 1989) 12.14
United Nations Universal
    Declaration of Human
    Rights (New York,
    December 10, 1948) 12.2

GLOSSARY OF COMMONLY USED TERMS

Adult at risk Sometimes used in a general sense, but also refers to people offered particular protection by the Adult Support and Protection Act. See para 2.3.

Adult protection committee The local committee responsible for developing adult protection strategies and policies for its areas. See para 3.4.

Attorney A person appointed under a power of attorney (see below) to take financial, welfare and/or medical decisions on behalf of another person. See paras 3.13, 9.24.

Continuing attorney A person with financial and/or property powers under a power of attorney.

The Convention The European Convention on Human Rights, now incorporated into Scottish law. See chapter 12.

Crown Office Procurator Fiscal Service The public body responsible for deciding whether a crime should be prosecuted. See para 3.18.

Council officer The local authority staff member with specific functions under the Adult Support and Protection Act. See para 3.3.

Curator ad litem A person (usually a solicitor) appointed by a court or tribunal to protect the interests of an individual who is unable to instruct a solicitor for the proceedings.

Guardian The sheriff court may appoint a guardian to take financial, welfare and/or medical decisions on behalf of an adult with incapacity. See paras 3.13, 10.2.

Independent advocate An independent advocate finds out an individual's views and makes sure they are properly expressed and taken into account. See chapter 9.

Intervention order   A one-off order under the Adults with Incapacity Act. It may relate to financial, welfare or medical matters. See paras 10.2-3.

Mental health officer   A social worker with special training and experience in issues relating to mental illness, dementia and learning disabilities.

Named person   A named person has a special role in representing the patient's interests in any compulsory proceedings under the Mental Health (Care and Treatment) Act. See paras 3.14, 9.26.

Power of attorney   The document appointing another person as attorney.

Procurator fiscal   A lawyer working for the Crown Office Procurator Fiscal service, who is usually the first point of contact where a criminal prosecution is being considered.

Welfare attorney   A person with welfare powers under a power of attorney.

Chapter 1

THE DEVELOPMENT OF ADULT PROTECTION LAW IN SCOTLAND

1.1 The landscape of adult protection in Scotland has changed significantly in the last decade. In particular, the Scottish Parliament has passed three important pieces of legislation, the Adults with Incapacity (Scotland) Act 2000, the Mental Health (Care and Treatment) (Scotland) Act 2003 and, most recently, the Adult Support and Protection (Scotland) Act 2007. This followed widespread recognition by lawyers, voluntary bodies and the Scottish Law Commission, among others, that Scotland needed modern and flexible legislation.

There have also been significant changes in the way community care is provided[1]. Services tend to be more person-centred and adults are supported within their local communities rather than in institutions.

While these changes have been welcomed, they also present new challenges to local authorities, social workers, private and voluntary care providers, health boards and individuals. The number of organisations involved in the delivery of services means that information sharing and cooperation has become more complicated. People expect to be consulted and involved in decisions about their lives, and this is recognised as being vital to the system's success. Those involved in adult protection are also expected to be familiar with, and able to apply, general principles enshrined in the legislation, including using the least restrictive option in any situation and making sure that any intervention benefits the adult.

This chapter aims to put what follows into a wider context and highlight some of the tensions inherent in any system of adult protection. Subsequent chapters explain the current legal position in Scotland, as well as highlighting some of the practical issues faced in adult protection today.

---

[1] For further information, see *Changing Lives: Report of the 21st Century Social Work Review* (2006). This is available from www.scotland.gov.uk.

INTRODUCTION TO ADULT PROTECTION

1.2   Adult protection is a general term covering the laws, policies and procedures that dictate and influence responses in situations where it is suspected, or known, that certain adults are experiencing harm or abuse. It deals with situations where harm is inflicted by a third party, as well as self-harm and neglect. It is also relevant to situations where harm is unintended, for example where it is as a result of a carer struggling to cope.

The range of situations those involved in adult protection can face means that the legislation needs to be flexible and provide appropriate responses. However, this also means that professionals, and particularly social workers, are required to use their judgement about the most appropriate way to proceed. As a result, it has become increasingly important that those involved understand the legal framework within which they are operating, and how to best utilise the various laws to achieve an acceptable outcome.

Adult protection is not just about protecting adults from harm. It is also about providing support, as reflected in the title of the most recent legislation. This means avoiding making assumptions about what is best for an individual. It also creates the need to look beyond simply avoiding harm and instead providing the support and help that people need to make their own choices about their lives.

SCOPE OF LEGISLATION

1.3   The system of adult protection does not automatically apply to all adults in Scotland. Instead, each piece of legislation applies to a defined group of adults, who are generally viewed as being more 'vulnerable' than the general population. This might be because they have a disability, mental health issue or are in ill health.

The idea of 'vulnerability' is controversial, and many people with disabilities object to the use of that terminology. They prefer the view that it is not any disability or health difficulty that makes them vulnerable, but rather external situations and attitudes.

In fact, the Adult Support and Protection Act was originally called the Vulnerable Adults Bill, but the title was changed, largely due to pressure from disability groups. Certainly, it is true that most people can imagine situations in which they would feel vulnerable, regardless of their mental or physical abilities, for example, when they are walking home alone late at night or about to be given the results of medical tests. In some cases, feeling 'vulnerable', or being at a higher risk of harm, actually adds quality to life, which is part of the reason some people enjoy activities from roller coasters to cliff-diving and rock climbing. So there is merit in the idea that situations create vulnerability rather than a person's inherent characteristics.

However, when we refer to adult protection measures it can generally be assumed that we are dealing with an adult who has a disability, mental health issue or illness. Cases involving assault, theft or abuse of people who do not fall within the scope of adult protection legislation will normally not result in investigation by the local authority and will instead be dealt with by the criminal justice system. The adult may also have civil remedies, as set out in chapter 10.

BALANCING RISK AND PROTECTION

1.4   Adult protection can inevitably involve balancing rights and duties that appear to be in conflict. This tension often arises because it is generally accepted that adults should make their own decisions about how they live their lives, provided they act within the law. However, society also has an obligation to provide an appropriate level of protection to those experiencing harm and abuse, particularly where they are considered as less able to make decisions and protect their interests.

In some cases, decisions by local authorities and other organisations about when to intervene will be very clear. In a situation where an adult who lacks capacity is being physically or sexually abused, there will be an overwhelming consensus that an intervention should take place swiftly.

However, those involved in adult protection will know that cases are not always so straightforward, especially where close, and often complicated, personal relationships are involved.

For example, there have been situations where an adult with a learning disability is found to be handing over almost all her income to another person, leaving her unable to pay for basic items or make choices. To the outsider, the relationship might seem exploitative. However, there may be aspects of the relationship that the adult values. She might enjoy attention and affection, friendship, social contact or even receive physical care and support. Regardless of what anyone else thinks, she might view these benefits as outweighing the negatives, and in such cases the decision about if, when and how to intervene is difficult.

Complex issues can also emerge where other people consider an individual's living arrangements unacceptable. Where conditions have deteriorated as a direct result of illness or disability, it will often be appropriate to intervene. However, the decision is more complicated where the living arrangements are a genuine lifestyle choice. For example, it can be difficult to set general rules about when to intervene where someone chooses to drink excessively, does not take medication, fails to take care of personal hygiene or lives in any other way outside society's norms.

Of course, robust mechanisms are needed to allow public authorities to stop harm or abuse. However, most adults generally take for granted the right to make their own decisions about their lives, even if they know those choices are unwise or increase the risk of harm. Taking risks, and experiencing the outcomes of choices, helps people find out what they want and value and is part of what makes life interesting and meaningful. It is important that those involved in adult protection are able to justify any action to remove or limit a client's right to personal autonomy and self-determination.

THE WIDER CONTEXT

1.5 One of the big issues for those involved in adult protection is achieving long-term success. Legislation can provide clear powers to intervene and, in particular, to remove an adult from an abusive situation in the short-term. However, the reality is that unless the adult has real alternatives, any intervention may have limited success. If the adult has no access to emotional support, alternative housing, advice about money and other appropriate services then she may well decide that returning to her original living situation is the best option.

There is a real need to view adult protection in this wider context and think seriously about what is available in terms of housing, support and community care services, as well as access to advice and advocacy. These services are explored further in chapter 9 and will inform decisions about when and how to intervene.

CONCLUSION

1.6 While the law provides a range of powers and duties, it does not necessarily offer a straightforward answer to individual situations. Even with the new legislation, cases will continue to be challenging and involve difficult decisions about intervention. However, while there will often be an element of discretion involved, those working in adult protection must be aware that their powers and duties are part of a definite legal framework and they must operate within set rules and apply specific principles to decisions. This book argues that respect for the principles underlying the legislation will, in many cases, help resolve the complex ethical issues underlying adult protection practice.

Chapter 2

THE LEGAL FRAMEWORK

2.1 This chapter introduces the main legislation relevant to adult protection as a foundation for later chapters. Some of the legislation overlaps, and this means that in individual cases, more than one legal remedy or approach may be available. This will mean a decision is required about which is most appropriate to use. In other cases, a number of laws might be relevant, depending on the interventions required, and a combination can be used.

The focus of this book is on provisions of direct relevance to adult support and protection. The intention is not to provide a comprehensive guide to all aspects of the legislation and so, where appropriate, reference is made to other sources for further information. In addition, it is always necessary to have regard to the general principles of each piece of legislation. These are set out and discussed in chapter 4.

ADULT SUPPORT AND PROTECTION (SCOTLAND) ACT 2007

2.2 The Adult Support and Protection (Scotland) Act 2007[1] was based on a draft Vulnerable Adults Bill proposed by the Scottish Law Commission in 1997[2]. Whilst its report dealt with adults who were vulnerable because of mental disorder or mental incapacity, the Scottish Law Commission also considered that certain other individuals might be vulnerable to abuse or harm, particularly some older people.

The Act was designed to make sure that the relevant authorities had the powers they needed to allow them to intervene to prevent harm or abuse. The focus in this book is on Part 1 of the Act, which came into force on 1 October 2008. Parts 2 and 3 amend other laws and are largely outside the scope of this book[3].

---

[1]   For full text of the legislation see www.opsi.gov.uk.
[2]   *Report on Vulnerable Adults* Scottish Law Commission No 158.
[3]   Parts 2 and 3 amended community care legislation and the Adults with Incapacity (Scotland) Act 2000.

Adults covered by Act

2.3 The legislation uses the term 'adults at risk'. These are adults who:

- are unable to safeguard their own well-being, property, rights or other interests,

- are at risk of harm, and

- because they are affected by disability, mental disorder, illness or physical or mental infirmity, are more vulnerable to being harmed than adults who are not so affected[4].

An adult might be at risk where another person's conduct is causing, or is likely to cause, harm. However, situations where the adult is causing, or is likely to cause, harm to himself are also covered[5]. Adults under this Act are defined as being individuals over the age of 16[6].

An adult must meet all three of the criteria set out above to fall within the definition of 'adult at risk'. However, this potentially includes a wide range of individuals, some already covered by existing laws about mental disorder and incapacity, as well as adults who have capacity but are considered vulnerable due to illness or disability.

The definition of 'adult at risk' was debated at length before the final version found in the legislation was agreed. The then Scottish Executive wanted to make sure that the definition was broad enough to cover those with capacity but who were viewed as more vulnerable to abuse. There was a lot of debate and discussion, particularly in the voluntary sector, on how this could be achieved. For example, at one stage the proposed definition included a reference to individuals who were 'in need of community care services'. However, this was removed, due to concerns it might contribute to assumptions that requiring support or assistance automatically makes a person more vulnerable[7].

The interpretation of the term may well develop through case law over the next few years.

---

4   Adult Support and Protection (Scotland) Act 2007, s3(1).
5   ASP(S)A 2007, s3(2).
6   ASP(S)A 2007, s53(1).
7   For further discussion, see the analysis of responses to the third Consultation on *Protecting Vulnerable Adults – Securing their Safety* published by the Scottish Executive, November 2005.

Scope of Act

2.4 The Act introduced new duties, powers and responsibilities explored in detail throughout this book. In very broad terms, the provisions cover the following areas:

Investigations

2.5 A local authority has a duty to make inquiries in cases where it believes harm is taking place or is likely to take place[8]. There are also new powers of entry to facilitate investigations where access is likely to be an issue[9].

Cooperation

2.6 Specific public bodies are required to cooperate about matters of adult protection, including suspected and actual harm. Currently, these are the Mental Welfare Commission, the Care Commission, the Public Guardian[10], local authorities, police chief constables and health boards[11]. There is provision for Scottish Ministers to specify other public bodies at a later stage.

New orders

2.7 The legislation provides for a range of orders to deal with harmful or abusive situations. These are granted by a court and allow the local authority to investigate harm, remove an adult at risk or ban an alleged abuser from a specific place. The new orders are called assessment orders[12], removal orders[13] and banning orders[14] and are dealt with in more detail in subsequent chapters. Applications for orders will generally be to the sheriff court, but justices of the peace can grant orders in an emergency.

---

[8]   ASP(S)A 2007, s4.
[9]   ASP(S)A 2007, s7(1) and (2).
[10]   These organisations and their functions are explored further in chapter 3.
[11]   See para 11.4 for a discussion about the position of general practitioners.
[12]   ASP(S)A 2007, s11.
[13]   ASP(S)A 2007, s15.
[14]   ASP(S)A 2007, s19. An application for a banning order can also be made by the adult or someone else living in the same house as the adult.

Adult Protection Committees

2.8   Local authorities are required to establish multidisciplinary adult protection committees to oversee adult protection in their area[15]. The role of these committees is explored in more detail in chapter 3.

Potential use of Act

2.9   When a local authority becomes aware that there is an adult at risk in the area, it has a duty to carry out an investigation. However, such an investigation will not necessarily end with the granting of a formal order. There may be informal resolution with the adult involved agreeing to a specific course of action. Cases might also result in a decision that no further action is needed or that the situation should be monitored for an agreed period. Sometimes an intervention under other legislation might be more appropriate.

However, in some cases an application for a court order will be necessary. Local authorities might use a formal order in adult protection cases where:

- Harm is suspected but the individual has the capacity to make decisions and refuses to cooperate. In such cases, the local authority might be able to take action if it believes the adult is being unduly pressured into not cooperating[16].

- A third party is obstructing the local authority's investigation. For example, a social worker may be continually told an adult believed to be at risk is on holiday, visiting relatives or otherwise unavailable. If this happens, the local authority can apply for a court order to gain access.

- There is real risk of harm if an adult at risk is not immediately removed. In this situation, the local authority can apply for an emergency removal order[17].

In addition, adult protection committees can deal with general and procedural issues and may become involved where a multi-agency approach is required.

---

[15]   ASP(S)A 2007, s42. Some local authorities are setting up joint committees with neighbouring authorities.

[16]   See chapters 6 and 12 for further discussion on consent and undue pressure.

[17]   Emergency measures are dealt with in detail in chapter 8.

Information needs of adults, relatives and carers

2.10 The majority of families, carers, friends and adults will not need to
know the provisions of the legislation in any detail unless they are part of
a specific investigation. However, a general awareness about some of the
signs of harm and abuse is important[18]. It may also be useful for them to
know that:

- Local authorities have a duty to investigate suspected abuse and
  may have the power to intervene even if the adult has capacity and
  is refusing to cooperate. This can happen if someone else is unduly
  pressuring the adult.

- There is an adult protection committee in their area and its remit.

- No one can be detained, compelled to cooperate with an interview
  or forced to have a medical examination against their will under this
  Act.

- Adults must always have their views taken into account.

- Adults should receive information about what is happening and can
  ask to see any court order; and

- Relatives, carers and those close to the adult should be consulted.

Information for service providers and advice agencies

2.11 Service providers and those delivering advice will need a general
awareness of the legislation and be able to provide the basic information
that individuals need. In some cases, where adult protection measures are
being considered, this might involve suggesting that a solicitor is
consulted. In addition, service providers and advice agencies will want to
consider:

- General training on recognising and dealing with harm and abuse.

- A review of policies on data protection, investigations and
  information sharing. Such policies should reflect the duty to hand
  over clients' records in certain circumstances. This is important,
  given it is an offence to obstruct anyone carrying out duties under
  the Act[19].

[18] This is explored further in chapter 5.
[19] ASP(S)A 2007, s49.

- Training and updating policies on harm and abuse. Although the legislation does not contain a specific duty to report abuse to the local authority, an organisation will often be under a duty to report in other ways[20].

MENTAL HEALTH (CARE AND TREATMENT) (SCOTLAND) ACT 2003

2.12 The Mental Health (Care and Treatment) (Scotland) Act 2003 largely implemented the recommendations of the Millan Committee, which reviewed mental health law in 2001[21]. The Act was designed to modernise and improve the use of compulsory measures in mental health care. It reflects the general move over the last two decades towards care and treatment in the community rather than in hospitals or other residential settings. The title was debated at length and the words 'care' and 'treatment' were deliberately included to reflect the philosophy behind the legislation.

The Act was also an opportunity to improve patient focus, and in some instances provides for support even when compulsory measures are not being used. An example of this approach is the inclusion of a right to access independent advocacy services[22].

It also contains mechanisms for dealing with offenders who have a mental disorder and so interacts with the criminal justice system. However, the details of these aspects of the legislation are not within the scope of this book[23].

People covered by Act

2.13 The Mental Health (Care and Treatment) Act covers individuals who are defined as having a 'mental disorder'. This term includes mental

---

[20] This is explored further in para 11.9.

[21] See *New Directions: Report on the Review of the Mental Health (Scotland) Act 1984* (Scottish Executive (2001)).

[22] Advocacy is covered by the Mental Health (Care and Treatment) (Scotland) Act 2003, s259.

[23] For further details see *Mental Health, Incapacity and the Law in Scotland*, Hilary Patrick, Bloomsbury Professional (2006).

illness, personality disorder and learning disability[24]. Certain behaviours or characteristics do not, in isolation, indicate a mental disorder. These include sexual deviancy, drug or alcohol dependence or the failure to act as a prudent person would in any particular situation[25]. Unlike other adult protection legislation, there is no prescribed age in the Act. However, as the focus in this book is on adult protection the particular issues around mental health and children are not examined.

The majority of cases involving compulsory measures have been in relation to people diagnosed with a mental illness[26], although clearly some of those individuals may also have a learning disability.

Scope of Act

2.14 In basic terms, the Mental Health (Care and Treatment) Act provides for the protection of people with a mental disorder in a hospital or community setting. The main provisions relate to the following areas:

Investigation of harm

2.15 The local authority is under a duty to investigate if it believes that a person aged 16 or over[27] has a mental disorder and may be suffering ill treatment, neglect or another deficiency in care and treatment[28]. The duty also applies where there is a risk of financial abuse or loss of the patient's property.

The similarity to the duty found in the Adult Support and Protection Act means the local authority may be obliged to investigate an individual case under both pieces of legislation. The local authority has the power to apply for a court order requiring entry for the purposes of an investigation[29]. It can also take emergency action where necessary[30].

The Mental Welfare Commission also has duties to investigate harm. These are explored further in chapter 7.

---

[24] Mental Health (Care and Treatment) (Scotland) Act 2003, s328(1).
[25] For a complete list see the MH(CT)(S)A 2003, s328(2).
[26] See annual statistics published by the Mental Welfare Commission.
[27] This particular duty only applies to adults. There is a different system for child protection.
[28] MH(CT)(S)A 2003, s33.
[29] MH(CT)(S)A 2003, s35.
[30] MH(CT)(S)A 2003, s293.

Cooperation

2.16 Specific public bodies are required to cooperate with the local authority in any investigation of harm[31]. This is similar to the duty contained in the Adult Support and Protection Act and currently covers the Mental Welfare Commission, the Public Guardian, the Care Commission and health boards[32].

Detention

2.17 The Act provides for various measures to allow an individual to receive medical care and treatment on a compulsory basis. These include emergency and short-term detention in hospital, as well as longer orders. Some treatment orders can be community based. These options are explored further in chapter 10 and other comprehensive resources are available[33].

Mental health tribunals

2.18 The Act introduced a new system of mental health tribunals with a number of functions, including considering applications for orders and appeals against orders. The details of the tribunal system are discussed further in chapter 13.

Advance statements

2.19 The Act provides for advance statements, which allow individuals to set out in advance how they want, and do not want, to be treated for a mental disorder[34]. The importance of such statements is explored further in chapter 9.

Relevance to adult protection

2.20 The local authority, or in many cases a health professional, is likely to consider using the Act in adult protection cases where the adult has a mental disorder and is at risk of harm. Such situations could include:

---

[31] MH(CT)(S)A 2003, s24.
[32] The role and responsibilities of these organisations are explored further in chapter 3.
[33] See *Mental Health, Incapacity and the Law in Scotland*, Hilary Patrick, Bloomsbury Professional (2006).
[34] MH(CT)(S)A 2003, s275.

- Where a person needs treatment for a mental disorder and is suffering harm. This could be where an individual is not able to take care of his personal well-being or property, because of a mental illness, and appropriate treatment would prevent the harm continuing.

- Where someone is already subject to, or in breach of, a compulsory treatment order. For example, the adult might be in breach of a condition that he takes prescribed medication or attends medical appointments; or

- Where someone has a mental disorder and needs to be detained for his own protection or the protection of others. This covers situations where the primary reason for detention is protection rather than treatment.

Information needs of adults, relatives and carers

2.21 Most people will not find themselves subject to a compulsory intervention under the Mental Health (Care and Treatment) Act. However, it is helpful to be aware that:

- Local authorities have a duty to investigate harm and abuse.

- When action is taken under this Act individuals have clearly defined legal rights to be heard and represented, as well as to appeal decisions.

- Families, carers and friends may also have an independent right to be heard[35].

- People with a mental disorder have the right to access independent advocacy services.

- Any individual can write an advance statement that expresses his views about how he wants to be treated; and

- The Mental Welfare Commission can investigate concerns.

---

[35] See paras 3.12–3.14 for further details.

Information for service providers and advice agencies

2.22   Agencies providing support and representation at tribunals will need to have a sound understanding of the operation and detail of the legislation. Other organisations should have a basic knowledge and be able to signpost those needing further information to an appropriate local solicitor or specialist organisation.

The primary role of advocacy organisations is to make sure the adult understands the process and is able to express his own views. However, advocacy workers are likely to be best placed to carry out their role if they have a reasonable knowledge of the procedures involved.

ADULTS WITH INCAPACITY (SCOTLAND) ACT 2000

2.23   A major report from the Scottish Law Commission formed the basis of the Adults with Incapacity (Scotland) Act 2000[36]. The Act created a new system regulating how decisions are made for individuals who lack capacity to make decisions in relation to an aspect of their welfare, property, financial affairs or medical treatment. It also established the office of Public Guardian, who has a major role in both monitoring and regulating interventions under the Act[37].

The Act was designed to provide an individual approach to decision-making and to recognise that, as far as possible, people should have autonomy and be able to control their lives. The ability to make specific decisions should only be transferred to someone else where this is justified and necessary in all the circumstances.

In terms of adult protection, the Adults with Incapacity Act contains a range of options to deal with situations of harm and abuse, where the adult involved lacks capacity. It can provide a longer-term solution and, even if not used immediately, may be useful after an initial intervention under another piece of legislation. For example, following an adult's removal under the Adult Support and Protection Act, it may become apparent that he is unable to make his own decisions and it is necessary to consider appointing a guardian.

---

[36]   *Incapable Adults* Scot Law Com No 151 (1995).
[37]   See chapters 3 and 7 for more information about the Public Guardian.

Adults covered by Act

2.24 The Adults with Incapacity Act applies to individuals over the age of 16 who lack the legal capacity to make some, or all, decisions about their lives. 'Incapacity' is defined in the Adults with Incapacity Act as including those who are unable to:

- act;

- make decisions;

- communicate decisions;

- understand decisions; or

- retain a memory of decisions[38].

The definition could include some people with learning disabilities or mental illness, as well as those who have impaired capacity for another reason, for example, following a head injury or as a consequence of an illness such as dementia.

Scope of Act

2.25 The Adults with Incapacity Act is a wide-ranging piece of legislation containing a number of options that can be used in individual cases. In basic terms, it includes provisions on the following:

Investigation of harm

2.26 The responsibility for investigating depends on the type of harm involved. The local authority is under a duty to investigate harm where the personal welfare of an adult seems to be at risk or where there are complaints about a welfare attorney or guardian or a person authorised under a welfare intervention order[39]. The Public Guardian investigates any circumstances where the property or financial affairs of an adult who might lack capacity seem to be at risk[40].

The duties overlap with those in both the Adult Support and Protection Act and the Mental Health (Care and Treatment) Act. This means a local authority might have a duty to investigate a single case

---

[38] Adults with Incapacity (Scotland) Act 2000, s1(6).
[39] AWI(S)A 2000, s10.
[40] AWI(S)A 2000, s6.

under all three pieces of legislation. In practice, only one investigation is likely to take place.

> ## PRINCIPLES AND PRACTICE
>
> The decision about which piece of legislation should be used is important, given there are differences in not just the duties and powers, but also the approach. The local authority should be clear which legislation it is acting under in any case, as this will affect the procedure it operates. For example, under the Adult Support and Protection Act an individual being interviewed should be advised that he does not need to cooperate. This is not the case under other adult protection legislation.

Attorneys

2.27   An individual can appoint an attorney to take decisions if, in the future, he becomes unable to make these decisions himself. Attorneys can be appointed to make financial decisions or welfare decisions or both[41] and must be appointed in accordance with the procedure set out in the legislation[42]. The attorney can be anyone the person chooses, although there is a legal requirement that the attorney formally accepts the position. For this reason, it is important to check that a potential attorney is prepared to take on this role. Powers of attorney are explored further in chapters 3 and 9.

Managing bank accounts

2.28   The Act allows an individual or organisation[43] to apply to the Public Guardian for authority to manage an existing bank account, or open[44] and manage a new bank account, for an adult who lacks capacity. This system is designed to deal with normal living expenses and is usually used by families or organisations providing support.

---

[41]   AWI(S)A 2000, ss15 and 16.
[42]   AWI(S)A 2000, Part 2.
[43]   AWI(S)A 2000, s25 (as amended).
[44]   AWI(S)A 2000, s24D (as amended). Previously a bank account could be operated but not opened.

Managing residents' finances

2.29 This allows managers of residential accommodation to manage funds for residents and can be useful for adults with incapacity living in, or moving to, residential accommodation[45]. This power is only available to managers of services that are registered with the Care Commission. More information about the scheme can be found in chapter 9.

Making medical decisions

2.30 The Adults with Incapacity Act regulates decisions about medical care and treatment[46]. Medical practitioners are responsible for assessing an individual's capacity to make a specific decision about medical care or treatment. If the individual involved has capacity, his decision about whether or not to have any treatment offered must be respected. If he lacks capacity, a statutory certificate is completed detailing the nature of the treatment needed[47]. Medical treatment is explored further in chapter 6.

Intervention and guardianship orders

2.31 Intervention orders and guardianship orders are mechanisms for making decisions for those who lack capacity (in whole or in part). The application process for both is very similar, although the purpose of each order is different. An intervention order is used to make a one-off decision, while a guardianship order is an ongoing order used where someone will need a number of decisions made over a period of time. Both orders can be used for financial and/or welfare decisions.

Relevance for adult protection

2.32 Consideration of the Act is likely in most adult protection cases where the adult involved appears to lack capacity. The types of situation where a local authority might use the Act include:

- Where an individual's personal welfare, finances or property are at risk and he lacks capacity to make his own decisions. The local authority must consider if any further action is necessary.

[45] AWI(S)A 2000, Part 4.
[46] AWI(S)A 2000, Part 5.
[47] AWI(S)A 2000, s47.

- In cases where a guardian or attorney has already been appointed with the power to make decisions to prevent harm. For example, another person might already have the power to decide where the adult should live. The local authority also monitors guardians to make sure they carry out their role properly.

- Where there is financial abuse or an individual is having difficulties managing his money. There are a number of options in such cases, explored further in chapter 9.

Information needs of adults, relatives and carers

2.33 As the population ages, more and more people will have to navigate the provisions of this Act. In specific cases, more detailed advice will be necessary but it may be helpful for individuals to know that:

- Local authorities have a duty to investigate suspected harm and abuse.

- Everyone should think about granting a power of attorney to provide for the possibility they might lose capacity at some point in the future.

- A range of options are available if an adult becomes, or is likely to become, unable to make decisions; and

- The general principles must be applied to all interventions or decisions not to intervene[48].

Information for service providers and advice agencies

2.34 Service providers and agencies providing advocacy, advice and supported living or employment services will need a general awareness of the legislation and should include this in staff training. Organisations providing services or advice to people who lack capacity or the families of such individuals may need a more detailed knowledge.

---

[48]   See chapter 4 for further details.

CODES OF PRACTICE

2.35 Codes of practice supplement the Adults with Incapacity Act, the Mental Health (Care and Treatment) Act and the Adult Support and Protection Act[49].

Whilst such codes of practice are not legally binding, they are statutory documents, and in any legal challenge or complaint about a person's performance of his functions under the legislation, his failure to have regard to the relevant code of practice could be relevant.

For this reason, this book contains frequent reference to the requirements of the various codes.

OTHER RELEVANT LEGISLATION

Vulnerable Witnesses (Scotland) Act 2004

2.36 The Vulnerable Witnesses (Scotland) Act 2004 was designed to provide additional support for certain categories of victim to help them give their best evidence in court. It recognises that, while giving evidence is a difficult experience for everyone, certain people face additional barriers. The Act introduced a range of measures to assist witnesses, and may be relevant to adult protection cases involving court proceedings. The provisions are discussed in more detail in chapter 13.

Social Work (Scotland) 1968

2.37 The Social Work (Scotland) Act 1968 sets out the duties of local authorities to provide social care and support for their areas. Local authorities have a duty to promote social welfare in their area by making available advice, guidance and assistance to those in need, as appropriate[50].

A local authority has a legal duty to make a formal assessment of the needs of anyone within its area appearing to require community care services[51]. This involves carrying out a community care assessment

---

[49]   Under provisions in AWI(S)A 2000, s13, MH(CT)(S)A 2003, s274 and ASP(S)A 2007, s48.
[50]   Social Work (Scotland) Act 1968, s12.
[51]   SW(S)A 1968, s12A.

identifying the person's needs, and then recording how it proposes to meet those needs. Where an intervention is made in an adult protection case there will often be a need to carry out a formal assessment of need. Carers have a right to a separate assessment[52].

The Adult Support and Protection Act amended this Act to clarify local authorities' powers to help incapable adults benefit from social services[53]. This amendment allows a local authority to take steps to move an incapable adult to residential accommodation. The amended provisions are discussed further in chapter 12.

Chronically Sick and Disabled Persons Act 1970

2.38 Under the Chronically Sick and Disabled Persons Act 1970, if the local authority thinks that a disabled person in its area needs specific services it must arrange to provide these[54]. These services are listed in the Act and include practical help at home, meals, telephone equipment, home adaptations and help with transport to services. In adult protection cases, where the adult has a disability, a formal assessment under this Act will often be necessary.

Housing (Scotland) Act 1987

2.39 The local authority is under a legal duty to provide housing and has particular duties to those who may be considered homeless in terms of the legislation[55]. Housing law is not covered in any detail in this book but adult protection cases may involve consideration of long and short-term housing options, for example, where it is unreasonable for an adult to return home.

---

[52] SW(S)A 1968, s12AA(1) (added by the Community Care and Health (Scotland) Act 2002).
[53] ASP(S)A 2007, s64 inserted s13ZA to the SW(S)A 1968.
[54] Chronically Sick and Disabled Persons Act 1970, s2(1) as amended by the Chronically Sick and Disabled Persons (Scotland) Act 1972 and the Disabled Persons (Services, Consultation and Representation) Act 1986.
[55] Housing (Scotland) Act 1987 as amended by the Housing (Scotland) Act 2001, and the Homelessness etc. (Scotland) Act 2003.

CONCLUSION

2.40 Various public bodies, and, in particular, local authorities, have duties and responsibilities under several pieces of legislation. In many cases, a local authority may be obliged to carry out an investigation under more than one piece of legislation as well as assessing the need for services. Subsequent chapters will provide further information about how these various laws can be used to help protect adults at risk.

Chapter 3

KEY ORGANISATIONS AND INDIVIDUALS

3.1 This chapter looks at the various individuals and bodies potentially involved in adult protection cases, including local authorities, health care providers, protective bodies and those involved in the criminal justice system.

LOCAL AUTHORITIES

3.2 Local authorities have a lead role in adult protection and have a number of legal duties. Adult protection legislation places a duty on them to investigate where a person may be at risk. Social care law requires them to assess people's needs for community care help and organise services where appropriate. They have additional important obligations under the Adults with Incapacity Act and the Mental Health (Care and Treatment) Act and coordinate the adult protection committees that are responsible for developing strategy and policies in each area.

The social work department will carry out the majority of this work. Some local authorities have now merged social work into a wider health and social care or children and families department.

Local authorities have a general duty to promote social welfare in their area, by providing advice, guidance, assistance and such facilities as they consider suitable and adequate[1]. They may provide services themselves or arrange for another organisation to provide them.

One of the most important changes brought about by the Adult Support and Protection Act was to set out very clearly the key role of the local authority in protecting adults at risk of harm[2]. Chapters 6 and 10 look at this in more detail and discuss local authorities' powers to take further action.

---

[1] Social Work (Scotland) Act 1968, s12(1).
[2] Adult Support and Protection (Scotland) Act 2007, s4.

Anyone concerned that an adult may be at risk should contact the local authority's health and social care department. If the person appears to have a mental disorder, it might be appropriate to contact a mental health officer. These are specialist social workers with extra training and experience in mental illness, dementia and learning disabilities and have the duty and authority to carry out certain functions under mental health and incapacity legislation.

Council officers

3.3 Local authority employees acting in an adult protection role must have special qualifications and training. The Adult Support and Protection Act describes them as 'council officers'.

Recognising that many disciplines can have a role in adult protection, councils may appoint registered social workers, nurses and occupational therapists to act in an investigatory role under the Adult Support and Protection Act. Registered social service workers (non-social workers working in care services and registered with the Social Services Council) may also carry out this role. All these professionals must have at least 12 months' post qualifying experience of identifying, assessing and managing adults at risk[3].

A social service worker who is not a qualified social worker cannot be responsible for initiating an assessment order, a removal order, moving an adult at risk or protecting the property of an adult moved under adult protection law[4].

ADULT PROTECTION COMMITTEE

3.4 The Adult Support and Protection Act requires all local authorities to establish and operate adult protection committees[5]. These are multi-agency committees with representation from various public bodies[6]. The core functions of these committees are set out in the legislation as[7]:

---

[3]   The Adult Support and Protection (Scotland) Act 2007 (Restriction on the Authorisation of Council Officers) Order 2008 SSI 2008 No. 306.
[4]   SSI 2008 No. 306, article 4.
[5]   ASP(S)A 2007, s42.
[6]   ASP(S)A 2007, s43(3).
[7]   ASP(S)A 2007, s42(1).

- To keep under review the procedures and practices of public bodies and office-holders relating to the safeguarding of adults at risk. This includes procedures to facilitate cooperation.

- To give information or advice or make proposals to public bodies and office-holders on the exercise of their functions under the Act.

- To make, or assist with, arrangements to improve the skills and knowledge of office holders and employees of public bodies; and

- Any other function specified by an order of the Scottish Ministers.

The way in which each committee operates is not set down by statute and will be decided by members in each area[8]. Some committees cover just one local authority area, but some of the smaller local authorities are setting up joint adult protection committees. Each local authority is, however, accountable for policies and procedures in its own area.

These committees have a very important role in establishing good practice in adult protection. An important part of their work is to improve cooperation between the various agencies involved. They must have regard to guidance issued by Scottish Ministers about how they operate[9].

Adult protection committees must review adult protection practice and procedures in their area and give information and advice to those involved in safeguarding adults at risk. This includes monitoring adult protection practice and auditing the performance of the various agencies involved[10]. They are also responsible for training. Scottish Ministers may make regulations extending these functions[11].

The code of practice for adult protection committees does not envisage that committees will become involved in individual cases[12]. However it says that staff should be encouraged to bring issues of concern from individual cases to the attention of the committee, if these raise issues of strategy or good practice. The code recognises that joint consideration of individual cases may help committee members develop greater joint understanding of service users' concerns and professional practice.

---

[8]   ASP(S)A 2007, s44.
[9]   *Guidance to adult protection committees* Scottish Government, January 2009. Issued under ASP(S)A 2007, s47.
[10]   Adult Support and Protection Act Code of Practice, chapter 13, para 3.
[11]   ASP(S)A 2007, s42.
[12]   *Guidance to adult protection committees* Scottish Government (above), chapter 2, para 18.

Membership

3.5 The local authority appoints the adult protection committee convener and members. The convener must be independent of the local authority. The relevant health board(s) and police force must nominate a representative, and the Care Commission (see below) may nominate a member if it chooses to do so[13].

Each local authority can invite those they consider to have relevant knowledge and skills to be part of the committee. This might include individuals from groups representing those most likely to be considered 'adults at risk' as well as local service providers and other experts. The code of practice recommends that committees make contact with representatives of the independent care sector and with service user and carer organisations[14].

The committee must allow certain other bodies to send a representative to meetings. These are the Mental Welfare Commission, the Public Guardian, (see below) and the Care Commission (if it does not have membership on the committee)[15]. Because of time and resource constraints, these bodies are unlikely to attend all the meetings of all the adult protection committees, but they will receive minutes of meetings and may attend at a committee's request. They should, of course, be consulted as appropriate in respect of individual cases.

One of the most important parts of adult protection is information sharing. The legislation underlines this, by providing that all the relevant public bodies must give the adult protection committee any information it may reasonably require to enable it to perform its functions[16]. More information about how this may work in practice can be found in chapter 11.

Adult protection committees will report every two years to the relevant bodies and Scottish Ministers[17]. They will be extremely important in developing good practice in Scotland and it will be interesting to see how they develop.

[13] ASP(S)A 2007, s43. There is a power to make regulations to add to this list.
[14] At paras 39 and 40.
[15] ASP(S)A 2007, s44.
[16] ASP(S)A 2007, s45.
[17] ASP(S)A 2007, s46.

HEALTH CARE PROVIDERS

3.6 General practitioners (GPs) provide primary health care in Scotland. GPs are self-employed and provide medical services under a contract with their local health board[18]. The form of contract is set out in regulations[19].

Health boards run hospitals[20]. Health boards also run community health partnerships, providing community based services, including community mental health services[21].

Health professionals who may be involved with adults at risk include not just GPs and hospital doctors, but nurses, (both hospital-based and those working in the community), health visitors, occupational therapists and other health professionals.

Health boards and their staff have new legal duties under the Adult Support and Protection Act and will need to ensure they understand these duties.

The adult protection legislation realises the need for all those involved to cooperate to protect adults at risk. As with child protection, in some cases rules of patient confidentiality may be waived where an adult is at risk. (See chapter 11.)

Health boards, and those working for them, must cooperate with a local authority making inquiries into any case involving an adult at risk. They must also cooperate with the other relevant parties to the investigation. However, the health board can refuse to cooperate if it does not regard this as consistent with the proper exercise of its functions, or if it does not consider such cooperation is likely to enable or assist the local authority with its inquiries[22].

Health professionals may be required to carry out medical assessments where a local authority is investigating a case and may also be required to hand over health records to a local authority official for the purposes of

---

[18] Primary Medical Services (Scotland) Act 2004, s4.

[19] Under the National Health Service (Scotland) Act 1978, s17J. The current form of contract is prescribed in the National Health Service (General Medical Services Contracts) (Scotland) Regulations 2004, SSI 2004 No. 115.

[20] Scottish NHS Trusts were abolished in the 2004 National Health Service Reform (Scotland) Act, s1.

[21] NHSR(S)A 2004, s2.

[22] ASP(S)A 2007, s5.

an inquiry[23]. At the time of writing, this duty applies only to doctors, nurses and midwives, but Scottish Ministers could extend the rules to cover, for example, occupational therapists and psychologists[24]. For more details on the position of GPs, see chapter 11.

PROTECTIVE BODIES

3.7 Three major national bodies have a role in protecting the welfare of people who may be at risk. These are the Care Commission, the Public Guardian and the Mental Welfare Commission. All these bodies may be involved in adult protection committees and can give advice and guidance in individual cases. Depending on the nature of the case, the person requesting advice might be referred to another body. For example, the Care Commission is likely to refer cases that do not involve registered services to the local authority for investigation.

With their national overview, these bodies could have an important role in the development of good practice. At the time of writing, the Scottish Government has introduced the Public Sector Reform Bill, which will make significant changes to how these protective bodies operate. This is discussed further in chapter 15.

Care Commission

3.8 The Care Commission was established in April 2002 and regulates all adult and child services and independent healthcare in Scotland[25]. It makes sure that care services meet the requirements of the Regulation of Care Act, associated regulations and Scotland's national care standards laid down by the Scottish Government. It does this through registration, inspection, complaints, investigations and enforcement activity.

Care services include residential services, day services and agencies providing care in the home. The Care Commission's healthcare remit covers independent hospitals, independent specialist clinics and nursing agencies that choose to opt in to registration[26]. In due course, the Scottish

---

[23]   ASP(S)A 2007, s10.

[24]   ASP(S)A 2007, s52.

[25]   Under the Regulation of Care (Scotland) Act 2001.

[26]   This is likely to be made compulsory by the Scottish Government at some stage.

Government is likely to require that private dental services are also registered.

The Care Commission should exercise all its functions in a way that ensures that the safety and welfare of people using care services is protected and enhanced[27]. It can become involved in adult protection issues at various stages[28]. When it registers a service, it carries out checks to ensure that those providing the service are fit to do so and that they have appropriate adult protection policies in place. It may also become aware of issues during a routine inspection of services or following a complaint from a service user, carer, worker or a member of the public.

In all such cases, the Care Commission will refer the allegations or concerns to the local authority, which has the primary role in investigating where an adult is at risk. However, the Care Commission will discuss the allegations and, in some cases, might be asked by the local authority to make initial inquiries. In addition, a joint investigation might be considered.

Adult protection issues may have an impact on the continued registration of a service. The Care Commission has powers to take enforcement action where services are inadequate.

The Care Commission can attend adult protection committees. It has said that it is unlikely that in the long-term it will be able to sustain a presence at the separate adult protection committees in the 32 local authority areas throughout Scotland[29], but for 12 months from October 2008, it will attend all the committees[30].

Public Guardian

3.9 The Public Guardian has important duties and powers in relation to adults who, because of a mental disorder, or an inability to communicate caused by a physical disability, may be unable to manage all or part of their property or financial affairs or safeguard or promote their interests or rights.

---

[27] ROC(S)A 2001, s59(2).
[28] For more detail, see the Care Commission's Adult Protection Policy and Procedure (2008). Available on its website.
[29] In its submission to the Scottish Parliament's Health Committee Adult Support and Protection (Scotland) Bill Inquiry.
[30] See its Adult Protection Policy and Procedure (2008).

The Public Guardian maintains the registers of powers of attorneys and appointments and interventions under the Adults with Incapacity Act. She monitors and supervises people appointed under Parts 3 and 6 of the Adults with Incapacity Act to manage the financial or property affairs of an adult who is unable to do this herself.

The Public Guardian can be extremely important if an adult is at risk of financial abuse or is otherwise unable to manage financial or property matters. She must investigate if she becomes aware that the property or financial affairs of an adult appear to be at risk[31]. Action taken could include applying for the removal of an attorney or guardian, freezing bank accounts, an application for a guardianship order, or reporting fraud or dishonesty to the police.

There is helpful information on the Public Guardian's website[32] and the office itself is very approachable for those needing information or advice.

Mental Welfare Commission

3.10 The Mental Welfare Commission is an independent organisation working to safeguard the rights and welfare of everyone in Scotland who has a mental illness, learning disability or personality disorder.

As well as a formal role in monitoring the operation of mental health and incapacity legislation, it can become involved in individual cases where adults are at risk. Such cases may come to its attention either on one of its regular visits or following a referral to the Commission. It may investigate itself, ask the local authority to investigate or, in some cases, hold a formal inquiry[33].

The Mental Welfare Commission has considerable experience in issues relating to the protection of adults with mental disorders[34] and has the potential to make a valuable contribution to the work of adult protection committees in providing advice on ethical, legal and practice issues.

---

[31] AWI(S)A 2000, s6(2)(d).

[32] www.publicguardian-scotland.gov.uk. Note that there is a separate Public Guardian for England and Wales, established in 2007.

[33] The Mental Welfare Commission has the authority to do so under Mental Health (Care and Treatment) (Scotland) Act, s12.

[34] See, for example, the report of its investigation into the care and treatment of Mrs T, November 2007.

It can be an important source of advice on good practice for professionals and has a user and carer advice line, open during office hours. More information is available on its website[35].

CARE PROVIDERS

3.11 While local authorities and health boards provide some welfare and support services, many other services are provided by the independent sector, including voluntary or charitable agencies[36]. These include support services, employment projects, day care services, advice agencies, and independent advocacy organisations.

These bodies will be required to have appropriate adult protection policies and may have to report matters of concern to the local authority. An employee of an independent organisation could report any concerns to the Care Commission or to the local authority, as well as informing the Mental Welfare Commission. The Scottish Government's adult protection training and awareness group has developed some useful training materials.

When a local authority carries out inquiries into possible risk to an adult, an independent agency may be legally required to hand over some or all of its records for examination. More information about this is found in chapter 11. The Adult Support and Protection Act code of practice stresses the importance of adult protection committees taking account of the views of service users, families, carer representatives and local voluntary and private providers when they develop their adult protection policies and strategies. It also points out that people from the voluntary sector with relevant skills and knowledge can be appointed onto adult protection committees[37]. This is also true of people from the independent sector.

The voluntary sector can be an important source of advice and expertise, both for professionals and for service users and carers. Further information about key organisations is available from ENABLE Scotland[38].

---

[35] www.mwcscot.org.uk.
[36] For example, in March 2008 of the 942 care homes for older people, 176 (18.7 per cent) were run by a local authority or by the NHS, 623 (66.1 per cent) were privately owned and 143 (15.2 per cent) were in the voluntary sector. *Scottish Government Statistical Bulletin* 2008.
[37] Adult Support and Protection Act Code of Practice, chapter 2, paras 13–15.
[38] See www.enable.org.uk.

INDIVIDUALS SUPPORTING AN ADULT

3.12 A family member, friend or neighbour may have concerns that an adult is at risk, as may a carer. This might involve the risk of harm from a third person, or the risk of self-harm or neglect.

In addition to considering contacting the person's general practitioner or other relevant health professional, anyone concerned about an adult at risk can contact the local authority social work department. It has overall responsibility for making the appropriate inquiries. If a crime may have been committed, anyone with information or concerns can contact the police.

It is clearly important that adult protection supports, and does not undermine an adult's family relationships, as well as existing social contacts and supports. Government guidance says that every effort should be made to ensure that any action taken to protect an adult at risk does not adversely affect these relationships[39].

Involvement of family and carers is a key principle of all adult protection legislation[40]. The Adults with Incapacity Act, Adult Support and Protection Act and the Mental Health (Care and Treatment) Act all require those intervening to take account of the views of relevant parties. The Mental Health (Care and Treatment) Act also requires consideration of the needs and circumstances of carers and of the importance of providing information to carers to help them to care[41].

Unfortunately the legislation does not contain a single definition of carers. The Adults with Incapacity Act requires the involvement of the 'primary carer'. This is the person, paid or unpaid, who is primarily involved in caring for the adult[42].

The Mental Health (Care and Treatment) Act excludes paid carers and volunteers employed by voluntary organisations from its definition of carers[43] and the Adult Support and Protection Act also uses this definition[44]. A paid carer or volunteer will not be considered the primary carer, even if she provides most of the care for the adult.

---

[39] Adult Support and Protection Act Code of Practice, chapter 2, para 6.
[40] See chapter 4 for information about the general principles.
[41] AWI(S)A 2000, s1(4), ASP(S)A 2007, s2, Mental Health (Care and Treatment) (Scotland) Act 2003, ss1(3), (5).
[42] AWI(S)A 2000, ss1(4), 87(1).
[43] MH(CT)(S)A 2003, s329.
[44] ASP(S)A 2007, s53.

This does not mean that arrangements made under these Acts will not require any discussions with paid carers or volunteers. Where care packages are being devised for people at risk, local authorities will have to establish what help is available to the adult from all sources, and all carers' input will remain valuable.

Attorneys, guardians and people authorised under intervention orders

3.13 Under the Adults with Incapacity Act, an individual may sign a power of attorney appointing someone to manage matters should she be unable to act on her own behalf in the future. The person appointed is called an attorney. The power of attorney may give the attorney power to manage money and property, and/or to have a role in welfare decisions, such as medical matters or where the person should live. More details about powers of attorney are in chapter 9.

Similarly, if someone becomes unable to take decisions and there is a need to protect her interests, the sheriff court may appoint a guardian to take financial or welfare decisions or both. If a one-off decision is required, for example, the sale of a house or signing a contract for residential care, the court may make an intervention order to authorise the transaction[45]. For more details on these orders, see chapter 10.

Any attorney, guardian or person with a relevant intervention order should be involved in any adult protection procedures as appropriate[46].

Nearest relative and named person

3.14 Mental health laws have for many years given a special role to the closest relative of the patient, whom it calls the nearest relative. The Mental Health (Care and Treatment) Act contains a detailed list identifying the nearest relative[47].

Under the previous Mental Health Act, it was not possible to remove an unsuitable nearest relative. However, this was in breach of the

[45] Although where there are ongoing obligations under a contract, such as a tenancy agreement, a guardianship order may be more appropriate.
[46] See, for example, the principles in s2 of the Adult Support and Protection Act.
[47] MH(CT)(S)A 2003, s254.

European Convention on Human Rights[48] and for this reason the Mental Health (Care and Treatment) Act allows someone to nominate another person to act in place of the nearest relative should the service user become subject to compulsory measures. The person nominated is called the 'named person'[49]. Anyone able to do so can nominate a named person[50].

Where there is no nomination, the primary carer will act as the named person[51]. If there is no primary carer, the nearest relative will be treated as the named person[52].

Under the Mental Health (Care and Treatment) Act, where the patient has a named person the nearest relative has no role, unless she is involved as a carer. By contrast, the Adults with Incapacity Act requires the involvement of the nearest relative, unless there has been an application to the sheriff to remove the nearest relative or reduce her powers[53].

It is perhaps unfortunate that the Adult Support and Protection Act refers to the involvement of the nearest relative rather than the named person and does not provide for the removal of a nearest relative where this is appropriate. This could face a challenge on human rights grounds. Anyone concerned about the inappropriate involvement of a relative should raise this with the local authority.

Independent advocacy

3.15 Independent advocacy is a way of helping people express their own wishes and needs and make their own decisions. Advocacy workers can help people speak up for themselves or can speak on behalf of them if necessary. They can also help with communication, although in some cases technical or other aids to communication may also be necessary[54]. For more information about advocacy and legal rights, see chapter 9.

---

[48]   *JT v the UK* 1998 Application No 26494/95, on the equivalent provision in the Mental Health Act 1983 for England and Wales.

[49]   MH(CT)(S)A 2003, s250.

[50]   For more detail, see *Mental Health, Incapacity and the Law in Scotland*, Hilary Patrick, Bloomsbury Professional (2006), para 4.02 ff.

[51]   MH(CT)(S)A 2003, ss251(1), 329.

[52]   MH(CT)(S)A 2003, s251(5).

[53]   Under AWI(S)A 2000, s4.

[54]   Adult Support and Protection Act Code of Practice, para 3.10.

CRIMINAL JUSTICE SYSTEM

3.16 Where an adult at risk may be experiencing harm that could constitute a criminal offence it is essential that local authority and health care staff consider the need to report concerns to the police. Crimes include physical or sexual assaults, including harassment, as well as financial or property crimes such as fraud or theft, as discussed in chapter 14.

The police

3.17 Responsibility for investigating crime in Scotland rests with the police. During inquiries into possible risk to an adult there may be occasions where it is important to involve the police. This is discussed in chapter 14. In addition, if there is a risk to investigating staff, the police should be involved

The police are key members of the local adult protection committee. They are likely to assist in establishing adult protection protocols with the local authority, health boards and others. The police, like the other relevant bodies, are under a legal duty to cooperate in relevant inquiries[55].

Moreover, if an adult protection issue comes to the police, for example from a member of the public, they must report this to the relevant local authority[56].

Crown Office Procurator Fiscal Service

3.18 The Crown Office and Procurator Fiscal Service is responsible for the prosecution of crime in Scotland. It also investigates any sudden or suspicious deaths (with a view to a possible fatal accident inquiry) and complaints against the police. The head of the service is the Lord Advocate, the principal law officer in Scotland. The Solicitor General is her second in command.

Where a crime may have been committed, the police carry out an initial investigation and then submit a report to the local prosecutor, who is known as the procurator fiscal.

Procurators fiscal deal with all investigations into crimes and carry out all prosecutions in the sheriff and district courts. The procurator fiscal

---

[55]   ASP(S)A 2007, s5.
[56]   ASP(S)A 2007, s5(3).

decides if a prosecution would be in the public interest and whether or not there is sufficient evidence to prosecute. The police and procurator fiscal will work closely in any future inquiries and the procurator fiscal may give the police instructions on how to conduct an inquiry.

The Crown Office and local prosecution services intend to cooperate with adult support agencies nationally and locally respectively. An experienced prosecutor will attend local adult protection committee meetings at least twice a year to discuss criminal justice matters. The local point of contact should be the local procurator fiscal service[57].

CONCLUSION

3.19 While the local authority takes a key role in adult support and protection, it will succeed in this role only if it has the cooperation of a wide variety of bodies and individuals. This will require changes in cultures and ways of working, including the need to share information and work across boundaries. The new adult protection committees will have a key role in developing good practice.

---

[57] Adult Support and Protection Act Implementation newsletter no. 4, February 2009.

Chapter 4

PRINCIPLES IN ADULT PROTECTION LAW

4.1 The main pieces of adult protection legislation contain a set of principles, set out in the initial sections. These principles have a crucial impact on how the law should work in practice. This chapter looks at the principles and examines their legal and practical effect.

Statements of principles in legislation in Scotland are a relatively new development, and are increasingly seen as helpful where a law deals with complex ethical issues affecting the rights of the individual[1].

BACKGROUND TO PRINCIPLES

4.2 Both the Adults with Incapacity Act and the Mental Health (Care and Treatment) Act are values-based laws. Those proposing reform had a clear view of the principles they felt should underlie the legislation[2]. The principles set out the ethical basis for the powers granted under the legislation and the values underpinning it. These principles clearly influenced the development of the Adult Support and Protection Act.

The principles also influenced the content of the new legislation. For example, the importance of respect for the wishes of the patient gave rise to the right to independent advocacy in the Mental Health (Care and Treatment) Act. The least restrictive principle was behind the hierarchy of financial interventions in the Adults with Incapacity Act.

But the principles have more than a historic interest. They have an ongoing day-to-day importance for the way people exercise statutory

---

[1] For example, the Children (Scotland) Act 1995 includes the principle that the welfare of the child should be paramount. The Adoption and Children (Scotland) Act 2007 lists matters for the court to consider in adoption proceedings.

[2] *Report on Incapable Adults*, Scottish Law Commission (1995), paras 2.47–2.73. *New Directions: Report on the Review of the Mental Health (Scotland) Act 1984* (2001), chapter 3.

powers. A court should not grant guardianship under the Adults with Incapacity Act unless it is satisfied that this is the least restrictive option necessary to protect the adult's interests. A doctor deciding about the use of compulsory medication under the Mental Health (Care and Treatment) Act must bear in mind the patient's wishes.

The principles inform practical decision-making and give those operating the relevant legislation guidance on how it should work. The principles cannot be applied mechanically, and it is not unusual for principles to conflict. For example, in mental health cases, a person may not want medical treatment, but there may be clear evidence this would benefit him. Those intervening will have to balance the different principles. This often involves very difficult questions of judgement.

PRINCIPLES IN ADULTS WITH INCAPACITY ACT

4.3 The Adults with Incapacity Act contains a clear statement of principles. These principles apply to any intervention in the life of an adult who is unable to take one or more decisions about financial, health or welfare matters. Anyone taking action under the Act has a clear legal duty to implement the principles[3].

This applies both to interventions and to decisions not to intervene[4]. This means a sheriff may decide not to grant an order if he judges that the benefit to an adult would not be sufficient to justify overruling the adult's wishes.

The Adults with Incapacity Act contains five key principles:

- **Benefit** There should be no intervention under the Act unless the person intervening or authorising the intervention is satisfied that this will benefit the adult, *and* that this is the only reasonable way of achieving the benefit. For example, where someone could remain at home with extra help, it may not be reasonable to move the person to residential care against his will.

    The Scottish Law Commission recommended that the principle be expressed in terms of 'benefit' rather than 'best interests', which

---

[3]   Adults with Incapacity (Scotland) Act 2000, s1(1).
[4]   See Adrian Ward, *Adult Incapacity*, W Green (2003), para 4.3.

it regarded as too paternalistic in questions of adult welfare. The Commission did not think 'best interests' gave enough emphasis to the wishes and feelings of the adult[5].

PRINCIPLES AND PRACTICE

Balancing benefit and risk in individual cases can be extremely difficult[6]. The most common example is where someone appears to be at risk but is adamant he does not need help. In such circumstances, the impact of intervening against his will could reduce any benefit to him.

Perhaps the person may be prepared to accept a less restrictive alternative, and this may reduce some risks, but not all. However, the benefit to him of not having arrangements forced on him may outweigh these risks.

One way of approaching benefit is to test it against the other principles in the Act. This is the approach used by the Mental Capacity Act for England and Wales[7]. It spells out that, in determining whether an intervention is in a person's best interests, the intervener must (among other things) encourage the adult to participate in decision-making and take account of his wishes and feelings, beliefs and values[8].

• **Least restrictive option** Any intervention should be the least restrictive option in relation to the freedom of the adult necessary to achieve the purpose[9].

• **Ascertaining views of adult** Anyone deciding whether to intervene, and if so, how, should consider the present and past wishes and feelings of the adult[10].

---

[5] *Report on Incapable adults*, para 2.50.

[6] *The AWI(S)A 2000: Learning from Experience* Jan Killeen, Fiona Myers and others, Scottish Executive (2004), para 5.131.

[7] Mental Capacity Act 2005, s4. For further discussion of how the courts interpret the principles, see the comments of Adrian Ward in his annotations of the *Adults with Incapacity Legislation* W Green (2008).

[8] MCA 2005, s4(6).

[9] AWI(S)A 2000, s1(3).

[10] AWI(S)A 2000, s1(4).

All reasonable means should be used to find out the adult's views and feelings, past and present. This may involve using communication or interpretation facilities, including advocacy. Enquiries should be made to establish whether the adult has expressed a view on the matter or has made an advance statement or living will.

The duty to show respect for the adult's present wishes and feelings applies even when an adult is unable to take a decision. This is a significant protection against the apparent paternalism of a benefit test and an important safeguard against a person being bound by past statements that may no longer reflect his feelings[11].

If the use of communication facilities reveals that the person can take the relevant decision, then the Adults with Incapacity Act cannot be used.

PRINCIPLES AND PRACTICE

Even people with significantly impaired capacity are usually able to find a way to communicate what they want, feel or think, by behaviour, facial expression, or gestures. Their preferences should be taken into account even if they are unable to make a decision.

In some cases, for example, it might be clear that someone is more content in one location than another, and this should be a factor in any decision made about where that person should live.

- **Respect for views of significant others** The views of the adult's nearest relative[12], named person and primary carer[13] must also be taken into account, if this is reasonable and practicable. In addition the views of any guardian or attorney with relevant powers and of any other person with an interest in the adult's welfare or the proposed intervention should be taken into account[14]. An interested individual (or organisation) can apply to the sheriff to be consulted.

  The requirement to have respect for the views of significant others does not necessarily mean that these people should receive

---

[11]   Ward annotations (above).
[12]   As defined in the Mental Health (Care and Treatment) (Scotland) Act 2003.
[13]   That is, the person or organisation primarily caring for the adult. This could include a paid carer. AWI(S)A 2000, s87(1).
[14]   AWI(S)A 2000, s1(4).

confidential information where the adult does not want this to happen. The courts in England have said that it may not be 'practicable' to consider another's views where the adult has said he does not want them involved[15]. Similar arguments could be advanced in such cases in Scotland.

- **Encouraging use and development of skills** A guardian, attorney, or person managing a resident's funds must encourage the adult to exercise whatever skills he has in connection with property, financial or personal welfare matters and to develop new skills, so far as reasonable and practicable[16].

MENTAL HEALTH (CARE AND TREATMENT) ACT PRINCIPLES

4.4 The principles contained in the Mental Health (Care and Treatment) Act largely mirror those recommended by the Millan Committee[17], which were widely welcomed. The principles apply to everyone exercising functions under the Act[18] (other than the patient and those representing the patient[19]) and require them to have regard to the following:

- **Participation** The need to take account of the patient's wishes and feelings, past and present[20]. Those involved must take appropriate means to establish the patient's views[21].

  People should consider how to enable the patient to participate as fully as possible in decisions, and should bear in mind the need to give the patient information and support[22].

[15] *R (E) v Bristol City Council* (2005) EWHC 74 (Admin).
[16] AWI(S)A 2000, s1(5).
[17] *New Directions* (above) para 3.3.
[18] MH(CT)(S)A 2003, ss1–3.
[19] That is the patient's named person or primary carer, any independent advocate or lawyer representing the patient, a curator *ad litem*, guardian or welfare attorney of the patient. MH(CT)(S)A 2003, s1(7).
[20] MH(CT)(S)A 2003, s1(3)(a).
[21] MH(CT)(S)A 2003, s1(8).
[22] MH(CT)(S)A 2003, ss1(3),1(10).

- **Respect for views of significant others** The importance of considering the views of the named person, any carer and any welfare guardian or attorney provided it is reasonable and practicable to do so[23]. This does not apply to decisions about medical treatment[24].

- **Respect for carers** The Mental Health (Care and Treatment) Act is the only adult protection law to include, as far as reasonable and practicable, considering the needs of any carer and the importance of giving a carer the information needed to help care for the person[25]. This principle could conflict with the principle of respect for the patient's wishes where a patient does not wish a carer to receive information. On the other hand, a carer may need certain information to be able to care. For more discussion, see chapter 11.

- **Least restrictive alternative**[26] People should carry out duties under the Act in the least restrictive manner necessary in the circumstances, bearing in mind the other principles, the needs of any carer, the duty of reciprocity (below) and any other considerations[27].

- **Benefit** The importance of providing the maximum benefit to the patient[28].

- **Child welfare** If the patient is a child or young person under 18, the need to intervene in the way that will best secure the child's welfare[29].

- **Non-discrimination and respect for diversity** The need to ensure the patient's treatment is no worse than what someone who is not a patient would receive in a similar situation, unless this is justified in the circumstances[30]. (This somewhat obscurely worded principle stems from the Millan Committee principle of equality, which said

---

[23]   MH(CT)(S)A 2003, s1(3)(b).
[24]   MH(CT)(S)A 2003, s1(9).
[25]   MH(CT)(S)A 2003, s1(5). For information on the definition of carers, see para 3.12.
[26]   MH(CT)(S)A 2003, s1(3)(e).
[27]   MH(CT)(S)A 2003, s1(4).
[28]   MH(CT)(S)A 2003, s1(3)(f).
[29]   MH(CT)(S)A 2003, s2(4).
[30]   MH(CT)(S)A 2003, s1(3)(g).

that powers under the Act should be exercised without any direct or indirect discrimination on grounds of age, sex, race, disability etc[31].)

The person's abilities, background and characteristics, including his age, sex, sexual orientation, religious persuasion and cultural and ethnic background should be also taken into account[32].

Effectively, this means not discriminating, treating people fairly and making positive attempts to meet people's individual needs.

• **Reciprocity** The importance of providing appropriate services to a person subject to compulsory measures, including providing continuing care when the person is no longer subject to such measures[33].

ADULT SUPPORT AND PROTECTION ACT

4.5 The Adult Support and Protection Act principles adapt the principles of the Adults with Incapacity Act and the Mental Health (Care and Treatment) Act, taking elements of both.

There is one overarching 'general principle'. A person should intervene, or authorise an intervention under the Act, only if he is satisfied that the intervention will provide a benefit to the adult not reasonably obtainable without the intervention *and* that the proposed intervention is the least restrictive option available[34].

Any public body or office-holder performing a function under the Act must have regard to this general principle (insofar as it is relevant)[35] and to the following:

• **The adult's wishes and feelings** (past and present), in so far as these are ascertainable. There is no explicit duty to make all reasonable efforts to ascertain the adult's views, (although this is clearly good practice) but there is a duty to consider the importance of providing independent advocacy services[36]. People with a mental

---

[31]   *New directions* (above), recommendation 3.3(3).
[32]   MH(CT)(S)A 2003, s1(3)(h).
[33]   MH(CT)(S)A 2003, s1(6).
[34]   Adult Support and Protection (Scotland) Act 2007, s1.
[35]   ASP(S)A 2007, s2.
[36]   ASP(S)A 2007, s6.

disorder have an entitlement to advocacy services under the Mental Health (Care and Treatment) Act[37].

- **The views of relevant other parties insofar as these are known** The list includes the adult's nearest relative or primary carer[38], any guardian or attorney and any other person with an interest in the adult's well-being or property known to the person carrying out the function. This could include a named person appointed under the Mental Health (Care and Treatment) Act or any other person who has been involved in helping the adult.

- **Participation** The importance of the adult participating as fully as possible in any decisions and of giving him such information and support as is necessary to facilitate this.

- **Non discrimination** The importance of ensuring that the adult is not, without justification, treated less favourably than the way in which any other adult who is not at risk might be treated in a similar situation.

- **Respect for diversity** The adult's abilities, background and characteristics (including age, sex, sexual orientation, religious persuasion, racial origin, ethnic group and cultural and linguistic heritage)[39].

Table 4.1 – The principles compared			
Principle	**ASP Act**	**MH(CT) Act**	**AWI Act**
Benefit	✓	✓	✓
Least restrictive option	✓	✓	✓
Find out and consider the adult's views	✓	✓	✓
Consider the views of significant others	✓	✓	✓
Encourage use and development of skills			✓
Involving carers		✓	
Child welfare		✓	
Non discrimination	✓	✓	
Reciprocity		✓	
Respect for diversity	✓	✓	
Support adult to participate in decisions	✓	✓	

---

[37] MH(CT)(S)A 2003, s259. See paras 9.2–9.5 for discussion on independent advocacy.

[38] As defined in the Mental Health (Care and Treatment) (Scotland) Act.

[39] ASP(S)A 2007, s2(f).

HUMAN RIGHTS CONCEPTS

4.6 Chapter 12 looks at how human rights law deals with adult protection issues. Human rights law includes important concepts that supplement the principles in the Scottish legislation and can usefully aid decision-making.

The human rights approach starts by setting out specific rights: to liberty, respect for family life etc. Any interference with those rights must be *lawful*. It must also be *necessary*. There must be no less restrictive alternative, and the risks must be such that the intervention is appropriate[40].

Similarly, any intervention must be *proportionate*, that is, it must be appropriate for the risk posed[41]. Decision takers must weigh up the relevant risks and benefits to the person at risk and others, and their response should be a balanced response to these risks and benefits.

LEGAL IMPACT OF PRINCIPLES

4.7 The principles in the Adults with Incapacity Act are clearly stated and impose binding legal obligations. These principles direct the way in which bodies must carry out their duties under the law. For example, a sheriff cannot grant an order unless he is satisfied that it will benefit the adult and is the least restrictive option[42].

Some people have argued that the Mental Health (Care and Treatment) Act principles are less clearly stated. Those involved must only 'have regard' to the principles. However, the courts will require evidence that those intervening have considered the principles[43]. It also appears that, in practice, the mental health tribunal gives serious consideration to the principles when it reaches decisions.

Anyone concerned that those intervening have not given due consideration to the principles could challenge this by means of judicial review[44].

---

[40] See, for example, *Witold Litwa v Poland*, no. 26629/95, para 78, ECHR 2000-III.

[41] See *Winterwerp v The Netherlands* [1979] ECtHR 4.

[42] As, for example, in *Application in respect of Mr DM* Glasgow Sheriff Court AW36/06.

[43] See Judgment of Sheriff Principal James A Taylor in *Peter Di Mascio against the Mental Health Tribunal for Scotland and the Named Person* Glasgow, 4 August 2008 B812/08.

[44] See *Mental Health, Incapacity and the Law in Scotland*, Hilary Patrick, Bloomsbury Professional (2006) para 51.02.

The Adult Support and Protection Act principles are similar to the Adults with Incapacity Act principles in that they are admirably clearly stated, but, like Mental Health (Care and Treatment) Act principles, the duty is only to 'have regard' to the principles.

The nature of the principles in each of the Acts reflects the complex issues raised in individual cases. We have seen that the principles may need to be balanced one against another, and the law recognises this.

Adults with Incapacity Act indemnity

4.8   The Adults with Incapacity Act specifically protects people acting in accordance with its principles. Where someone acting under the Act can show that his actions were reasonable, in good faith and in accordance with the principles, he will not be liable for any breach of duty of care[45]. A person who has not acted in accordance with the principles does not have the benefit of this limitation of liability. This protection is unique to that Act.

Promoting the principles

4.9   The Mental Health (Care and Treatment) Act gives the Mental Welfare Commission a legal duty to promote the principles of that Act, as part of its general duty to promote best practice in relation to the Act[46].

The Commission provides guidance and monitors good practice. It has set up a 'Principles into Practice Network', to share information about good practice.

CONCLUSION

4.10   The principles contained in adult protection legislation generally represent agreed good practice. Human rights law principles add an extra dimension.

Balancing the different principles and applying them to individual circumstances is a question of judgement. The principles require different emphasis in different situations. For example, the risks to an adult may be so serious that it is appropriate to overrule his wishes. Similarly, there

---

[45]   AWI(S)A 2000, s82(1).
[46]   MH(CT)(S)A 2003, s5.

may be situations where taking account of the views of a carer or relative may cause an adult grave distress.

The principles should help professionals making difficult decisions involving balancing human rights and risk, by providing a framework for decision taking. Adrian Ward has said, in connection with the Adults with Incapacity Act, that *'reference to the principles will usually assist – often decisively – in resolving points of difficulty in the application of the Act's provisions to particular circumstances, or of interpretation'*[47].

---

[47]   Ward, *Adult Incapacity*, para 4.2.

Chapter 5

HARM AND ABUSE

5.1 This chapter provides an introduction to the common types of harm and abuse encountered in adult protection cases. Abuse and harm can take place in a variety of settings and concerns may become apparent in a number of ways. It is vital that the response is effective and proportionate. The need to protect an individual must always be balanced with her right to make her own decisions about her life – even when others might think those choices are not in her best interests. The most appropriate approach in individual cases will need careful consideration and adequate support must be provided[1].

LEGAL DEFINITIONS OF HARM AND ABUSE

5.2 The definition varies depending on the legislation being considered, although several laws cover some types of harm and abuse. For example, a physical assault might justify intervention under the Adult Support and Protection Act or the Adults with Incapacity Act, as well as the criminal law. In this section, how the law defines and approaches harm and abuse is examined.

Adult Support and Protection Act

5.3 The Adult Support and Protection Act defines 'harm' as all harmful conduct and, in particular, includes:

- Conduct that causes physical harm;

- Conduct that causes psychological harm (for example: by causing fear, alarm or distress);

---

[1] Supporting the adult is covered in chapter 9.

- Unlawful conduct that appropriates or adversely affects property, rights or interests (for example: theft, fraud, embezzlement or extortion); and

- Conduct that causes self-harm[2].

  An adult is considered 'at risk of harm' where:

- Another person's conduct is causing (or is likely to cause) the adult to be harmed, or

- The adult is engaging (or is likely to engage) in conduct that causes (or is likely to cause) self-harm[3].

A local authority is under an obligation to investigate where it thinks an adult is at risk of harm. Where a statutory order is being considered it is necessary to show not just harm but 'serious harm'[4]. This is because a protection order is a significant intervention in an adult's life[5]. The word 'serious' is not defined in the legislation and will depend on the circumstances of each case. The code of practice states that what constitutes 'serious harm' will be different for different people[6].

Mental Health (Care and Treatment) Act

5.4 Compulsory measures under the Mental Health (Care and Treatment) Act can be used where there is a significant risk to an individual's health, welfare or safety or to the safety of others. The decision as to what is a 'significant risk' is a matter for the clinical judgement of doctors and other health professionals.

Where longer-term detention is being considered the mental health tribunal will need to be satisfied the risk is significant before granting a compulsory treatment order[7]. The tribunal can also look at the issue of risk when it hears appeals.

---

[2] Adult Support and Protection (Scotland) Act 2007, s53(1).
[3] ASP(S)A 2007, s3(2).
[4] The statutory orders are assessment, removal and banning orders. These are covered in detail in chapter 6.
[5] Adult Support and Protection Act Code of Practice, para 1.11.
[6] Para 1. 12.
[7] Mental Health (Care and Treatment) (Scotland) Act 2003, s64(5).

It is generally agreed that it is not necessary to prove that there is an immediate life threatening risk. For example, an intervention may be possible where a person's illness has recurred and there is evidence that early compulsory intervention will prevent a serious deterioration in her health.

Adults with Incapacity Act

5.5 The Adults with Incapacity Act does not specifically define harm but instead refers to situations where an adult's finances, property or welfare are at risk. In such cases, the local authority, the Public Guardian and Mental Welfare Commission all have a role in investigations[8]. Where, as a result of an investigation, it becomes clear that a guardianship or intervention order is necessary, the local authority is under a legal obligation to apply[9].

The Adults with Incapacity Act has a different approach to other adult protection legislation and can be used to take decisions, not just to prevent harm, but also for the benefit of an adult lacking capacity. For example, there could be clear evidence that an individual living in a group setting would benefit from being supported in her own tenancy. A guardianship order might allow the local authority, or a family member, to move her to a better living arrangement[10]. The primary purpose of this action is to provide a positive benefit to the adult rather than to remove her from a situation of harm or abuse.

COMMON CATEGORIES OF HARM AND ABUSE

5.6 Abuse and harm can happen to anyone at any age and is a significant and serious issue for society. In this section, some of the common types of harm and abuse are outlined.

Physical abuse

5.7 Physical abuse normally involves deliberately inflicting pain or suffering on another individual. This can include behaviour such as

---

[8] For further information about investigations, see chapter 7.
[9] Adults with Incapacity (Scotland) Act 2000, ss53(3) and 57(2).
[10] It may also be possible to move the adult using s13ZA of the Social Work (Scotland) Act 1968. See chapters 2, 10 and 12.

punching, slapping, hitting, kicking, shaking, burning, scalding or forcing an individual to take substances that are likely to cause harm.

It includes providing support or assistance in a way that causes physical injury. It would cover situations where a carer was rough and caused injury when helping an adult in or out or the bath. Inappropriate medication, sedation for the convenience of a carer or administering covert medication without proper authority, can also be classed as physical abuse[11].

Sexual abuse

5.8 Sexual abuse covers a variety of behaviours, including non-consensual touching or penetration, exposure and showing another individual sexually explicit material. Generally, sexual abuse is any sexual activity to which an individual has not consented, or cannot[12] consent. It is also a specific criminal offence for a care worker to have a sexual relationship with someone she supports[13]. This is the case even if the relationship is apparently consensual. Sexual abuse is a criminal offence and should be reported to, and investigated by, the police[14].

Neglect by a third party

5.9 Neglect describes an ongoing lack of appropriate care and attention. It can be intentional or unintentional and includes a lack of stimulation, safety, nourishment or nutrition, warmth or medical attention. Neglect can happen in any setting in which an adult is dependent on someone else for care and attention, including family homes and formal care settings.

In some cases, neglect is not deliberate but an indication that a carer is not coping. It can be very difficult for a carer to admit she is struggling and there may be concerns or guilt about what might happen if she asks

---

[11] Inappropriate medication may also be an assault.
[12] MH(CT)(S)A 2003, ss311–313 (due to be amended by the Sexual Offences (Scotland) Act) 2009. See chapter 14.
[13] MH(CT)(S)A 2003, s313. This provision has been restated in the Sexual Offences (Scotland) Act 2009, which is expected to come into force in 2010.
[14] See para 14.10 for information on criminal prosecutions.

for help. This can include worries that a spouse will be required to move to residential accommodation against her express wishes. In such cases, an assessment of the adult's needs, as well as the needs of the carer[15], followed by the provision of appropriate support might be a more appropriate response than the use of adult protection legislation.

Self harm, neglect or abuse

Self neglect

5.10 Self-neglect happens when an individual does not take appropriate care of her physical and mental health or needs. It can include behaviour such as a failure to wash clothes, deal with personal hygiene, eat properly or keep her home in a reasonable condition. This may be the result of a physical difficulty or a mental disorder or illness.

Local authorities are under a duty to investigate and consider an intervention where an individual lacks capacity, is an adult at risk or has a mental disorder. They may also have duties to take action where property is not maintained to an acceptable standard[16].

PRINCIPLES AND PRACTICE

Cases of self-neglect can be challenging, as they involve the need to balance individuals' rights to choose how they live with the protection of those who are unable to cope due to a mental impairment or illness. In every case, consideration about how an individual will respond to any intervention will be necessary before a decision is made on how to proceed.

Self-harm or injury

5.11 Self-harm or injury occurs when an individual causes a direct physical injury to herself. Injury can be inflicted in a number of ways,

---

[15] Carers are entitled to a separate assessment under the Social Work (Scotland) Act 1968, sections 12A and 12AA(1) (added by the Community Care and Health (Scotland) Act 2002).

[16] For example, under environmental health legislation. Contact the local environmental health department for further information.

including cutting, burning, scalding, hair pulling, using blunt objects or interfering with wounds healing. Self-harm or injury is a complex topic and any intervention requires to be carefully managed. However, it may fall within the scope of adult protection legislation in some cases, for example:

- Where the individual involved lacks legal capacity, the use of powers under the Adult with Incapacity Act may be appropriate.

- Where a mental disorder is present and the person does not consent to treatment, compulsory measures under the Mental Health (Care and Treatment) Act can be considered.

- Self-harm or injury falls within the definition of 'harm' in the Adult Support and Protection Act[17]. However, action cannot be taken under this Act if the adult refuses to consent unless she has been unduly pressured into that refusal[18].

Eating disorders

5.12 Eating disorders are often indicated when an individual's eating patterns or behaviours cause her significant physical or mental harm. Common examples are bulimia and anorexia. Some eating disorders will amount to, or be a symptom of, mental disorder. As with the issues around self-harm, dealing with eating disorders is complicated and the benefits of any action need careful consideration. Direct intervention is a serious step and must be balanced with the individual's right to make decisions about her body. It might be appropriate to use the legislation in serious or life threatening cases in a similar way to situations of self-harm or neglect.

Domestic abuse

5.13 Domestic abuse normally describes any type of abuse that happens between two people in a relationship (or who have been in a relationship together in the past). It is an extremely complex problem and is generally outside the scope of this book.

---

[17] ASP(S)A 2007, s3(2)(b).
[18] See paras 6.27–6.28 for further discussion on the concept of 'undue pressure'.

However, where someone is experiencing domestic abuse and falls within the terms of the Adults with Incapacity Act[19], the Mental Health (Care and Treatment) Act[20] or the Adult Support and Protection Act[21] there will be a duty on the local authority to investigate and consider an intervention. The police may also take action where a crime has been committed. The role of the criminal justice system is explored in chapter 14.

Financial abuse

5.14   Financial abuse involves an inappropriate use of an individual's money or other property without her agreement or consent. It might involve withholding benefit or other income, obtaining credit in another person's name or transferring ownership of property under false pretences. Such abuse may also be a criminal offence.

WHERE HARM AND ABUSE HAPPEN

5.15   Abuse or harm can happen anywhere but the response might be different depending on the setting in which it takes place.

At home

5.16   Harm or abuse can happen in the family home, a group home or another community care setting, such as supported living. The local authority, Mental Welfare Commission and Public Guardian are all under duties to investigate abuse or harm believed to be happening within an individual's home[22]. There are powers to enter and investigate if access to the adult is denied or an investigation is otherwise obstructed.

Where there is suspicion that a support worker is the cause of abuse or harm, the employer will have power to suspend the worker pending an

---

[19]   AWI(S)A 2000, s1(6).
[20]   MH(CT)(S)A 2003, s328(1).
[21]   ASP(S)A 2007, s3(1).
[22]   See chapters 2 and 7 for further details of the duties to investigate under relevant legislation.

investigation. Organisations should follow internal procedures and have regard to the duty to report to external bodies such as the local authority.

It will also be appropriate to involve the Scottish Social Services Council where harm or abuse happens within a day service or centre. The SSSC registers social care workers and has responsibility for raising standards in the social care workforce.[23] The Care Commission has relevant powers, and duties, to investigate harm or abuse in residential or nursing homes[24].

In the community

5.17   The community is another potential setting for abuse, for example, where an individual suffers antisocial behaviour from neighbours or others who live in the community. Although this may be a criminal offence, rather than an adult protection issue,[25] adult protection legislation might be used. In some cases, a guardianship order may be necessary to provide appropriate protection[26]. Additional remedies, including banning orders, interdicts and anti-social behaviour orders may also be available[27].

RECOGNISING HARM OR ABUSE

5.18   Harm and abuse can become apparent in a number of ways and because reactions vary from person to person, it is important to take any disclosures, allegations, concerns, injuries or changes in behaviour seriously and investigate in an appropriate manner.

Disclosure by adult

5.19   In some cases, an adult may report abuse or harm directly by telling a social worker, carer, family member, support staff or the police. In some cases, those who become aware of harm will be under a legal duty to disclose that information to the appropriate authority. The issues around the disclosure of information are looked at in detail in chapter 11.

---

[23]   www.sssc.uk.com.
[24]   Regulation of Care (Scotland) Act 2001.
[25]   See chapter 14 for further information on criminal prosecution.
[26]   AWI(S)A 2000, Part 6.
[27]   See chapter 10 for more information.

Disclosure by a third party

5.20   Information about abuse or harm can come to light because a third party has witnessed the abuse or has been abused by the same person or in the same institution or setting.

Concerns raised following behaviour changes

5.21   A person who knows the adult well and who has noticed significant changes may report concerns. This could be a relative, friend, neighbour, teacher, colleague or support worker worried about an adult's appearance, lack of funds, increasing debts or changes in behaviour and mood.

Other indicators can be disrupted sleeping patterns or frequent nightmares, a loss of personal modesty, a fear of being alone, or someone becoming prone to angry and aggressive outbursts. There may also be the development of psychological difficulties, including depression, obsessive behaviour, and a loss of confidence or panic attacks. Such changes can be a way of communicating emotions and as such should be taken seriously and investigated.

Medical care and treatment

5.22   The adult may have unexplained physical injuries, such as cuts, bleeding or bruising, that indicate abuse. In some cases, urgent action might be necessary to make sure the individual gets the medical care and treatment she needs.

Where the adult refuses to cooperate, and lacks capacity, consideration might be given to using the powers under the Adults with Incapacity Act. Otherwise, any care or treatment against the wishes of a competent adult can constitute an assault, unless it is covered under the common law doctrine of necessity or the Mental Health (Care and Treatment) Act[28]. Issues around medical treatment are examined in chapter 9.

Abuse may also become apparent when an adult with reduced capacity becomes pregnant or is diagnosed with a sexual transmitted disease.

---

[28]   This can only authorise treatment for a mental disorder.

CONCLUSION

5.23 In some cases, the harm will be of a degree that an intervention is undoubtedly necessary. However, in other cases there may be a number of factors to consider before deciding how to proceed. It is clear that the issues around abuse and harm are complicated and decisions about when and how to respond are difficult. There may also be issues around confidentiality and, in particular, the situations in which information can, or must, be disclosed[29].

---

[29] The disclosure of information and duties of confidentiality are discussed in detail in chapter 11.

Chapter 6

LOCAL AUTHORITIES' ROLE AND RESPONSIBILITIES

6.1 This chapter looks at the duties and powers of local authorities where formal measures are necessary in relation to the investigation of harm. These powers and duties arise under various pieces of legislation, each of which has a different emphasis, although inevitably some of the provisions overlap. The role of other organisations is explored in chapter 7, while criminal investigations are covered in chapter 14.

The local authority will generally be the first point of contact where there is suspicion of harm or abuse. It should take seriously any report that an adult may be at risk of harm, even when it is from an anonymous source[1]. The social work department should carry out the inquiry in accordance with local adult protection procedures and may work with other agencies as necessary[2].

In many cases, initial investigations will be relatively informal and will not involve applications for court orders. It is hoped that the adult will often be prepared to accept assistance[3]. However, there will be situations in which the adult refuses to cooperate, despite the fact he is suffering, or is likely to suffer, harm. In other cases, a third party might deliberately obstruct an investigation by insisting that an adult is unavailable, continually refusing to answer the door or failing to attend appointments. This will mean the local authority needs to consider the use of statutory powers.

A decision about such a course of action will be influenced by a number of factors, including the specific circumstances of the case, the relevant legal powers, the adult's capacity and the benefit of an intervention.

---

[1]   Adult Support and Protection Act Code of Practice, para 4.4.
[2]   Adult Support and Protection Act Code of Practice, para 4.7.
[3]   Although this might not be possible in emergencies. See chapter 8 for further details.

POWERS AND DUTIES UNDER ADULT SUPPORT AND PROTECTION ACT

Duty to investigate

6.2 Local authorities have a key role in adult protection under the Act, with wide ranging duties to make inquiries. The legislation now makes it clear that the primary responsibility for investigating any risk to adults is with the local authority.

A local authority must make inquiries wherever it considers an adult protected by the legislation is at risk of harm[4] (from others or from self harm) and that action may be necessary to protect his well-being, property or finances[5]. This duty extends to people living in their own homes, in residential care and in hospital and healthcare settings.

The Act also provides the local authority with powers of compulsion in certain circumstances, where the adult or a third party is obstructive or refuses to cooperate with the investigation. The local authority can apply for an order to authorise an assessment of the adult or for an order to remove him to a place where he can be interviewed or examined.

However, these powers will normally only be used when other methods have failed. The code of practice recognises that the system should be *'flexible and professional in its approach'* and that interventions must be *'person centred and based on an individual's personal circumstances'*[6].

Other organisations are obliged to cooperate in any investigations[7] and the police should also be involved at the earliest possible point where it appears a crime has occurred.

PRINCIPLES AND PRACTICE

The general principles, as outlined in chapter 4, must be applied whenever the legislation is considered or used. Any intervention must be the least restrictive alternative, must offer a benefit to the individual and should maximise the participation of the adult in the decision making process.

---

[4]   See chapter 5.
[5]   Adult Support and Protection (Scotland) Act 2007, s4.
[6]   Adult Support and Protection Act Code of Practice, para 4.7.
[7]   For further information see chapters 7 and 11.

In line with this last principle, the code of practice states the local authority should keep the adult informed at every stage of the process unless this would risk prejudicing investigations[8]. The code recognises, however, that there may be situations where the local authority will have to weigh up the need to involve the adult against the ultimate benefit a successful investigation might produce.

In line with the principle of participation, if the local authority considers it may need to intervene, it should consider whether the adult should be referred to an independent advocacy organisation or provided with other appropriate services[9].

Allocation of inquiries

6.3 While the primary legal responsibility for making inquiries rests with the local authority, adult protection committees will need to establish local procedures for allocating inquiries among the various organisations and professionals involved.

For example, where a local authority receives a report that a health worker is abusing a vulnerable person in a long-term ward, it may be sensible for the health board to carry out the inquiry and report to the local authority. Similarly, if the local authority has concerns about financial risk to an adult who has a financial guardian, the Public Guardian might be best placed to carry out the inquiry.

In sexual abuse cases involving children, government guidance recommends joint inquiries involving the police, social work and health services[10]. This model may be helpful in adult protection cases.

Visits

6.4 The Adult Support and Protection Act gives the local authority the formal power to enter any place if this is considered necessary as part of an investigation to establish whether an adult in the premises is an adult

---

[8] See, for example, Adult Support and Protection Act Code of Practice, para 4.12.

[9] ASP(S)A 2007, s6.

[10] See *Child Abuse, Child Protection and the Law*, Alison Cleland, W Green & Son Ltd (2008), chapter 2, para 027.

at risk and whether the council needs to take any action (under the Adult Support and Protection Act or otherwise) to protect him from harm[11].

A visit must be at a reasonable time and the officer must state the objective of the visit and produce evidence of his authority to visit[12]. Good practice will be to provide notice of a visit where possible, although it is recognised that in some cases an unannounced visit might maximise the chances of getting access to the adult[13].

Another person can accompany a council officer on the visit[14]. Some examples of circumstances in which this might be helpful are listed in the code of practice:

- **To facilitate joint investigation of concerns.** For example allowing the council officer to investigate concerns jointly with a key worker, a police officer, health professional or a representative from the Care Commission or Office of the Public Guardian.

- **To help assess the risk to the adult.** A general practitioner, community nurse, key worker or other person already known to the adult and any other members of the household might be involved.

- **To assist with communication.** For example, in cases where English is not the adult's first language or he uses British Sign Language[15].

If there is concern that the council officer might risk violence or threats at the premises, consideration should be given to how the visit will take place, including involving the police, if necessary[16].

If the council officer is refused entry, he may not use force to gain entry[17], but the local authority may apply for a warrant for entry.

---

[11] ASP(S)A 2007, s7(1). This includes a right to enter any adjacent place for the same purpose. ASP(S)A 2007, s7(2). See chapter 3 for the definition of council officer.
[12] ASP(S)A 2007, ss36(1) and (2).
[13] Adult Support and Protection Act Code of Practice, para 5.15.
[14] ASP(S)A 2007, s36(3).
[15] Adult Support and Protection Act Code of Practice, para 5.6.
[16] Adult Support and Protection Act Code of Practice, para 5.8.
[17] ASP(S)A 2007, s36(4).

Warrant for visit

6.5   Where a council officer has been refused entry, the local authority should consider whether a different approach might be more successful[18]. However it has the option of applying to sheriff court for a warrant for entry to carry out a visit[19].

The sheriff may grant a warrant for entry if he is satisfied that a council officer has been (or reasonably expects to be) refused entry or unable to enter the premises or that any attempt by a council officer to visit the place without a warrant would defeat the object of the visit[20].

The warrant for entry authorises a council officer to be accompanied by a police constable. The police constable can use reasonable force to gain entry[21]. The code of practice emphasises that force is '...*an absolute last resort, to be used in very exceptional circumstances, and only when all other options have been exhausted*'[22].

The warrant must be used within 72 hours of being granted[23]. In urgent cases the local authority can apply to a justice of the peace for a warrant[24].

Interviews

6.6   During the course of a formal visit the council officer may interview anyone over the age of 16 who is in the premises[25]. This includes both the adult who may be at risk and any carers, relatives or friends or other service users.

The officer can insist that the interview be held in private[26] but should, of course, ask the adult whether he wishes another person to be present, such as a family member, carer or independent advocate[27].

[18]   Adult Support and Protection Act Code of Practice, para 5.20.
[19]   ASP(S)A 2007, s37(1)(a).
[20]   ASP(S)A 2007, s38.
[21]   ASP(S)A 2007, s37.
[22]   Para 5.27.
[23]   ASP(S)A 2007, s37(2).
[24]   ASP(S)A 2007, s40(1). See chapter 8 for additional information about dealing with emergencies.
[25]   ASP(S)A 2007, s8(1).
[26]   ASP(S)A 2007, s8.
[27]   Adult Support and Protection Act Code of Practice, para 6.10.

The council officer should consider how to maximise the adult's participation in the interview and whether any communication assistance would facilitate the interview[28].

No one is required to answer any questions during an interview and people must be informed of that fact before the interview begins[29]. If an adult at risk (or any other adult in the place being interviewed) refuses to answer questions, the local authority has no power to override the refusal and compel participation[30]. The concept of undue pressure (explained below) cannot be used in these circumstances.

Medical examinations

6.7   In some cases it will be desirable for a medical examination to take place, in particular, where the adult has suffered injuries that need to be treated. An examination might also provide evidence of harm that will help an application for a banning order or criminal prosecution.

The Adult Support and Protection Act provides that a health professional[31] visiting an adult with a council officer may examine anyone in the place who is believed to be an adult at risk[32]. The examination may be held in private.

The adult has the right to refuse to consent to a medical examination and he must be informed of this before any medical examination takes place[33].

The code of practice suggests that if an adult is not able to give informed consent to the medical examination, the local authority should establish whether there is a welfare attorney with relevant powers who may be able to consent on his behalf. If not, it suggests that consideration should be given to the use of the Adults with Incapacity Act or Mental Health (Care and Treatment) Act[34].

---

[28]   Adult Support and Protection Act Code of Practice, para 6.8.
[29]   ASP(S)A 2007, s8(2).
[30]   ASP(S)A 2007, s35(6).
[31]   This means a doctor, nurse or midwife. ASP(S)A 2007, s52(2). Scottish Ministers have powers to extend this list to include, for example, occupational therapists.
[32]   ASP(S)A 2007, s9.
[33]   ASP(S)A 2007, s9(2).
[34]   Adult Support and Protection Act Code of Practice, para 7.6.

It would clearly be good practice, and in accordance with Adult Support and Protection Act principles, to involve any welfare attorney, named person or other person with powers under the Adults with Incapacity in any requests to carry out a medical examination. However, the Adult Support and Protection Act does not specifically require the informed consent of the adult to the examination. It simply gives the adult the right to refuse.

In such situations a healthcare professional might consider that, where the adult did not appear to object to or refuse the examination, he could carry out the examination using the general authority under s47 of the Adults with Incapacity Act or, in an emergency, under the common law of necessity (see below). Alternatively, if the adult has a mental disorder, it may be helpful to consider the use of the warrant provisions of the Mental Health (Care and Treatment) Act (see below).

Access to records

6.8   A council officer may require anyone holding health, financial or other records relating to someone whom he believes to be an adult at risk to make the records (or copies of them) available to him[35].

The legislation does not prescribe the form a request should take, although if it is not made in the context of a visit, it must be in writing[36]. Email requests are permissible[37].

The council officer should be able to demonstrate he is authorised to access records and each local authority should have agreed procedures in place for obtaining and verifying authorisation[38]. This could involve specifying post holders at certain grades have authority to make requests.

Any other person the council officer considers appropriate can also inspect the records[39].

Health records can only be inspected by a health professional[40]. These are records relating to an individual's physical or mental health made by

---

[35]   ASP(S)A 2007, s10.
[36]   ASP(S)A 2007, s10(2).
[37]   ASP(S)A 2007, s10(6).
[38]   Adult Support and Protection Act Code of Practice, para 8.22.
[39]   ASP(S)A 2007, s10(4).
[40]   This means a doctor, nurse or midwife. ASP(S)A 2007, s52(2).

or on behalf of a health professional in connection with the care of the individual. Records made, for example, by a psychologist or occupational therapist do not, at present, come within these rules, as such professions are not currently regarded as health professions for the purposes of the Adult Support and Protection Act. They could be inspected, but it would not be necessary for a health professional to do this.

It is an offence to refuse or otherwise fail to comply with a request to make records available without reasonable excuse[41]. This is punishable by a fine not exceeding level 3 on the standard scale and/or three months' imprisonment.

That said, it is unlikely that criminal law would be used other than in highly exceptional circumstances. A reasonable belief that the person did not have appropriate authority is likely to be a legitimate defence. The code of practice anticipates that compulsion will be a last resort and states that *'[c]ouncils should make reasonable efforts to resolve disagreements when record holders refuse to disclose them. Informal or independent conciliation might be considered, depending on the circumstances and reasons given for refusal'*[42].

It is good practice for agreements to be reached with the record holder about the length of time records should be kept and how they are returned or destroyed[43]. Some of these issues are likely to be decided locally by adult protection committees.

Chapter 11 discusses the confidentiality issues these provisions raise.

PRINCIPLES AND PRACTICE

While it is essential that any adult protection concerns are taken seriously, with the results of any investigation recorded, this does not mean that every investigation must follow formal procedures. A less restrictive intervention may be appropriate, provided this is consistent with the overall aim of protecting the adult.

The Adult Support and Protection Act code of practice suggests that where an adult is known to services it may be appropriate for him to have an initial discussion with someone known to him, such as an

[41]   ASP(S)A 2007, s49(2).
[42]   Adult Support and Protection Act Code of Practice, para 8.27.
[43]   Adult Support and Protection Act Code of Practice, para 8.25.

adult support worker, rather than a professional with whom he has had no previous contact[44]. Such an interview may suggest ways of supporting the adult or a carer and remove the need for further interventions.

This approach is clearly in accordance with the principle of minimum necessary intervention, although it would also be important for the local authority to review the situation in the future, to ensure that the issues remain resolved.

It is also important that this approach does not detract from the importance of taking questions of risk very seriously, and, in particular, of ensuring that those who are victims of crime receive access to justice. If a crime is suspected, the police should be involved. It may be necessary to seek advice from them if there is concern about preserving evidence needed for a subsequent prosecution.

Assessment orders

6.9 If it is not possible to interview or examine an adult at risk during a visit, the local authority can apply to the sheriff court for an assessment order. This authorises moving the adult to a specified place so that the interview or medical examination can take place[45].

An assessment order may be appropriate if the local authority needs to establish if the person is an adult at risk and whether or not the local authority needs to take action (under the Adult Support and Protection Act or otherwise) to protect him from harm[46].

Grounds for order

6.10 The sheriff will only grant an assessment order if satisfied that:

- There are reasonable grounds to suspect that the person is an adult at risk who is being or is likely to suffer serious harm;

- The order is necessary to establish this;

[44]   Adult Support and Protection Act Code of Practice, para 4.7.
[45]   ASP(S)A 2007, s11(1).
[46]   ASP(S)A 2007, s11(2).

- The adult consents to the order or has been unduly pressured to refuse consent;

- An interview or medical examination cannot take place during the course of a visit without the adult being moved; and

- The place to which the adult will be moved is suitable and available[47]. (This place could be a friend or relative's house or a care home, hospital or GP surgery. In light of the minimum necessary intervention principle, the place chosen should be that which is least disruptive for the adult, while still able to facilitate the interview or medical examination.)

It should be noted that the sheriff must be satisfied that there is a risk of 'serious harm' rather than 'harm'. This is required because the granting of a protection order is considered a serious intervention in an adult's life[48]. There is no definition of 'serious harm' in the legislation, so an assessment will need to be made in individual cases. The code of practice acknowledges that what constitutes serious harm will be different for different people[49].

An assessment order will only be granted if it is not practical to interview or examine the adult without removing him. This might be necessary where a third party is thought to be pressuring the adult or otherwise obstructing the investigation.

This does not mean that the council must have previously tried and failed to examine the person during the course of a visit. There may be circumstances, perhaps where an adult or carers are known to services, where the council officer will be aware that he will not be able to obtain access to the adult during the course of a visit. In such circumstances it might be pointless for the council officer to attempt to visit without an order.

Making the application

6.11 The local authority's legal department will generally make the application. The court will require evidence on oath and generally both the local authority's solicitor and the authorised council officer will appear before the sheriff. For court procedure, see chapter 10.

---

[47]   ASP(S)A 2007, ss12, 13.
[48]   Adult Support and Protection Act Code of Practice, para 1.11.
[49]   Adult Support and Protection Act Code of Practice, para 1.12.

Limits to powers

6.12 The adult cannot be compelled to participate in an interview or a medical examination even if he is thought to be under undue pressure (explained below). Therefore, if it is known that the adult will refuse to participate, an assessment order might be of limited use and the local authority should consider other formal and informal approaches. Where the adult lacks capacity, or requires treatment for a mental disorder, it may be possible to use other legislation. (See below.)

An assessment order does not carry the power to detain the adult, who can choose to leave at any time[50].

Impact of order

6.13 An assessment order is valid from the date specified in the order and must be used within seven days, after which it lapses[51]. The local authority continues to have a duty of care and so must provide reasonable assistance to allow the adult to return to the place from where he was removed, or another suitable place.

The adult must only be taken to the place specified on the order, but may agree to go to some other place. The assessment should be carried out in the shortest time practicable, so as to minimise any possible distress or confusion to the adult[52].

An anomaly in the legislation relates to the protection of the adult's property. When an adult is moved under a removal order, the local authority is under a duty to protect his property[53]. However, there is no corresponding legal obligation where the move is authorised by an assessment order.

However, it is possible that an obligation to protect property could be implied from the European Convention on Human Rights, which provides that an individual is entitled to peaceful enjoyment of his possessions[54]. A public authority cannot place restrictions on an individual's ability to enjoy his property without good reason and any interference must be legal, legitimate, necessary and proportionate.

---

[50]   Adult Support and Protection Act Code of Practice, para 9.14.
[51]   ASP(S)A 2007, s11(3).
[52]   Adult Support and Protection Act Code of Practice, para 9.35.
[53]   ASP(S)A 2007, s19.
[54]   Protocol 1, article 1 of the European Convention on Human Rights.

Where the sheriff grants an assessment order, a warrant for entry is automatically attached to the order[55]. (See above.)

Appeals

6.14   There is no appeal against the granting of, or the sheriff's refusal to grant, an assessment order.

Removal orders

6.15   There may be a situation where the local authority is concerned that an adult at risk needs to be protected from harm. In some circumstances, it may be appropriate for the local authority to apply to the sheriff for a removal order. This authorises the local authority to move an adult at risk to a specific place to allow steps to be taken to protect him from harm[56].

A removal order includes the power to enter premises to move the adult[57]. This could be the adult's home or any public, private or commercial premises. A removal order is primarily aimed at protecting the adult, not at assessing his needs or carrying out a medical examination[58].

As a removal order is a serious intervention in an adult's life, the code of practice suggests it should be only used when all other options have been explored and exhausted[59]. However, protecting the adult from harm will provide a benefit to the adult within the terms of the Act's principles. Undue delay in applying for an order while all other options are investigated may not be appropriate in some cases involving serious harm or risk of serious harm.

Making the application

6.16   As with assessment orders, the local authority legal department will need to become involved. See chapter 10 for court procedure.

---

[55]   ASP(S)A 2007, s38(1).
[56]   ASP(S)A 2007, s14(1).
[57]   ASP(S)A 2007, s16.
[58]   Adult Support and Protection Act Code of Practice, para 10.2.
[59]   Adult Support and Protection Act Code of Practice, para 10.13.

Emergency applications

6.17 In urgent situations, the local authority can ask a justice of the peace to grant an emergency removal order[60]. The time limits for emergency orders are different and are discussed in more detail in chapter 8.

Grounds for order

6.18 The sheriff will only grant a removal order if satisfied that:

- There is reasonable cause to believe that the person is an adult at risk who is likely to suffer serious harm if not moved to another place[61];

- A removal order is necessary to protect the adult;

- The adult consents to the order or has been unduly pressured into refusing consent[62]; and

- The place to which the adult is to be moved is suitable and available[63]. (There is no legal requirement that a removal order specify the place from where adult is to be removed. However, it must always specify the place to which the adult will be moved. If a decision is made to move the adult somewhere else, either a fresh application for a removal order will be necessary, or it may be possible to apply to vary the order.)

Impact of order

6.19 The removal order authorises a council officer (or someone nominated by the local authority) to move the adult to the place specified in the order. It also authorises the local authority to take such reasonable steps as it thinks fit to protect the adult from harm[64].

---

[60]   ASP(S)A 2007, s40(1)(a).
[61]   As with assessment orders 'serious harm' rather than 'harm' must be established.
[62]   ASP(S)A 2007, s35. This is discussed further below.
[63]   ASP(S)A 2007, s15.
[64]   ASP(S)A 2007, s14(1).

A removal order must be used within 72 hours of the date it is issued[65]. This means the adult must be moved within that time. A warrant for entry is automatically attached to the order[66]. (See above.)

If the adult moves to a different address before any action is taken under the removal order, and a warrant is required for entry to the premises, the previous warrant will not be valid and a new application will be necessary. The removal order will remain valid, unless it specified the place from where the adult was to be removed.

No detention

6.20 Although a removal order includes no power to detain the adult, the legislation is not explicit about what happens if the adult chooses to leave. However, the local authority will continue to have a duty of care and should make reasonable arrangements to return the adult to the place from where he was removed, or indeed any other appropriate place.

Expiry of order

6.21 The legislation specifies that the removal order expires after a period of seven days[67]. However, the significance of these seven days is limited, because the legislation does not carry any powers of detention. The adult must be allowed to leave the specified place at any time if he wishes to do so, unless he can be detained under the Mental Health (Care and Treatment) Act.

The code of practice says that a further application for a removal order should not be made on the expiry of the order with the intention of extending the order. The removal period should aim to be for as short as possible a time, in line with the general principles of benefit, least restriction and the adult's wishes[68].

Contact conditions

6.22 The removal order may contain specific provisions allowing certain person(s) to have contact with the adult at risk at certain times during the

---

[65]   ASP(S)A 2007, s14(1)(a).
[66]   ASP(S)A 2007, s39(1).
[67]   ASP(S)A 2007, s14(2).
[68]   Adult Support and Protection Act Code of Practice, paras 10.47–48.

currency of the order. The order may spell out the conditions attaching to such contact[69].

Before making such a requirement the sheriff must consider any representations made by the local authority, the adult at risk or any other interested party[70]. (The sheriff can waive this rule in exceptional cases[71].)

Variation or recall

6.23 A sheriff can vary or recall an order within the seven-day period. This can be on the application of the adult at risk, the local authority or any other interested party. A variation cannot be used to extend the order beyond the original seven-day duration[72].

If the sheriff recalls the removal order, he may direct the council to return the adult to the place from where he was removed or to some other place. The sheriff should have regard to the adult's wishes before specifying some other place[73].

Protection of property

6.24 The local authority is under a duty to take reasonable steps to protect and secure the property of an individual moved under a removal order if the adult is unable to deal with it, and no other suitable arrangements have been, or are being, made. A council officer may enter any premises (and any adjacent place) where he knows or believes such property is situated[74]. The costs of doing this cannot be recovered from the adult[75].

Appeals

6.25 As with assessment orders, there is no appeal against a removal order, or against the refusal of the sheriff to grant an order. However either the adult at risk, or anyone else with an interest in the adult's well

---

[69]   ASP(S)A 2007, s12(2).
[70]   ASP(S)A 2007, s15(3).
[71]   ASP(S)A 2007, s41(2).
[72]   ASP(S)A 2007, ss17(2) and (4).
[73]   ASP(S)A 2007, s17(3).
[74]   ASP(S)A 2007, s19.
[75]   ASP(S)A 2007, s18(5).

being or property can apply to the sheriff for a variation or recall (cancellation) of an order[76].

Banning orders

6.26 In some situations, the local authority might consider applying for a banning order. This is granted by a sheriff and bans a third party from a specified place or places[77]. The order can prohibit the third party from moving anything from the specified place as well as requiring him to do, or refrain from doing, anything else considered necessary. Banning orders are explored in more detail in chapter 10. Emergency orders are also available. See chapter 8.

The adult's consent

6.27 Under the Adult Support and Protection Act, the sheriff must not make an order if it is known that the affected adult at risk has refused to consent to the granting of an order[78]. Similarly a person cannot take any action authorised by an order if he knows the affected adult at risk has refused to consent to the action[79].

The legislation clearly envisages the adult at risk will be advised of the proposed order and asked whether he consents. What this means in practice for local authorities (or for any individual making an application for a banning order) is not yet clear. It could certainly be implied that the local authority should actively seek the adult's views.

The legislation does not prohibit the sheriff from granting an order where the views of the adult are not known and cannot reasonably be ascertained. However, it is likely that sheriffs will inquire into the position of the adult at risk and so the local authority should be in a position to explain the steps it has taken to obtain the adult's views and what those views are.

There is also an issue about what happens in situations where the adult refuses to consent to an order but it is believed that he lacks the capacity to make that decision, perhaps because he is not fully able to protect his

[76]   ASP(S)A 2007, s17(1).
[77]   ASP(S)A 2007, s19.
[78]   ASP(S)A 2007, s35(1).
[79]   ASP(S)A 2007, s35(2).

own interests. The code of practice suggests that in such circumstances there is no need to prove undue pressure and that the adult's refusal to consent can be disregarded[80].

However, the legislation states that an order must not be made if the adult has refused to consent, unless undue pressure is established. The concept of undue pressure is explained below. Therefore, it could be argued that a sheriff, or person using an order, would have to respect a refusal to consent, regardless of the adult's capacity. A person may have the capacity to refuse an order even where he lacks the capacity properly to safeguard or promote his own welfare or property interests within the meaning of the Adults with Incapacity Act.

If undue pressure cannot be established and the adult is believed to lack capacity then it would be possible to make an application under the Adults with Incapacity Act for the appointment of a guardian with the power to consent, or refuse consent, to an order under the Adult Support and Protection Act. Alternatively, if the adult with incapacity has a mental disorder, it may be more appropriate to consider the use of a warrant or order under the Mental Health (Care and Treatment) Act, which can permit an assessment, medical examination and, if necessary, the removal of the person at risk to a place of safety without his consent.

Some people may, of course, lack the capacity either to consent or to refuse an order. For example, they might be unable to express or communicate a preference at all, because of profound learning disabilities. Where the sheriff is satisfied that this is the case, and that a person is unable to express a view either way, he may make an order regardless of the adult's consent.

Undue pressure

6.28 There is a major exception to the requirement that the adult must consent. The Act specifies that an order can be granted, or used, without consent in situations where either the sheriff, or the person seeking to enforce the order, reasonably believes that:

• The affected adult at risk has been unduly pressured to refuse consent; and

---

[80] Adult Support and Protection Act Code of Practice paras 9.25 and 10.24.

- That there are no steps that could reasonably be taken with the adult's consent which would protect the adult from the harm which the order or action is intended to prevent[81].

The Act provides an example of a situation in which 'undue pressure' is present[82]. It states that an adult at risk can be considered to be under undue pressure if:

- The person causing the harm that the order, or action, is intended to prevent, is someone in whom the adult at risk has confidence and trust; and

- The adult at risk would consent to the order or action if he did not have confidence and trust in that person.

This is primarily intended to cover situations where an adult refuses to consent to action because someone else is pressuring him. This could be a family member, partner, spouse, friend or anyone else with a close personal relationship to the adult.

There will be cases where the adult is afraid of the consequences of cooperating because he has been threatened or told that something will happen. Someone might have convinced the adult that he will not be believed, will be blamed or even be removed and held in custody or a hospital.

A refusal to participate in an interview or to consent to a medical examination cannot be overridden by the concept of undue pressure[83].

The concept of undue pressure can, in theory, apply to applications for orders in cases involving self-harm or abuse. However, this would only be the case where a third party is the cause of the undue pressure. Where there is no third party an adult's refusal to consent to an order cannot be overridden.

While the concept of undue pressure will be useful in some cases, it is not thought that it will be often used as overriding the wishes of an adult is a significant intervention. There is always a need to balance the right of the adult to make his own choices with the local authority's obligation to protect those experiencing harm or abuse. Some of these issues are

---

[81]   ASP(S)A 2007, s35(3).
[82]   ASP(S)A 2007, s35(4).
[83]   ASP(S)A 2007, s35(6).

explored further in chapter 12. Interventions might also have more chance of success in the longer term if the adult agrees they should happen.

Outcome of inquiries

6.29   In some cases the local authority's inquiries may suggest further action is needed. In other cases no further action will be needed. In all cases proper recording is essential, because events may indicate that a concerning situation is worsening. If no further action is required, the local authority should place a note on the adult's case file on the circumstances giving rise to the initial inquiries, the action taken and why no further action was required[84].

ADULTS WITH INCAPACITY ACT POWERS AND DUTIES

6.30   The Adults with Incapacity Act will be of relevance in some cases where an adult is incapable of making some or all decisions about his welfare, medical matters or his property or finances[85]. It imposes duties on the local authority to investigate and provides a regime for authorising such decisions. These remedies are discussed in chapters 9 and 10.

Duty to investigate

6.31   The local authority has a general duty to investigate any circumstances where it is aware that the personal welfare of an adult with incapacity appears to be at risk[86].

It must also investigate complaints about welfare attorneys, welfare guardians and people with welfare powers under intervention orders[87]. (Concerns about risk to the person's property and finances can be passed to the Public Guardian, see chapter 7.)

The local authority should consult with the Public Guardian and/or

---

[84]   Adult Support and Protection Act Code of Practice, para 4.14.
[85]   Adults with Incapacity (Scotland) Act 2000, s1(6).
[86]   AWI(S)A 2000, s10(d).
[87]   AWI(S)A 2000, s10(1)(c).

the Mental Welfare Commission if they have an interest in the case[88]. These bodies are legally obliged to cooperate with the local authority[89].

The Adults with Incapacity Act code of practice gives guidance on good practice[90]. The local authority should generally arrange to visit the adult, and must consider the principles of the Act when carrying out its investigations. Following its investigations, the local authority will consider whether it is necessary to make an application to the sheriff to safeguard the property, financial affairs or personal welfare of the adult[91]. It should copy its investigation report to the Mental Welfare Commission[92].

Emergencies

6.32   The use of the Act in emergencies is explored further in chapter 8 and guardianship and intervention orders are discussed in chapter 10.

Medical examinations and treatment

6.33   In some cases an adult may agree to seek care and treatment in a residential care home or hospital, either temporarily or permanently. Complex legal issues arise where the person lacks the capacity to consent to care or treatment. This section looks at the issues.

Where a medical examination is considered necessary the adult should be asked for his consent. If the adult has capacity and is able to make decisions, a medical examination or treatment cannot be carried out without such consent[93].

The concept of undue pressure under the Adult Support and Protection Act does not apply to a refusal to consent to medical examination or treatment.

---

[88]   AWI(S)A 2000, s10(1)(b).
[89]   AWI(S)A 2000, s12(2).
[90]   *Code of Practice for local authorities exercising functions under the Act* Scottish Executive (2001) ('the local authority code'), Part 4.
[91]   AWI(S)A 2000, s12(1).
[92]   Local authority code, para 4.38.
[93]   ASP(S)A 2007, s35. In addition, a medical examination or treatment without consent can be considered an assault.

Where a patient is unable to consent to treatment, a medical practitioner may treat the patient under the general authority in the Adults with Incapacity Act[94]. A doctor relying on the general authority to treat must issue a certificate in the prescribed form[95]. Other health professionals, including dentists, opticians and registered nurses, may sign certificates for treatment within their area of expertise provided they have undergone prescribed training on assessing capacity[96].

The certificate can cover a specific treatment, such as an operation, or a range of treatments, as set out in a treatment plan. A treatment plan avoids the need for excessive certification for an adult with various predictable health-care needs[97].

The general authority does not allow the use of force or detention, other than in an emergency[98] or the admission of an adult to hospital for psychiatric treatment against his will[99].

Where a guardian or attorney has been appointed, he will be asked for consent. However, the statutory certificate must still be completed, as it is the completed certificate that provides the authority to treat rather than the consent of another person. Where a guardian or attorney disagrees with proposals for medical treatment, the decision can be referred to an independent medical practitioner. The Mental Welfare Commission can provide additional information about this procedure.

In an emergency, where the patient is unable to consent to or refuse treatment, a health professional can treat him under the common law doctrine of necessity in order to save life or prevent serious injury[100].

POWERS AND DUTIES UNDER MENTAL HEALTH (CARE AND TREATMENT) ACT

6.34 The Mental Health (Care and Treatment) Act put into effect some of the recommendations of the Scottish Law Commission's *Report on*

---

[94] AWI(S)A 2000, s 47(1).
[95] The form is on the Scottish Government's Adults with Incapacity website.
[96] AWI(S)A 2000, (as amended), s47(1A).
[97] See Adults with Incapacity Act Part 5 Code of Practice, Scottish Executive (2002), paras 2.19–2.26.
[98] AWI(S)A 2000, s47(7)(a).
[99] AWI(S)A 2000, s47(7)(b).
[100] For more detail see *Adult Incapacity*, Adrian Ward, W Green (2003), para 14.30.

Vulnerable Adults, insofar as it related to adults with mental disorders[101]. It was thus the forerunner of the Adult Support and Protection Act, and can be relevant in adult protection, particularly in cases involving individuals with a mental disorder who are at risk of self-harm, abuse or neglect.

As well as giving local authorities clear powers and duties to investigate where someone with a mental disorder in their area may be at risk, the Act also provides that if necessary a local authority can obtain a warrant to enter premises, to authorise a medical examination or to gain access to medical records. It can apply to move someone to hospital or a care home for assessment and medical examination.

Where an adult at risk has a mental disorder and may need medical treatment for the disorder, further intervention may be sought under the Mental Health (Care and Treatment) Act to provide care and treatment to him[102]. (See chapter 10.) The Act also includes the possibility of criminal charges where a local authority is obstructed in an investigation (see chapter 14).

Duty to inquire

6.35 The Act places a local authority under a clear duty to investigate where it believes that a person aged 16 or over has a mental disorder and may be at risk. The risk might be:

- Ill-treatment, neglect or inadequate care (other than care in hospital), either currently or in the past.

- Where someone appearing to be living alone or without care appears unable to look after himself or his property or finances.

- Risk to other people because of the person's mental disorder (unless he is already in hospital).

- Risk of loss or damage to someone's property because of his mental disorder.[103]

The local authority should bear in mind the principles of the Mental Health (Care and Treatment) Act. It should not seek formal powers if a

---

[101] Scottish Law Commission (1997) No. 158.
[102] Under sections 36, 44 or 63 of the Act.
[103] Mental Health (Care and Treatment) (Scotland) Act 2003, s33.

less restrictive alternative is possible. It should try to involve the person at risk and any carers as far as possible when carrying out investigations and bear in mind the wishes of the person at risk.

The Code of Practice gives further advice on how these powers should operate in practice[104].

Cooperation with local authority

6.36 A wide range of bodies should cooperate with a local authority carrying out a Mental Health (Care and Treatment) Act investigation. These include the Mental Welfare Commission, the Public Guardian, the Care Commission and any relevant health board[105]. These bodies must cooperate, except where the organisation believes that this would prejudice their other duties[106].

Warrants for entry

6.37 If the local authority is unable to, or has reasons for believing it will be unable to, gain access to the adult, it can apply to a sheriff or justice of the peace for a warrant to enter any premises for the purpose of its investigation[107]. The mental health officer generally makes the application

A warrant authorises the mental health officer and anyone named in the warrant to enter the premises within eight days of the warrant, and authorises a police constable accompanying the mental health officer to force entry[108]. Before granting such a warrant, the sheriff or justice of the peace must have evidence on oath that the mental health officer is likely to be denied access.

If forced entry is used, the mental health officer must take steps to protect the person's premises and belongings[109]. The code of practice contains guidance to minimise the impact on the person[110].

[104] Mental Health (Care and Treatment) Act Code of Practice, vol 1, chapter 15.
[105] MH(CT)(S)A 2003, s34.
[106] MH(CT)(S)A 2003, s34(4).
[107] MH(CT)(S)A 2003, s35.
[108] MH(CT)(S)A 2003, s35(2).
[109] Mental Health (Care and Treatment) Act Code of Practice, vol 1, para 15.24.
[110] Mental Health (Care and Treatment) Act Code of Practice, vol 1, para 15.25.

Medical examinations and access to records

6.38 The Mental Health (Care and Treatment) Act also provides that a mental health officer can apply to a sheriff or justice of the peace for a warrant to allow a medical practitioner to carry out a medical examination of an adult with a mental disorder who is believed to be at risk. The mental health officer must demonstrate that such an examination is necessary and that the adult involved will not consent[111]. (This could be either because the mental health officer has been unable to speak to the person or because the person has refused consent.)

The application is to the sheriff or justice for the area where the person is living[112].

If the order is granted, it allows the adult to be detained for up to three hours so that a medical examination can take place. The three hours runs from the time of the detention, not the time of the warrant. The procedure should be in accordance with the local psychiatric emergency plan[113]. This examination can happen without the adult's consent.

Access to records

6.39 The mental health officer may also apply for a warrant to allow access to someone's medical records[114]. The application is to the sheriff or justice for the area where the person is living.

The mental health officer must satisfy the court that it is necessary for a doctor to see the records and the mental health officer cannot obtain the person's consent[115].

If the court grants the warrant, any person who has the medical records must allow the doctor named in the warrant to inspect them[116].

Making the application

6.40 A mental health officer may apply for all or any of the warrants.

---

[111] MH(CT)(S)A 2003, s35(4).
[112] MH(CT)(S)A 2003, s35(6).
[113] Mental Health (Care and Treatment Act Code of Practice, vol 1, para 15.28.
[114] MH(CT)(S)A 2003, s35.
[115] MH(CT)(S)A 2003, s35(7).
[116] MH(CT)(S)A 2003, s35(8).

For a warrant to enter premises, a mental health officer employed by the local authority where the premises are situated should make the application. For other warrants, the mental health officer must be an employee of the local authority conducting the enquiries[117].

The mental health officer will be required to attend the hearing and to give evidence on oath[118].

There are prescribed forms for the application and warrant[119]. These are available on the Scottish Government's mental health law website.

As soon as possible after the hearing, the mental health officer must notify the Mental Welfare Commission of the outcome[120].

It is not possible to appeal against the decision of the sheriff or justice to grant or refuse a warrant[121].

Removal orders

6.41 Removal orders available under the Mental Health (Care and Treatment) Act[122] are somewhat different from those available under the Adult Support and Protection Act. This section attempts to highlight the differences.

A removal order is suitable only if someone is a risk to themselves or at risk from others. Short-term (or emergency) detention might be appropriate where someone may pose a risk to others. A removal order does not authorise the giving of medical treatment to the person.

The application is to the sheriff of the area where the person at risk is living. In an emergency, a justice of the peace may grant an order.

Making the application

6.42 The mental health officer making the application should be an employee of the local authority for the area where the person is living[123].

---

117   MH(CT)(S)A 2003, s35(12).
118   MH(CT)(S)A 2003, s35(1).
119   Mental Health (Form of Documents) (Scotland) Regulations 2006 SSI 2006/12.
120   MH(CT)(S)A 2003, s35(10).
121   MH(CT)(S)A 2003, s35(11).
122   Under MH(CT)(S)A 2003, s293.
123   MH(CT)(S)A 2003, s293(8).

The application is to the sheriff for that area[124]. A statutory form[125] is available on the Scottish Government's mental health law website.

The mental health officer must satisfy the sheriff that the person is aged over 16 and has a mental disorder, that he is likely to suffer significant harm if he does not go to a place of safety, and that one or more of the grounds in para **6.35** above apply to the person[126].

The sheriff may dispense with a hearing if he considers this would cause delay likely to prejudice the interests of the person at risk[127].

Effect of order

6.43 A removal order authorises the mental health officer and anyone named in the order to enter the place specified in the order within 72 hours of the making of the order. A police officer may accompany them and may use reasonable force to gain access. The person can be taken to a place of safety (see below) within 72 hours of the order.

Unlike an Adult Support and Protection Act order, a person subject to a Mental Health (Care and Treatment) Act removal order can be detained under the order. The detention can last for up to seven days, as specified in the order[128]. In line with the principles of the Act, if less than seven days is sufficient, the mental health officer should apply for a shorter period.

Appeal

6.44 There is no appeal against the sheriff or justice's decision to make or refuse to make a removal order[129], but the person subject to the order and anyone with an interest may apply for a variation or recall.

---

[124] MH(CT)(S)A 2003, s293(4). For procedure, see Act of Sederunt (Summary Applications, Statutory Applications and Appeals etc. Rules) Amendment (Mental Health (Care and Treatment) (Scotland) Act 2003) 2005 Scottish Statutory Instrument 2005/504.

[125] Under the Mental Health (Form of Documents) (Scotland) Regulations 2006 SSI 2006/12.

[126] MH(CT)(S)A 2003, ss293(1), 293(2).

[127] MH(CT)(S)A 2003, s293(7).

[128] MH(CT)(S)A 2003, s293(3). The European Convention of Human Rights permits detention of people with 'unsound mind'. See chapter 12.

[129] MH(CT)(S)A 2003, s296.

The mental health officer must notify all relevant parties of the outcome of the application and advise them of their rights to apply for variation or recall[130]. The mental health officer must also notify the Mental Welfare Commission of the making of the order.

Place of safety

6.45 The removal order will specify the address of the place of safety to which the person is to be taken. The place of safety should be a hospital, a care home service[131] or any other suitable place[132]. A police station should not be used as a place of safety (although it may be necessary to do so in an emergency).

An accident and emergency department is not a suitable place unless the person has significant physical health problems, perhaps because of self harm. A place of safety should have qualified mental health staff. It should generally be a specialist assessment unit linked to, or with access to, a psychiatric hospital or clinic[133]. Unlike the removals under the Adult Support and Protection Act, the Mental Health (Care and Treatment) Act does not envisage the use of private homes for removal orders, and this would not be suitable where someone is to be detained under the order.

Cancellation or variation of removal order

6.46 A person subject to a removal order and any person with an interest in his welfare may apply to a sheriff (not a justice of the peace) to set the order aside or to move the person to a different place[134].

There is a form on the Scottish Government's website[135] that should be submitted to the sheriff court for the area from where the person was moved[136].

The sheriff must give the relevant people a chance to make representations and to lead or produce evidence. These people are the

---

[130] Mental Health (Care and Treatment) Act Code of Practice, vol 1, paras 15.44–15.45.
[131] As defined in the Regulation of Care (Scotland) Act 2001, s2(3).
[132] MH(CT)(S)A 2003, s300.
[133] Mental Health (Care and Treatment) Act Code of Practice, vol 1, para 15.86.
[134] MH(CT)(S)A 2003, s295.
[135] Form MHO7.
[136] MH(CT)(S)A 2003, s295(3).

mental health officer who applied for the removal order, the nearest relative of the person, any guardian or welfare attorney of the person and the person's primary carer[137]. The sheriff cannot dispense with this requirement on grounds of urgency[138].

If the sheriff cancels the order, he may order the local authority to return the person to the place from where he was removed or to another suitable place chosen by the person[139].

It is not possible to appeal against a sheriff's decision to cancel or vary a removal order or to refuse to do so[140].

CHOICE OF PROCEDURES

6.47 There may be cases where it is not clear to a local authority whether to take action to protect an adult at risk under adult protection legislation, the Adults with Incapacity Act or mental health legislation.

The authors understand that some local authorities are advising their staff that if initial inquiries reveal that an adult at risk lacks capacity, or if the adult is already known to services as lacking the capacity to protect his interests, it is not appropriate to intervene under the Adult Support and Protection Act. They advise that action should be taken under the Adults with Incapacity Act or Mental Health (Care and Treatment) Act.

On the other hand, it may be that the investigatory and other powers available under the Adult Support and Protection Act could be appropriately used in a particular case despite the adult's apparent incapacity or mental health issues and even though further long-term measures might be sought under other legislation. For example, the formal visiting powers in section 7 of the Act may provide sufficient authority to enable a council officer to gain access to the adult and others living with him. Under the principle of the least restrictive alternative, this would be preferable to, for example, seeking a warrant under the Mental Health (Care and Treatment) Act.

The authors suggest that all decisions about the appropriate use of legislation should be made on a case-by-case basis. In complex situations, a local authority may need to seek legal advice.

---

[137] Mental Health (Recall or Variation of Removal Order) (Scotland) Regulations 2006 SSI 2006/11.
[138] MH(CT)(S)A 2003, s295(4)–(5).
[139] MH(CT)(S)A 2003, s295(6).
[140] MH(CT)(S)A 2003, s296.

Table **6.1** contrasts the duties of the local authority to investigate the various types of risk an adult might experience and Table **6.2** summarises their investigatory powers.

TABLE 6.1 – Risk to be investigated		
Act	**Person at risk**	**Nature of risk**
ASP(S)A	Person unable to safeguard interests	Physical/psychological harm
	At risk of harm	Fraud/theft etc
	Vulnerable because of disability, illness etc	Self-harm
AWI(S)A	Person with mental disorder (or person unable to communicate) unable to protect welfare/finances/property	Personal welfare Complaints about welfare attorney/guardian/person acting under intervention order
MH(CT)(S)A	Person with mental disorder	Ill treatment/neglect/risk to property/finances Person living alone unable to protect welfare/property/finances

TABLE 6.2 – Powers to investigate		
Act	**Powers given**	**Can adult refuse?**
ASP(S)A	Visit	Yes
	Warrant for visit	No
	Medical examination	Yes
	Access to records	No
	Assessment order + warrant	Yes unless undue pressure
	Removal order + warrant	Yes unless undue pressure
	Banning order	Yes unless undue pressure
AWI(S)A	Medical examination/treatment	Yes if capacity
MH(CT)(S)A	Warrant for entry	No
	Warrant for medical examination	No
	Warrant for assessment	No
	Removal order	No

CONCLUSION

6.48 The local authority has a number of statutory powers to investigate and deal with abuse or harm with, or without, the adult's consent. In some cases, a single piece of legislation will be used, while in others more than one will be necessary to achieve the desired outcome. It is important, where possible, to consider carefully the merits of using each piece of legislation. This will depend on issues such as the nature of the harm, the adult's ability and the desired outcome. Adult Support and Protection Act procedures should be seen as only a part of the legislation available in Scotland to protect adults at risk.

Chapter 7

POWERS AND DUTIES OF OTHER ORGANISATIONS

7.1 While chapter 6 looked at local authorities' powers to gain access, interview and assess adults at risk, the law also gives other bodies powers to intervene in certain circumstances. This chapter looks at the adult protection duties of other organisations, including the police, the Care Commission, the Mental Welfare Commission, the Public Guardian and the police. It also looks briefly at the role of professional regulators.

Adult protection committees will need to develop good practice so that the work of the various agencies is properly co-ordinated and information shared, where appropriate.

CARE COMMISSION

7.2 All local authority care services and all other services offering personal care and/or support are registered with the Care Commission[1]. These include services providing care in the home, residential care, short breaks, respite and day care services. A person employing a carer herself (not through an agency) does not need to register with the Care Commission.

The Care Commission has important powers and duties where an adult using a registered care service might be at risk.

Investigating risk

7.3 An inspection of a service may indicate to the Care Commission that a service user is, or has been, at risk. In addition, anyone can complain to the Care Commission about a service, including a service user receiving a registered service or a carer or family member[2]. Such complaints may raise adult protection concerns.

---

[1]   Regulation of Care (Scotland) Act 2001, s2.
[2]   ROC(S)A 2001, s64.

The Care Commission will refer the allegations or concerns to the local authority, which has the primary role in investigating where an adult is at risk. It will discuss the issues with the local authority and agree on appropriate action. This is the case whether or not the service user has requested such involvement[3]. Under a Memorandum of Understanding between the Care Commission and the Mental Welfare Commission, information may be shared with the Mental Welfare Commission where the adult in question has a mental disorder.

If the Care Commission considers that another body (such as the police or the local authority) has the primary duty to investigate, it will generally await their report before taking further action[4]. However, it will discuss and agree this with the other body and may continue to monitor progress.

Care service providers are legally obliged to notify the Care Commission about adult protection issues, including the death of a service user, any serious injury to a service user, any theft or accident, any allegations of misconduct by the provider or employees and a summary of any complaints made to the provider[5].

However, there is nothing in the legislation requiring notification if a local authority applies for an adult protection order or the court grants an order in a case relating to a registered service. The Care Commission has put in place a system where local authorities can notify it if adult support and protection referrals arise in any registered service[6]. A form of e-notification is available for local authorities to do this[7]. Communication between the organisations and agreement on appropriate action is important in such cases.

Investigatory powers

7.4 Care Commission inspectors have power to enter and inspect premises used for a care service at any time[8]. The inspectors can inspect

---

[3]   Care Commission's Adult Support and Protection Policy and Procedure (2008).
[4]   Care Commission Complaints Procedure (2008), para 2.2.
[5]   The Regulation of Care (Requirements as to Care Services) (Scotland) Regulations 2002 SSI 2002 No 114, regulations 21 and 25.
[6]   See Care Commission's website.
[7]   See Complaints Procedure (above).
[8]   ROC(S)A 2001, s25(2).

records and interview staff and users of the care service. The Care Commission can also interview and seek views from family members, carers, advocacy workers and other relevant parties.

Anyone, including a service user, may refuse to take part in an interview.

Enforcement

7.5   The Care Commission can intervene wherever the health, safety or welfare of anyone using a registered care service might be at risk. It can take enforcement action, such as requiring improvements of a service or imposing conditions[9], for example prohibiting the admission of any new clients, or requiring that a member of staff is replaced. If there is not adequate improvement, it may cancel a service's registration[10].

In urgent situations, where it considers the quality of service is so poor that there is serious risk to life, health or well being, the Care Commission can apply to the sheriff for the immediate cancellation of registration or the variation of conditions of registration[11]. It can also hold a formal inquiry into the operation of care services[12].

It is appropriate to contact the Care Commission about any concerns that a provider is not fit to provide a service, regardless of the possibility of a criminal prosecution[13]. It will liaise with the local authority and the police, if the procurator fiscal decides to proceed with a criminal prosecution.

Contacting the Care Commission

7.6   The Care Commission has a duty to investigate if anyone raises a concern, comment or complaint about the quality of a care service which it registers. This includes service users and people acting on their behalf. A complaint can still be made even where someone has made or is making a complaint to the service provider, or has notified the local

---

9   ROC(S)A 2001, ss10, 13.
10   ROC(S)A, s12.
11   ROC(S)A 2001, s18.
12   ROC(S)A 2001, s65(2).
13   Care Commission's *Adult Protection Policy and Procedure* (2008).

authority about a complaint[14]. Complaints can be made by email, telephone or online and it is possible to complain anonymously or confidentially where this is appropriate.

MENTAL WELFARE COMMISSION

Duty to investigate

7.7 The Mental Welfare Commission's remit extends to everyone (children as well as adults) who has a mental illness, a learning disability or a personality disorder. If such a person is at risk, it can carry out investigations in a wide range of settings.

For example, it can investigate care in prisons and young offenders' institutions, residential care and day services and healthcare (in both community and hospital settings[15]).

The Mental Welfare Commission can inquire into the situation of anyone who is subject to a compulsory order under the Mental Health (Care and Treatment) Act or who is being treated in hospital under the Adults with Incapacity Act[16].

It also has a legal duty to carry out investigations as it considers appropriate where it believes that someone with a mental disorder may be (or has been) at risk. The risk could be:

- That the person is unlawfully detained in hospital.

- Ill-treatment, neglect or inadequate care or treatment, either currently or in the past.

- That someone who appears to live alone or without care is unable to look after herself or her property or finances.

- Loss or damage to a person's property because of her mental disorder, or the risk of such loss in the future[17].

Where the local authority has an overlapping duty to investigate, the Commission generally passes the enquiry on to the local authority. In such cases, it asks that the local authority advise the Commission of the

---

[14] ROC(S)A 2001, s6(2).
[15] Mental Health (Care and Treatment) (Scotland) Act 2003, ss11, 17.
[16] MH(CT)(S)A 2003, s11(2)(b).
[17] MH(CT)(S)A 2003, s33.

results of the investigation. Depending on the outcome, it may then decide to carry out its own investigation. In other cases, it will make informal enquiries or may require the health or social care provider to investigate. Many cases will not result in a formal investigation and report by the Commission, but it can carry out formal inquiries in cases raising particularly important issues.

Following inquiries, it may make recommendations to any body that it considers appropriate, including Scottish Ministers, local authorities, health boards, care homes, individual social workers and doctors and the police[18].

If there is a complaint about a welfare attorney, welfare guardian or a person with welfare powers under an intervention order and the Commission is not satisfied with the local authority's investigation, or the local authority has not investigated, the Commission must receive and investigate the complaint[19]. It should consult with any relevant local authority with an interest in the case[20].

Formal inquiries

7.8 In addition to its ability to make inquiries into any case and to investigate further, as it considers appropriate, the Mental Welfare Commission can carry out a formal inquiry into any case. This can be a semi-judicial process, with witnesses being required to attend and give evidence on oath[21].

Although the Commission has never had to use these formal powers, they remain available should less formal investigations fail to satisfy its requirements. It has carried out a number of 'deficiency of care' inquiries, sometimes at the request of Scottish Ministers[22].

Visiting powers

7.9 The Commission has wide powers to visit people subject to compulsory orders under the Mental Health (Care and Treatment) Act

---

[18]   MH(CT)(S)A 2003, s8.
[19]   Adults with Incapacity (Scotland) Act 2000, s9(1)(d).
[20]   AWI(S)A 2000, s9(1)(c).
[21]   MH(CT)(S)A 2003, s12.
[22]   For details, see its Annual Reports and website.

and the Adults with Incapacity Act. It can also visit people with a mental disorder in hospitals (in both the national health service and independent sector), care home services, secure accommodation, local authority services, prisons and young offenders institutions to inspect the services and facilities. Such visits may be pre-arranged or unannounced[23].

The Mental Welfare Commission can visit people subject to welfare guardianship, intervention orders and welfare powers of attorney[24] and may make further inquiries if the adult appears to be at risk.

Interviews and access to records

7.10 During the course of its visits, the Commission should offer people using the service an opportunity to have a private meeting with Commission staff and discuss any concerns[25].

To carry out its investigations into people at risk, it may need to interview the adult, carers or people who have raised concerns. A Commissioner or other member of its staff can be authorised to interview a service user or indeed anyone else, as considered appropriate. The interview may be in private if the Commission requests this[26].

A medical Commissioner or an appropriately trained member of the Commission's staff can also carry out a medical examination of the adult[27] and an authorised person may inspect any relevant records[28].

Access to facilities

7.11 Various bodies are required to give the Mental Welfare Commission all the help that is necessary to enable it to carry out its functions under the Mental Health (Care and Treatment) Act, including its investigatory functions. They are the Scottish Ministers, local authorities, health boards, including special health boards, the police, the managers of registered care services, prisons and young offender's institutions, the Care Commission and the Public Services Ombudsman[29].

---

[23]   MH(CT)(S)A 2003, s13.
[24]   MH(CT)(S)A 2003, s13.
[25]   MH(CT)(S)A 2003, s13(5).
[26]   MH(CT)(S)A 2003, s14(1).
[27]   MH(CT)(S)A 2003, s15.
[28]   MH(CT)(S)A 2003, s16.
[29]   MH(CT)(S)A 2003, s17.

If the Commission has concerns about the safety of an adult with mental disorder, it can seek the cooperation of these bodies in granting access to facilities and records, or facilitating an interview or medical examination of the adult.

Overlap with local authorities' role

7.12   Some of the Mental Welfare Commission's duties are very similar to those of local authorities. But there are differences. For example, the Commission may inquire into situations arising in hospital, where the local authority has no remit.

The Commission does not have a duty to investigate where a person's mental disorder poses a risk to others. This is the responsibility of the local authority, through its mental health officers.

However if a local authority has failed to act, the Commission could investigate whether there has been a deficiency of care. The Commission may choose to investigate such situations where the risk is a consequence of the deficiency in care and treatment or if the person is living alone or without care. In most cases, however, it would await the outcome of the local authority's investigation.

There remain situations where it is appropriate to raise adult protection concerns with the Commission rather than the local authority. An example could be concerns about the care or treatment of a person staying on a long-term hospital ward.

Overlap with other bodies

7.13   The Commission has signed memorandums of understanding with the Public Guardian and the Care Commission, which explain how they deal with their overlapping functions. For example, the Commission has a duty to investigate if a person's property or finances are at risk. However, unless financial or property concerns are part of a wider welfare problem, it will generally leave such matters to the Public Guardian. Similarly, the Commission will share information and concerns with the Care Commission where appropriate.

OFFICE OF THE PUBLIC GUARDIAN

Duty to investigate

7.14   The Public Guardian has important duties and powers in relation to adults who, because of a mental disorder or an inability to communicate because of a physical disability, may be unable to manage all or part of their property or financial affairs. As well as supervising people with financial powers under parts 2 (when directed by a sheriff), 3 and 6 of the Adults with Incapacity Act, she can also intervene in any case where an adult's property or finances may be at risk.

As with local authorities' duties, there are two parts to her duties. She must investigate any complaint about a financial attorney, a financial guardian, a person with financial powers under an intervention order or a person operating an access to funds scheme (see para 9.16)[30]. She must also investigate wherever she is aware that the property or finances of an adult who might be incapable of managing them appear to be at risk[31]. She may initiate or take part in any legal proceedings needed to safeguard the affairs of an adult whose finances are at risk[32].

Anyone with concerns in such a situation may bring these to the attention of the Public Guardian.

The Public Guardian consults with any relevant local authority and/or the Mental Welfare Commission if they have an interest in the case[33].

Powers to investigate

7.15　When the Public Guardian's staff are carrying out an investigation into possible risk to an adult's property or finances, she may require anyone with financial or property powers under the Adults with Incapacity Act to provide her with the relevant records and with such other information relating to the exercise of the powers as she may reasonably require. She may also require anyone who holds (or has held) funds belonging to an adult, for example a bank or building society, to hand over records and other information[34].

Enforcement

7.16　If a person with powers under the Adults with Incapacity Act misuses those powers and/or the adult's property or financial affairs

---

[30]　AWI(S)A 2000, s6(2)(c).
[31]　AWI(S)A 2000, s6(2)(d).
[32]　AWI(S)A 2000, (as amended by Adult Support and Protection (Scotland) Act 2007), s6(2).
[33]　AWI(S)A 2000, s6(2)(f).
[34]　AWI(S)A 2000, s81A.

seem to be at risk, the Public Guardian may take any steps thought necessary to safeguard those affairs. This may involve making an application to the sheriff for any order deemed necessary. She will also involve the police if she suspects criminal activity. Chapters 10 and 14 look at this in more detail.

Overlap with local authorities' role

7.17   The Adults with Incapacity Act authorises the Public Guardian, rather than the local authority, to investigate financial or property concerns about an adult with mental incapacity. However, the Adult Support and Protection Act gives local authorities a duty to investigate financial risk where the adult is not deemed to be incapable as defined by the Adults with Incapacity Act.

Local adult protection committees will need to work with the Public Guardian to develop protocols for investigations where there may be a question over an adult's capacity. These are likely to vary from area to area, according to local needs and priorities.

At present, where the Public Guardian undertakes an investigation, she usually advises the local authority to see if any relevant department has had contact with the person[35]. If the Public Guardian investigates and the individual appears to have capacity but remains vulnerable, the Public Guardian informs the local authority. The local authority will have a duty to investigate under the Adult Support and Protection Act.

Similarly, if the local authority investigates a vulnerable adult who appears to be incapable as defined by the Adults with Incapacity Act, it should contact the Office of the Public Guardian for information and advice where the concerns relate to finances or property.

Where appropriate following an investigation, the Public Guardian has specific legal powers to commence proceedings to safeguard the property or financial interests of an adult unable to do this herself. The local authority has the power (and a duty) to apply for a financial intervention order or financial guardianship in some situations (see chapter 10) but does not have power to take such wide-ranging proceedings as the Public Guardian[36].

---

[35]   Information to the authors from the Office of the Public Guardian.

[36]   See Adrian Ward's comments on the powers of the Public Guardian in *Adults with Incapacity Legislation*, W Green (2008).

Overlap with Care Commission

7.18 The authors understand that the Public Guardian and the Care Commission are, at the time of writing, developing a formal memorandum of understanding about managing any overlapping responsibilities and the ability to work jointly where needed.

THE POLICE

Role in adult protection

7.19 The police may be the first people with whom a vulnerable person comes into contact. They may receive reports of a disturbance at the person's home, or reports of misappropriation of funds. A person may be in the street in a disorientated state or may commit crimes indicating that she is at risk.

The police have clear duties to cooperate in adult protection and there will be occasions where the police will need to consider whether a person coming to their attention is an adult in need of protection because of her vulnerability[37].

People at risk in public

7.20 The police have special powers where a person with a mental disorder is at risk in a public place. If a police officer reasonably suspects that someone in a public place has a mental disorder and needs immediate care and treatment, the officer can remove the person to a place of safety[38]. There need be no immediate danger to the public. The police officer can remove the person either because there is a risk to the public or because it is in the person's interests to do so.

A place of safety is a hospital, a care home service or any other suitable place willing to take the person temporarily[39]. A police station should be a last resort, if no suitable place of safety is immediately available[40]. If the

---

[37] ASP(S)A 2007, s5(3).
[38] MH(CT)(S)A 2003, s297.
[39] MH(CT)(S)A 2003, s300.
[40] MH(CT)(S)A 2003, s297

police do take the person to a police station, they should take her to a more suitable place of safety as soon as possible[41].

These powers apply only where the person is in a public place, that is, any place to which the public have access. It includes places that charge for entry, such as cinemas and football grounds, and common stairs and hallways[42].

Arranging medical examination

7.21   The police may keep the person in the place of safety for up to 24 hours from the time they remove her from the public place. The police can return an individual to the place of safety, should she attempt to abscond[43].

The police officer should arrange for a doctor to examine the person as soon as possible to make any necessary arrangements for her care or treatment[44]. Each area of Scotland should have a plan for psychiatric emergencies[45]. The plan will ensure that the police know how to contact police surgeons and mental health professionals, such as mental health officers, community psychiatric nurses and psychiatrists.

Notifications

7.22   As soon as possible after the person has arrived at the place of safety, the police officer should contact the patient's nearest relative and the local authority for the area where the place of safety is situated[46]. The police officer should inform these people when and why the person was removed by the police, where the place of safety is and if a police station has been used, the reason why[47].

If it is impractical to inform the nearest relative, or if the nearest relative does not live with the person, the police officer should inform anyone living with the person, or a carer[48].

---

[41]   Mental Health (Care and Treatment) Act Code of Practice, vol 1, paras 15.82, 15.63.
[42]   MH(CT)(S)A 2003, s297(4).
[43]   MH(CT)(S)A 2003, s297(3).
[44]   MH(CT)(S)A 2003, s297(2). Code of Practice, vol 1, para 15.67.
[45]   Mental Health (Care and Treatment) Act Code of Practice, vol 2, para 7.58.
[46]   MH(CT)(S)A 2003, s298(2).
[47]   MH(CT)(S)A 2003, s298(3).
[48]   MH(CT)(S)A 2003, s298(5).

The police officer should notify the Mental Welfare Commission within 14 days[49]. The Commission's Annual Reports state that they have received very few notifications and the Commission believes that it is not being advised in all cases. The Commission is currently working with the Association of Chief Police Officers in Scotland (ACPOS) to try to increase the awareness of these procedures by the police in Scotland[50].

People not in public place

7.23 When someone is at risk in a private place, such as the home, the police must rely on their common law powers[51]. They can enter only if there is a serious disturbance, or to prevent a breach of the peace or if they are in active pursuit of someone they suspect of having committed a serious crime[52]. If the local authority needs the help of the police to gain access to someone in a private place, it must apply to a sheriff for a warrant. See chapter 6.

PROFESSIONAL REGULATORS

7.24 Most health and social care professionals are registered with a professional body. The General Medical Council registers doctors, the Nursing and Midwifery Council nurses and the Health Professions Council regulates professions allied to medicine, including occupational therapy, physiotherapy, radiography, speech and language therapy etc.

The Scottish Social Services Council is responsible for social service workers, including professionally qualified social workers and other staff, such as care staff and support workers, working in care services[53]. In some cases an employer may have a duty to notify the Council about staff misconduct. For example, where someone employing a social service

---

[49] MH(CT)(S)A 2003, s298(2)(b). There is a form on the Scottish Government's mental health law website.
[50] The website for ACPOS can be found at www.acpos.police.uk.
[51] *Halliday* v *Nevill* (1984) 155 CLR 1. See also *Gillies against Procurator Fiscal, Elgin* [2008] HCJAC 55.
[52] Alison *Criminal Law*, II.118. For a more recent discussion see D McFadzean, 'Police' in Niall R Whitty et al (eds), *The Laws of Scotland: Stair Memorial Encyclopaedia* (Wiltshire, 2008), paras 86, 99.
[53] ROC(S)A 2001, s44.

worker dismisses her on the grounds of misconduct or would, or might, have done so had the person not resigned first, the employer must notify the Scottish Social Services Council and give details of the circumstances[54].

Duty to investigate

7.25 All professional regulators have powers to investigate misconduct and questions of fitness to practise. An adult who has suffered harm caused by a care professional or a person with an interest could make a complaint to a professional regulator. Each profession has its own procedure, but sometimes this will involve attending a formal hearing, with evidence given on oath and cross-examination of witnesses.

Powers

7.26 Each body has different powers, but these usually include removing a person unfit to practise, imposing conditions on her registration or suspending the professional.

Contacting a professional regulator

7.27 A person complaining may need legal representation if a formal hearing takes place. More information is available from the professional organisations themselves, or their websites.

CONCLUSION

7.28 While the primary responsibility for investigating risk to adults rests with the local authority, a wide variety of other bodies have a role to play. All can offer advice and assistance to service users and carers where appropriate. Clearly the protection of adults at risk requires effective cooperation between the various agencies.

---

[54]   ROC(S)A 2001 (as amended by the Smoking, Health and Social Care (Scotland) Act 2005, s57A).

Chapter 8

EMERGENCIES

8.1 Ideally, any intervention where an adult is at risk would follow careful consideration of all the options and comprehensive discussion between the professionals involved. The adult and other interested parties would be fully consulted and have their opinions taken into account.

However, the reality is that detailed planning is not always possible and situations inevitably arise that need immediate action. This chapter examines the range of options available to deal with urgent situations.

ADULT SUPPORT AND PROTECTION ACT

8.2 The Adult Support and Protection Act anticipates that urgent action will sometimes be required to remove an adult at risk from a situation of harm or abuse[1]. Provision is made for emergency applications for either a warrant for entry to carry out a visit or a removal order[2].

Where the local authority considers an order is needed within a short timescale, it can make an application to the sheriff court. This can normally be done within a matter of days. However, if the situation is very urgent, the local authority can apply to a justice of the peace at any time during the day or night.

Application to justice of the peace

8.3 Where the local authority makes an application to a justice of the peace for an emergency warrant for entry to carry out a visit or a removal order it must be able to demonstrate that:

---

[1] The term 'adult at risk' is defined in the Adult Support and Protection (Scotland) Act 2007, s3.
[2] Under the ASP(S)A 2007, s40. Removal orders and warrants for entry are discussed in chapter 6.

- It is not practical to apply to a sheriff.

- The adult at risk is likely to be harmed if there is any delay in granting the order or warrant[3]. (The criteria here is 'harm' rather than 'serious harm'); and

- The usual criteria for an order are, on the evidence available, met[4].

A strict time limit of 12 hours is set within which an emergency order, or warrant for entry to carry out a visit, must be used[5]. This is to reflect the intent that they be used for urgent situations.

Involving the adult

8.4   Where an order is needed within a short timescale there may be less, or indeed no, opportunity to find out the adult's views and, in particular, whether or not he consents to the order. In some circumstances, the adult's views might be known because there have been previous investigations. However, this will not always be the case, and if the local authority does not know the adult's views, it should be prepared to explain to the justice of the peace the reasons why these cannot be obtained.

Where emergency orders are granted, there might still be a difficulty if the adult refuses to comply. This is because the requirement to respect the adult's wishes applies to both the granting, and the exercise, of the order. Therefore, any council officer acting under an order must respect the adult's refusal unless he believes there has been undue pressure. This might be difficult to determine in urgent situations.

Another reason for careful consideration of an order where an adult is not likely to accept help is that there is no right of detention, even where undue pressure can be established. This means orders are of limited use where the adult is likely to be very resistant and unwilling to accept any help. However, where there is a reason to believe the adult would accept help if removed from a specific situation, an order might still be appropriate.

---

[3]   ASP(S)A 2007, s40(2).
[4]   ASP(S)A 2007, s15 (removal order) and s38(2) (warrant for entry).
[5]   ASP(S)A 2007, ss40(7) and (8).

Temporary banning order

8.5 Another option available in an emergency is an application for a temporary banning order. This means a temporary order can be put in place while the application for a full banning order is considered[6].

The purpose of any banning order is to ban the person believed to be causing harm from a specific place or places to prevent future harm. Banning orders can also include specific conditions and are discussed further in chapter 10.

Banning orders are different to the other orders available under the Act, as applications are not restricted to local authorities. An adult at risk, as well as anyone living in the place to which an application relates, may apply[7].

Using the emergency measures

8.6 The emergency procedures of the Adult Support and Protection Act are most likely to be used where an adult is believed to be at risk of harm if immediate action is not taken and:

- There are reasonable grounds to believe that access will be obstructed by a third party;

- The adult is believed to be under undue pressure and it is thought he may cooperate if moved from the harmful situation; or

- There are reasonable grounds to believe the adult is at risk of harm and lacks capacity to take decisions about his welfare. In such cases, access to the adult might be needed to allow the position to be determined.

ADULTS WITH INCAPACITY ACT

8.7 The Adults with Incapacity Act is generally less useful than other legislation in emergencies. This is because the procedures are more complicated and preparation for an order takes time. However, in some cases, interim guardianship might be a useful option.

---

6   ASP(S)A 2007, s20.
7   ASP(S)A 2007, s22.

Interim guardianship

8.8   When an application is made to the sheriff court for the appointment
of a guardian, it can include a request for the appointment of an interim
guardian[8]. An interim (or temporary) appointment lasts until a
permanent guardian is appointed, or until three months have passed,
whichever happens first[9].

The application still needs to be submitted with two medical
certificates, as well as a report from a mental health officer. Where the
powers sought are solely financial, a report from someone with financial
expertise replaces the mental health officer's report[10].

An interim guardian can be appointed with some, or all, of the powers
requested in the full application. For example, the interim guardian could
be given the power to decide where an adult lives pending consideration
of the full application. This could allow the adult to be moved from a
situation of harm in the short term.

An important advantage of using an interim guardianship order is that
the guardian has a continuing power to make decisions about the adult's
welfare and life. This can be useful where an adult lacks capacity and
refuses to consent to any intervention. It allows the guardian to consent
on his behalf, provided the power to do so has been granted. However,
the guardian would obviously need to have regard to the general
principles[11], including taking account of the adult's views, as well as
respecting the adult's human rights[12].

The Act can also be used to authorise medical treatment using the
procedure set out in part 5 of the Act. This is discussed further below.

However, the Act is not appropriate in all adult protection cases. It can
only be used when dealing with adults who, because of mental disorder
(or, rarely, communication difficulties) lack the capacity to make some or
all of their own decisions[13] or to safeguard or promote their interests (or
where there are reasonable grounds to believe that this is the case).

---

[8]   Adults with Incapacity (Scotland) Act 2000, s57.
[9]   AWI(S)A 2000, s57(6).
[10] AWI(S)A 2000, s57(3).
[11] See chapter 4 for details of the general principles.
[12] Powers of guardians to detain or restrain are considered in the human rights
context in chapter 12.
[13] As defined in the AWI(S)A 2000, s1(6).

Guardianship and intervention orders inevitably take time, so are not always of use in very urgent situations. The Adults with Incapacity Act is most likely to be relevant where:

- The situation involves an adult with incapacity and requires action within days or weeks rather than hours; and

- The adult lacks capacity and is not likely to agree voluntarily to leave a harmful situation. In such a case, guardianship or an intervention order can be sought instead of, or following, a removal order; or

- An incapable adult requires immediate medical treatment (see below). (Though the Act cannot authorise the adult's admission to a psychiatric hospital against his will[14].)

MENTAL HEALTH (CARE AND TREATMENT) ACT

8.9   The Mental Health (Care and Treatment) Act provides a framework for the care and treatment of people with a mental disorder. It can be used to authorise urgent investigations or action and may be relevant in some adult protection cases where the adult involved has a mental disorder and falls within its terms.

The Mental Health (Care and Treatment) Act gives the local authority a duty to investigate possible harm and abuse to a person with a mental disorder[15]. If it is refused entry, or has reasonable grounds to believe this may happen, a sheriff or justice of the peace can grant a warrant for entry[16]. This allows the local authority to attend with the police, who can use reasonable force to gain entry. A warrant in these terms can be obtained at very short notice and so this can be useful in emergencies to assess situations of harm or abuse.

Removal to a place of safety

8.10   The Act also allows a sheriff or justice of the peace to grant a removal order under the Mental Health (Care and Treatment) Act if

---

[14]   AWI(S)A 2000, s47(7).
[15]   Mental Health (Care and Treatment) (Scotland) Act 2003, s33. This is discussed further in chapter 6.
[16]   MH(CT)(S)A 2003, s35. See chapter 6.

satisfied that an adult has a mental disorder and is likely to suffer significant harm if he is not moved[17]. A removal order under this Act is different to a removal order under the Adult Support and Protection Act. For more details, see chapter 6.

A removal order under the Mental Health (Care and Treatment) Act allows a mental health officer to attend with the police and remove the adult to a place of safety[18]. It also allows the adult's detention for a period of up to seven days[19]. The adult, or anyone else with an interest in his welfare, can appeal to a sheriff against the order[20].

The police also have a power to remove a person with a mental disorder from a public place to a place of safety, if he appears to be in immediate need of care or treatment[21]. The person can be detained for up to 24 hours to allow a medical examination to be carried out. (See para 7.20ff.)

Emergency detention

8.11 Even in an emergency, it may be possible to arrange for a psychiatrist and mental health officer to see a patient and arrange his short-term detention in hospital. This is often the preferred route because of the safeguards for patients.

However, there may be situations where a doctor believes that using these provisions will cause undue delay and that emergency detention is necessary. A registered medical practitioner can sign an emergency detention certificate if he believes that a person's ability to make decisions about medical treatment is significantly impaired because of a mental disorder[22]. This authorises the removal of the individual to a specified hospital, if he is not already in a hospital and for his detention there for up to 72 hours.

Before signing a certificate the medical practitioner must be satisfied that:

---

[17]   MH(CT)(S)A 2003, ss293 and 294.
[18]   As defined by MH(CT)(S)A 2003, s300.
[19]   MH(CT)(S)A 2003, s293(3)(c).
[20]   MH(CT)(S)A 2003, s295.
[21]   MH(CT)(S)A 2003, s297.
[22]   MH(CT)(S)A 2003, s36(3)(b).

Fig 8.1 An example of the decision making process that might be followed when dealing with an emergency situation where harm is caused by a third party

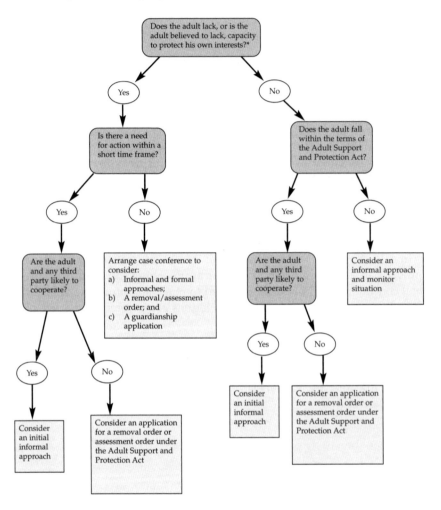

* Note that where the adult falls within the terms of the Mental Health (Care and Treatment) Act there will also be a duty to investigate under that legislation. Where the cause of harm is a mental disorder rather than a third party then action under the Mental Health (Care and Treatment) Act might be more appropriate.

- There is an urgent need to detain the person in hospital to assess the medical treatment he needs;

- If the person was not detained, there would be a significant risk to his health, safety or welfare, or the safety of any other person[23]; and

- Any delay caused by starting the short-term detention procedure is undesirable[24].

The person can be detained in a hospital for up to 72 hours, if necessary[25].

However, an emergency detention certificate does not authorise any medical treatment. If any treatment is needed the short-term detention procedure must be used. The other options for detention are discussed further in chapter 10[26].

CRIMINAL INVESTIGATIONS

8.12   The police have powers to enter and take action in cases where a crime is suspected. In addition, bail conditions can often be used to prevent an abuser returning home or approaching the adult. The use of bail conditions might remove the need to make an immediate application for a banning order. Criminal investigations are covered in chapter 14.

ANTISOCIAL BEHAVIOUR ORDERS

8.13   Chapter 10 looks at situations where an antisocial behaviour order may be appropriate. The sheriff can make interim orders where there is immediate risk[27].

---

[23]   Public protection was a reasonable ground for detention from the human rights perspective in *Anderson, Reid and Docherty v. the UK* 2002 3WLR 1460.

[24]   MH(CT)(S)A 2003, s36(3)(c).

[25]   MH(CT)(S)A 2003, s36(8).

[26]   For a comprehensive guide to detention under the Mental Health (Care and Treatment) (Scotland) Act see *Mental Health, Incapacity and the Law in Scotland*, Hilary Patrick, Bloomsbury Professional (2006).

[27]   Antisocial Behaviour (Scotland) Act 2004, s7.

URGENT MEDICAL TREATMENT

8.14 In some cases, an adult may require immediate medical attention. For example, he might have significant physical injuries or require treatment following an overdose.

In general, medical treatment can only be carried out with an individual's consent[28]. However, there will be some situations where it is not possible to obtain consent because the adult is unconscious or otherwise incapacitated. Medical treatment can be carried out without the patient's consent in the following circumstances:

- The common law doctrine of necessity permits medical treatment in an emergency to prevent loss of life or significant injury.

- The Adults with Incapacity Act authorises medical treatment when an adult is unable to consent. In such cases, the medical practitioner completes a statutory certificate, which provides the necessary authority to treat. If a welfare guardian or attorney has been appointed he will be asked for consent as part of this process[29].

- Treatment for a mental disorder may be authorised by the Mental Health (Care and Treatment) Act.

The General Medical Council and the Mental Welfare Commission have issued extensive guidance for medical practitioners about treatment and consent[30].

CONCLUSION

8.15 The law provides a range of options allowing for interventions in urgent or emergency situations. In many cases, it will be clear which is the most appropriate provision to use. For example, if an adult needs urgent medical treatment for a mental disorder and refuses consent, use of the Mental Health (Care and Treatment) Act may be appropriate.

---

[28] Medical treatment in general is discussed in chapter 6.
[29] Under part 5 of the Adults with Incapacity (Scotland) Act 2000.
[30] *Consent: Patients and doctors making decisions together* (2008) – available from www.gmc-uk.org. *Consent to medical treatment: A guide for medical practitioners* – available from www.mwcscot.org.uk.

In other cases, a combination of measures might be used. The adult might be removed under the Adult Support and Protection Act with a view to carrying out medical and other assessments in relation to a potential application for guardianship.

It is recognised that where urgent action is taken there is often less opportunity to explore the options with the adult and seek consent. However, it is vital that the adult is as fully involved in decisions as possible following any action, and that he is given the opportunity to contribute to ongoing decisions about his personal or financial welfare.

Chapter 9

SUPPORTING THE ADULT

9.1   Where an adult is experiencing abuse or harm, there are a number of ways of providing support while, or instead of, using statutory powers. Some of these supports are specifically provided for by legislation.

This chapter provides an introduction to the ways in which adults can, and should be, supported. Providing appropriate support is a crucial part of making sure the adult's views are known and considered. It may also improve the likelihood of the adult avoiding situations of harm and abuse in the longer-term.

The provisions of the Vulnerable Witnesses (Scotland) Act 2004 include specific support to give evidence in court. These are explained in chapter 10.

INDEPENDENT ADVOCACY

9.2   Independent advocates provide assistance to those who have difficulty understanding situations, or telling others what they think. The advocacy worker finds out an individual's views and makes sure these are properly expressed and taken into account.

An individual might struggle to participate in decisions about her life for a number of reasons. She may lack the confidence or ability to express her views or find it difficult to ask for the information she needs to make an informed choice. This can particularly be the case for individuals who are not used to being asked what they think or having their opinions taken seriously.

An individual may also feel inhibited or pressured by other people to provide specific responses. This can happen even when the person she is dealing with is trying to help.

The consequences of not involving and consulting adults in decisions can include frustration for all involved, as well as creating a lack of confidence in the system. This may in turn, reduce the prospects of achieving a satisfactory outcome. Therefore, the role of the independent advocate can be vital.

Different models of advocacy are available in Scotland. Citizen advocacy is normally provided by people who know the adult or by volunteers, while professional advocacy involves the use of paid advocacy workers. Group advocacy refers to situations where people with similar issues get together to support each other to express their views, often with the help of a facilitator. Self-advocacy involves building the capacity of individuals to speak for themselves.

Legal right to advocacy

9.3 The Mental Health (Care and Treatment) Act gives a legal right to advocacy. The Act states that 'every person with a mental disorder shall have a right of access to independent advocacy'[1]. Health boards and local authorities have a duty to work together to secure the provision of independent advocacy. There is also a duty to take appropriate steps to make sure individuals have the opportunity to use such services.

The Mental Health (Care and Treatment) Act defines advocacy services as being 'services of support and representation made available for the purpose of enabling the person to whom they are available to have as much control of, or capacity to influence their care and welfare, as is, in the circumstances, appropriate'[2]. An advocacy service is considered to be independent where the local authority or health board for that particular area does not provide it[3].

The right to access advocacy services, and the corresponding duty to provide these services, is not restricted to those subject to compulsory measures under the Act. In a sense, the right and duty are freestanding. Everyone with a mental disorder is entitled to access independent advocacy, regardless of which piece of legislation is being considered, and indeed, when no legislative intervention is being considered at all.

A local authority should be able to provide information about the services available in its area. The Scottish Independent Advocacy Alliance also produces useful information about advocacy[4].

[1]   Mental Health (Care and Treatment) (Scotland) Act 2003, s259(1).
[2]   MH(CT)(S)A 2003, s259(4).
[3]   MH(CT)(S)A 2003, s259(5).
[4]   See www.siaa.org.uk.

Adult Support and Protection Act

9.4 Under the Adult Support and Protection Act, local authorities are required to 'have regard to the importance of the provision of appropriate services (including, in particular, independent advocacy services)' to the adult concerned[5].

At the time of writing, the extent of the obligation 'to consider' the provision of advocacy had not been tested. However, if an adult has a mental disorder, she has an automatic right to access advocacy services under the Mental Health (Care and Treatment) Act. This means that in cases involving adults with a mental disorder the duty on local authorities goes beyond simply having regard to the importance of advocacy services.

Advocacy and the principles

9.5 The general principles of all the adult protection legislation include a duty to consult the adult and take account of her wishes[6]. The provision of independent advocacy can have an important role in this process.

There may also be a duty to provide access to advocacy where someone whose views must be taken into account has a mental disorder. This could be a friend, family member or other person with an interest in the affairs of the adult involved, rather than the adult herself.

COMMUNITY CARE SERVICES

9.6 Each local authority has duties to provide community and residential care services for those living within its area. The law relating to such services is lengthy and largely outside the scope of this book[7].

However, it does have some relevance, as a local authority may have a duty to carry out a community care assessment and provide services as well as, or in place of, an adult protection intervention.

---

[5] Adult Support and Protection (Scotland) Act 2007, s6(2).

[6] Adults with Incapacity (Scotland) Act 2000, s1(4)(a), MH(CT)(S)A 2003, s1(3)(a) and ASP(S)A 2007, s2(b). See chapter 3.

[7] For further details see Community Care, Nicola Smith, *Scottish Older Client looseleaf service* (Bloomsbury Professional).

In some instances the local authority will charge for the provision of community care services on the basis that the recipient can afford to pay. The position varies and a copy of the charging policy should be requested from the relevant local authority in individual cases[8].

Community care assessments

9.7 The Social Work (Scotland) Act 1968 creates a duty on each local authority to assess the needs of any person living within its area who appears to require community care services[9]. In many instances, individuals subject to adult protection investigations or measures will have a need for such services.

In the first instance, the local authority must carry out a formal community care assessment identifying a person's needs. The local authority then records how it intends to meet that need.

A community care assessment should take place along with any adult protection measures. In some cases, the provision of such services may reduce or prevent harm or abuse. For example, services to assist an individual diagnosed with dementia to remain safely at home may remove the need for her to be moved.

Carers' assessments

9.8 Where a carer provides 'a substantial amount of care on a regular basis'[10] for an adult, this must be taken into account when assessing the need for services. The local authority should also take into account the views of both the adult and the carer, provided it is reasonable and practical to do so[11].

---

[8] For further discussion see the Child Poverty Action Group publication, *Paying for Care Handbook: A guide to services, charges and welfare benefits for adults in need of care in the community or in residential or nursing care homes* (2009).

[9] Social Work (Scotland) Act 1968, s12A.

[10] This term is not defined. The Scottish Government issued guidance to local authorities in Scottish Executive Circular, CCD2/2003.

[11] SW(S)A 1968, s12A (as amended by Community Care and Health (Scotland) Act 2002, s8).

Carers have a right to their own separate assessment of their ability to care[12]. Such an assessment can be requested at any time and can be carried out independently of any community care assessment.

A carer's assessment will be very relevant where harm is the result of the carer struggling, physically, mentally or emotionally, to cope with caring responsibilities. An assessment of needs and subsequent provision of services may help the carer to cope and allow the relationship to continue.

Services under Chronically Sick and Disabled Persons Act

9.9 Under this Act, a local authority must arrange to provide specific services if it assesses a disabled person in its area as needing them[13]. The services include practical help at home, meals, telephone equipment, home adaptations and help with transport to services.

When an intervention is made in an adult protection case and the adult falls within the terms of this Act, a formal assessment may be required. Where an individual is being assessed under other legislation, such as the Social Work Act, and it becomes apparent she falls within the terms of the 1970 Act, a disabled person's assessment should be carried out.

Mental Health (Care and Treatment) Act entitlements

9.10 This Act places a duty on local authorities to provide care and support services for individuals with a mental disorder living in their area[14]. These are services to minimise the effect of the mental disorder and to allow the person to lead a life that is as normal as possible[15].

There is a further duty on local authorities to provide services that promote the well being and social development of those with a mental

---

[12] SW(S)A 1968, s12AA(1) (added by the Community Care and Health (Scotland) Act 2002, s9).

[13] Section 2 (1), Chronically Sick and Disabled Persons Act 1970 as amended by the Chronically Sick and Disabled Persons (Scotland) Act 1972 and the Disabled Persons (Services, Consultation and Representation) Act 1986.

[14] MH(CT)(S)A 2003, s25. Under s25(3), this includes residential accommodation and personal care and support services (as defined by the Regulation of Care (Scotland) Act 1968, s59(1)).

[15] MH(CT)(S)A 2003, s25(2).

disorder residing in their area. These services include social, cultural and recreational activities, as well as training and assistance in obtaining employment for those over school age[16].

Where adult protection measures are being considered in relation to an adult with a mental disorder, it may be necessary for the local authority to consider providing services under this Act.

Free personal and nursing care

9.11 Since July 2002, personal and nursing care has been free to everyone in Scotland over the age of 65 assessed as needing such care. In addition, nursing care is free to individuals of any age regardless of income or capital[17]. The rules apply to people living in their own homes and to those in residential care or nursing homes. Local authorities can still charge for care that does not fall within the definition of personal care.

Personal care includes care that relates to the day-to-day physical needs of the person. It also covers care in relation to the mental processes related to those needs and tasks[18]. Eating and washing are examples of physical tasks, while remembering to eat is an example of a mental process. This test could also cover a person with short-term memory loss who is at risk when using a cooker or someone with depression who lacks the motivation to cook.

The provision of free personal or nursing care may be of relevance in adult protection cases, where an individual is unable to care for herself in appropriate ways. The provision of support following an assessment may often be the most appropriate intervention.

Provision of suitable housing

9.12 The Housing (Scotland) Act 1987 places local authorities under a duty to provide housing. They have particular duties to those who may be considered homeless in terms of the legislation[19]. In some cases, an

---

[16] MH(CT)(S)A 2003, s26.
[17] Community Care and Health (Scotland) Act 2002, Schedule 1, paragraph 1(d).
[18] Regulation of Care (Scotland) Act 2001, s2(28).
[19] Housing (Scotland) Act 1987, sections 31 and 32.

adult will be suffering harm or abuse in her home. This might mean that she is unable to return home, particularly when the individual causing the harm continues to reside there.

In some cases, there will be a need to find the adult alternative accommodation in the short term. In addition, where there are no reasonable prospects of the adult returning home, she might need permanent re-housing. In these circumstances, the individual could be considered to be homeless and this creates a legal duty on the local authority to provide housing.

FINANCIAL SUPPORT AND ADVICE

9.13 An adult might need financial advice for a number of reasons. She may have suffered financial abuse or be leaving a relationship in which finances were dealt with jointly. Any change in living arrangements will normally have consequences for welfare benefits. In such cases, assistance from a welfare rights officer[20], Citizens Advice Bureau[21] or other money advice agency might be needed.

Some of the ways to provide financial support are set out below. Formal court applications are looked at in chapter 10 and the use of attorneys is explored later in this chapter.

The Office of the Public Guardian can give advice and may investigate if an adult's finances appear to be at risk.

Appointees

9.14 Where a person is unable to manage her welfare benefits, the Department for Work and Pensions can appoint someone to manage them for her[22]. The person who is appointed is normally referred to as an 'appointee'.

Before the appointee system is used, it is necessary to have evidence that the person cannot manage her own affairs, because of mental

---

[20]   Contact the relevant local authority for further information about services in a specific area.

[21]   www.cas.org.uk.

[22]   For more details, see the *Agents, Appointees, Attorneys and Deputies guide* on the DWP's website.

disability or, for example, following a stroke[23]. An appointee can be put in place even where an adult objects, if the Department is satisfied she cannot manage benefits and that the appointee is acceptable[24].

The appointee receives benefits and manages these for the adult. This can include welfare benefits, housing and council tax benefits as well as tax and pension credits.

Where the sole source of an adult's income is welfare benefits, the appointee system may avoid the need for more cumbersome procedures, such as financial guardianship.

Concerns about appointee

9.15 Anyone who has concerns that an appointee is misappropriating funds or otherwise not using them to benefit the adult can notify the Department for Work and Pensions. The Department can remove an appointee who is not acting in the claimant's best interests at any time[25]. If a claimant becomes able to manage benefits, the appointment can be cancelled.

Access to funds

9.16 The access to funds scheme is intended to be a simple way to manage the financial affairs of a person who is unable to do this herself[26]. The scheme is also sometimes referred to as 'the withdrawers scheme' or 'intromission with funds'. It allows the Public Guardian to authorise an individual or organisation to access an adult's bank or building society account to pay bills and meet regular expenses. The use of the access to funds scheme may mean financial guardianship is not necessary.

It is also possible to receive authority from the Public Guardian to obtain information about any existing bank accounts of the adult[27].

---

[23] Social Security (Claims and Payments) Regulations 1987 SI 1987/1968, reg 33, Housing Benefit (General) Regulations 1987 SI 1987/1971, reg 71(3), Council Tax Benefit (General) Regulations 1992 SI 1992/1814, reg 61(3).
[24] Personal experience of one of the authors.
[25] Social Security (Claims and Payments) Regulations (above), reg 33.
[26] Set out in Part 3 of AWI(S)A 2000, as amended by ASP(S)A 2007.
[27] AWI(S)A 2000, s24C (as amended).

The application is made on a standard form on which the applicant sets out the adult's income and projected expenditure. These details can be amended at a later date if the adult's circumstances change. The form includes a certificate of incapacity for completion by a medical practitioner. If the Public Guardian is satisfied that the applicant is a suitable person to be authorised she will issue a certificate. This provides the authority to open, or access, a bank account in the adult's name.

Access to funds is not available if a guardian or attorney with relevant powers has already been appointed[28].

Concerns about withdrawer

9.17 Anyone with concerns about the way in which an authorised withdrawer is acting should contact the Public Guardian. The Public Guardian can carry out appropriate investigations and, if necessary, terminate the authority[29].

Management of funds in residential homes and hospitals

9.18 In some situations it may be appropriate for a care home or hospital to manage the financial affairs of an adult who is unable to do this herself. The Adults with Incapacity Act allows authorised bodies to operate such a scheme[30]. This may be the most appropriate option, in preference to financial guardianship, where:

- An adult needs support with managing finances; or

- There has been financial abuse; and

- The adult is living in, or moving to, residential accommodation.

However, there are financial limits on the amount that can be managed. The limit, at the time of writing, is £10 000[31]. In addition, the scheme cannot be used if a guardian or attorney has been appointed with relevant financial decision-making powers[32].

---

[28] AWI(S)A 2000, s24B.
[29] AWI(S)A 2000, s31A.
[30] AWI(S)A 2000, Part 4.
[31] The Adults with Incapacity (Management of Residents' Finances) (No. 2) (Scotland) Regulations 2003, SSI 2003/266.
[32] AWI(S)A 2000, s46.

The Care Commission supervises the scheme for registered care homes, while local health boards supervise hospitals.

Concerns about management of funds

9.19 Anyone with concerns about the way in which either a care home or hospital are managing an adult's funds should contact the Care Commission or the health board, as appropriate. If necessary, following an investigation, the powers can be revoked[33].

PLANNING FOR THE FUTURE

9.20 A key principle of adult protection legislation is respect for the past and present wishes of the adult. There are three main ways in which an adult can make her views clear in the event of future incapacity. These are of particular relevance to those who have been subject to compulsory measures or who have a progressive illness.

- A person can speak to those providing her with health and social care to explain her wishes. These should be recorded in her records.

- She can make a formal advance statement or living will.

- She could appoint an attorney to take decisions during any future incapacity.

Advance directives

9.21 An advance directive sets out a person's wishes about future health care should she become incapable of taking treatment decisions in the future. Where these deal with end-of-life situations they are commonly called living wills.

An advance directive may consent to, or request, future treatment, or, more commonly, refuse certain treatments. A living will may envisage a refusal of treatment leading to the person's death.

Despite the recommendation of the Scottish Law Commission,[34] the Adults with Incapacity Act did not give advance directives legal force.

---

33   AWI(S)A 2000, s45.
34   *Report on Incapable Adults* (1995), recommendation 68.

This means their legal status in Scotland is unclear[35], although the law in England and Wales now recognises them[36].

It is probable that Scottish courts would regard a valid advance directive as binding under the common law[37]. At the very least Adults with Incapacity Act principles would regard an advance directive, or living will, as a clear expression of the adult's past wishes.

Advance statements in psychiatry

9.22 An advance statement about psychiatric treatment has a special status where a patient is subject to compulsory measures under the Mental Health (Care and Treatment) Act. Such a statement must be made in accordance with the prescribed procedure[38].

Anyone intervening under the Act must have regard to any valid advance statement the person has made. A person acting in conflict with the terms of an advance statement must report this to the Mental Welfare Commission[39].

In order to be valid, the individual must have capacity at the time she makes the statement, and the statement must be in writing, witnessed and signed. The witness must be a clinical psychologist, medical practitioner, occupational therapist, registered nurse, social worker, solicitor or person employed in the provision of (or in managing the provision of) a care service[40]. This is because the witness also has the role of certifying that the individual understands the content of the statement.

---

[35] For further discussion see *Report on Incapable Adults*, Scottish Law Commission above, paras 5.41–5.50.

[36] Mental Capacity Act 2005, s24.

[37] See the English cases of *Re T (Adult: refusal of treatment)* [1992] 4 All ER 649 and *Re C (Adult: Refusal of Medical Treatment)* [1994] 1WLR 290. *Airedale NHS Trust v. Bland* [1993] AC 789 HL at paras 860 and 866. See also discussion by Adrian Ward in *Adult Incapacity* at para 7.5.

[38] MH(CT)(S)A 2003, s275.

[39] MH(CT)(S)A 2003, s276.

[40] The Mental Health (Advance Statements) (Prescribed Class of Persons) (Scotland) Regulations 2004, SSI 2004 No. 387.

Statement of wishes and feelings

9.23 A statement of wishes, feelings and values can be an alternative to an advance statement and can help inform decision-making. It sets out in general terms the person's attitudes to such matters as life-prolonging treatments and future care. Although it would not bind doctors or other healthcare professionals, the principles of the Adults with Incapacity Act would require it to be considered.

There is no particular form for such a statement[41].

Appointing an attorney

9.24 A power of attorney is useful for an adult who has someone she trusts to act on her behalf. In basic terms, it is a legal document used by an individual to authorise another person to take financial, medical or welfare decisions on her behalf. Where an individual is diagnosed with a progressive or degenerative condition it is particularly important to discuss the options for future decision-making, and thinking about a power of attorney should be part of that process.

Financial powers can come into effect straight away while the person making the appointment retains capacity, but perhaps needs some help managing her finances. They then normally continue after capacity is lost. For this reason, financial attorneys are referred to as 'continuing attorneys'. Welfare powers can only ever come into force when capacity is lost.

It is not necessary to use a solicitor to draw up a power of attorney, although many people now grant powers of attorney at the same time as drawing up a will. However, a solicitor, doctor or member of the Faculty of Advocates must certify both the person's capacity to sign and that there was no undue influence[42]. Sample powers of attorney are available on the Office of the Public Guardian's website.

Only individuals who have capacity to understand the powers being granted can grant powers of attorney. They are normally used to provide for the possibility of capacity being lost on a permanent or temporary basis, at some point in the future, because of illness or injury. If an

---

[41]   For an example, see Ward *Adult Incapacity*, Appendix 5, Part 5.
[42]   AWI(S)A 2000, ss15, 16, as amended.

individual does not understand the legal documents needed to appoint an attorney she will not be able to make an appointment[43]. In such cases other mechanisms, including guardianship, are available and may be appropriate.

Concerns about attorneys

9.25 There is an assumption that an adult will choose someone she trusts as her attorney. As a result, attorneys are not subject to regular supervision and do not routinely report to the Public Guardian or the local authority. However, a financial attorney must keep records, which the Public Guardian may examine[44].

The Office of Public Guardian can give advice if there are concerns about how a financial attorney is operating. In some cases, informal measures, such as offering extra support to the attorney, might resolve the matter. The local authority or the Mental Welfare Commission can give advice if there is concern about a welfare attorney.

An adult can revoke a power of attorney, if she retains the capacity to do so[45]. The test is whether the person is able to understand the effect of the cancellation[46].

The adult, the local authority or anyone with an interest (including the Public Guardian) can make an application to the sheriff court for binding directions to an attorney[47].

The sheriff can also change or cancel an attorney's powers or order an attorney to accept supervision from the Public Guardian (for a financial power of attorney) or the local authority (for welfare matters). The sheriff may order a financial attorney to submit regular accounts to the Public Guardian. A welfare attorney may be required to report to the sheriff[48].

---

[43] This does not mean that the person has to be able fully to manage her own affairs. The test is whether she understands the nature of the power of attorney document *Re K, Re F* [1988] Ch 310.
[44] See Adults with Incapacity Act Code of Practice for Attorneys, para 5.70.
[45] AWI(S)A 2000, as amended by ASP(S)A 2007, s22A.
[46] AWI(S)A 2000, s22A(2).
[47] AWI(S)A 2000, s3(3).
[48] AWI(S)A 2000, ss20(2).

Named person

9.26 A person may wish to appoint a named person to act in connection with any compulsory measures under the Mental Health (Care and Treatment) Act[49]. The named person is consulted by professionals, can make appeals on the patient's behalf and can appear at the tribunal. The role of named persons is discussed generally at para 3.14.

COUNSELLING AND MEDIATION

9.27 An adult who has experienced harm or abuse might need some practical or emotional support. In many cases, it will be important to consider counselling services. These will often be accessed through the adult's general practitioner. Where the harm or abuse is also a criminal offence then specific services might be available[50].

Where a criminal investigation is ongoing, counselling, and mediation must be carefully considered and managed. This is discussed further at para 13.28.

Counselling may also be appropriate where a banning order sets out the circumstances in which contact is allowed between the adult and the subject of the order. In addition, supervised contact or mediation might be used to maintain the relationship, if this is in the adult's best interests.

CONCLUSION

9.28 There are clearly a number of formal and informal ways to offer support to an adult at risk. It is unlikely that an adult protection case will have a successful outcome unless the adult's wider needs are taken into account and she is supported and included to the maximum degree possible in all aspects of the decision making process, bearing in mind any impairments she may have.

---

[49] MH(CT)(S)A 2003, s250.
[50] www.victimsupportsco.org.uk

Chapter 10

COURT MEASURES OF PROTECTION

10.1 Chapter 9 looked at ways to support an adult at risk. This chapter looks at legal remedies which may be appropriate where informal support does not provide a solution that appropriately balances the risk to an adult and respect for his autonomy. It considers the use of guardianship and intervention orders, and orders against an abuser, including court orders (interdicts), family orders, banning orders and antisocial behaviour orders. The thresholds for using compulsory measures under the Mental Health (Care and Treatment) Act are also explained.

In some situations, the risk to the adult may be such that the use of court measures needs to be considered. This will depend on a number of factors, including the harm the adult faces, his needs and his ability or willingness to take action himself. For example, compulsory treatment under the Mental Health (Care and Treatment) Act or measures under the Adults with Incapacity Act may be appropriate. The tables below set out when the various measures may be appropriate.

TABLE 10.1 – Available remedies

Adult at risk of self-harm or self-neglect
Possible legal procedures include:
- Assessment and/or removal order under Adult Support and Protection Act (Chapter 6)
- Application under Mental Health (Care and Treatment) Act
- Guardianship or intervention order under Adults with Incapacity Act

Adult unable to manage aspects of finances or welfare
- Planning for the future, by signing power of attorney, advance statement or living will (Chapter 9)
- Appointment of appointee, guardian or attorney with relevant powers
- Compulsory measures under Mental Health (Care and Treatment) Act

---

Risk from another person
The following options are available:
- Criminal prosecution
- Order against abuser, including:
  - Interdict
  - Banning order under Adult Support and Protection Act
  - Remedies under matrimonial legislation
  - Antisocial behaviour order
- Removal of Department for Work and Pensions appointee
- Removal or supervision of person with powers under Adults with Incapacity Act
- Reporting health or social care professional to professional body
- (In the future) placing a worker on local authority list prepared under Protection of Vulnerable Groups (Scotland) Act

Some remedies require the consent or co-operation of the adult at risk, whereas in some situations the local authority or other person concerned can act even if the adult is unwilling to seek help. Table 10.2 sets out the rules.

TABLE 10.2 – Who can act

Either local authority or adult at risk may act
- Banning order
- Anti-social behaviour order
- Adults with Incapacity Act interventions
- Reporting to professional bodies
- Appointing DWP appointee or changing appointee

Requires action by adult
- Interdict
- Remedies under matrimonial legislation
- Appointing an attorney

Similarly, some remedies do not require the adult's consent, and in some circumstances are available even if an individual refuses consent. An example would be where an adult has a mental disorder and impaired capacity and is at risk of harm.

TABLE 10.3 – Where adult's consent not required

- Remedies under the Adult Support and Protection Act where adult is under undue pressure to refuse consent
- Measures under Mental Health (Care and Treatment) Act
- Measures under Adults with Incapacity Act
- Appointment of and changes to Department for Work and Pensions appointee
- Antisocial behaviour order
- Reporting to professional body
- Criminal prosecution. (Criminal prosecution may not be practical if adult is not willing or able to give evidence.)
- Action under Protection of Vulnerable Groups Act

This chapter looks at remedies where wider issues emerge and the roles of the Mental Welfare Commission, the Public Guardian and the adult protection committees.

GUARDIANSHIP AND INTERVENTION ORDERS

10.2 Where mental disorder means that a person is unable to act to promote his welfare, property or finances, formal measures to protect the person's interests may be appropriate. The Adults with Incapacity Act provides for intervention orders and a form of flexible guardianship, tailored to the needs of the individual[1].

The local authorities is under an obligation to apply for a guardianship or intervention order where it appears an order is necessary for the protection of the property, financial affairs or personal welfare of an adult and no other person has applied, or is likely to apply, for an order[2].

The application is to the sheriff court, and requires two medical certificates confirming incapacity. Where the application involves welfare powers, a mental health officer also provides a report. Where financial

---

[1]   Adults with Incapacity (Scotland) Act 2000, ss53, 64.
[2]   AWI(S)A 2000, s53(3) contains the duty to apply for an intervention order while s57(2) contains the duty to apply for a guardianship order.

powers are sought, a report from an individual with expert financial knowledge is needed[3].

In adult protection cases, a guardianship order can contain a range of powers to prevent continuing harm or abuse. The order might contain powers to decide where the adult lives, with whom he has contact and the terms of that contact, as well as the authority to consent to medical treatment. These powers must always be exercised in line with the general principles of the Adults with Incapacity Act[4].

Intervention order

10.3   An intervention order can authorise a specific one off procedure or transaction, such as a medical procedure or the sale of a property[5]. An intervention order is not considered appropriate to move an adult to residential care, which requires some ongoing supervision of the adult[6]. It may not be appropriate to seek an intervention order to authorise the signing of a contract for care, where there are doubts about the adult's capacity to comply with the terms of the contract. In such cases, guardianship will be the preferred option.

Guardianship

10.4   A guardianship order contains specific powers, granted according to the adult's needs and the principle of least restrictive intervention. Guardianship should not be used if other, less restrictive options could offer the same benefits to the adult. However, there are situations where guardianship can help protect an adult at risk.

Guardianship may be used to move an adult from an unsuitable living situation, to protect someone from abuse, or to prevent him from consorting with certain individuals. If the adult and his relatives and carers cannot reach agreement with the local authority, a guardianship application will allow the sheriff to decide whether the person is able to protect his own interests and can take his own decisions.

---

[3]   The criteria for granting reports are found in AWI(S)A 2000, s57.
[4]   See chapter 4 for further discussion on the general principles.
[5]   AWI(S)A 2000, s53.
[6]   Adults with Incapacity Act Code of Practice for Local Authorities, Scottish Executive (2001), chapter 5, para 34.6.

Guardianship can also be used to authorise community care arrangements for an adult's protection, even where the adult resists such care. This could be less restrictive than an unwelcome move to residential care, which may become inevitable if the person is at serious risk[7].

Guardianship may also be appropriate where an individual or local authority is actually exercising a significant degree of informal control over the adult's life. In such circumstances, it may be appropriate to consider seeking formal powers to give the adult legal protection[8].

A local authority (or individual) may apply for guardianship where someone is unable to protect his own interests because of mental disorder, even, in some circumstances where the person is able to state clearly where he wishes to live and what care he wants to accept. The sheriff may grant an order either because an adult is unable to take decisions about an aspect of his welfare, property or finances, or where someone is unable to safeguard or promote his interests[9].

A guardianship order lasts for up to three years, or indefinitely if the sheriff is satisfied there is a case for this[10]. Despite the principle of least restrictive intervention, in the year 2007–8, over 70 per cent of all welfare guardianships were for indefinite terms[11].

Complaints about guardian or intervener

10.5 The Public Guardian supervises everyone with financial powers under both guardianship and intervention orders[12]. She has wide powers and can cancel a guardianship order if there are grounds to do so[13]. Anyone with concerns should contact the Public Guardian for advice.

---

[7]   See Annual Report of the Mental Welfare Commission (2001–2), page 49.

[8]   See, for example, the case of Ms A, highlighted in the Mental Welfare Commission's investigation, *Justice Denied* (2008).

[9]   AWI(S)A 2000, s58(1)(a). See case quoted in the Mental Welfare Commission's Annual Report (2004–5), pages 5–6. The Commission found major deficiencies the care of a vulnerable woman with learning disabilities. It said that guardianship could have protected her from serious abuse. The fact that the woman had the legal capacity to state where she wished to live did not mean that she was able to take action to protect her own interests.

[10]   AWI(S)A 2000, s58(4).

[11]   Figures from Mental Welfare Commission.

[12]   AWI(S)A 2000, s6(2)(a).

[13]   AWI(S)A 2000, s73.

The local authority supervises welfare guardians. Either the local authority or the Mental Welfare Commission can cancel a welfare guardianship order if there are grounds to do so[14]. The local authority and the Commission can give advice if there are concerns about a welfare guardian.

The sheriff has wide powers, including giving directions to a guardian or person acting under an intervention order[15]. The sheriff can cancel financial and welfare guardianship and can replace a guardian or change the terms of an order[16].

Misappropriation of funds

10.6 The sheriff may order anyone with powers under the Adults with Incapacity Act who misuses the adult's funds or acts outside the scope of his authority, to repay the adult together with interest[17].

MENTAL HEALTH (CARE AND TREATMENT) ACT MEASURES

10.7 In some cases, the compulsory procedures under the Mental Health (Care and Treatment) Act may be appropriate.

The Act provides for both compulsory detention in hospital and community based treatment orders[18]. The usual means of admission to hospital is via a short-term detention certificate[19] but the Act also provides for emergency admission[20] and longer-term orders, either in hospital or in the community[21].

This topic is discussed in detail in *Mental Health, Incapacity and the Law in Scotland*[22]. Briefly, a person could be subject to compulsory measures under the Act where:

- The person has a mental disorder (mental illness, learning disability or personality disorder).

---

[14]   AWI(S)A 2000, s73(3).
[15]   AWI(S)A 2000, s3(3).
[16]   AWI(S)A 2000, ss71, 74.
[17]   AWI(S)A 2000, s81.
[18]   Mental Health (Care and Treatment) (Scotland) Act 2003, Parts 5–7.
[19]   Under s44 of the Act.
[20]   MH(CT)(S)A 2003, s36. See chapter 8.
[21]   See Part 7 of the Act.
[22]   Hilary Patrick, Bloomsbury Professional (2006).

- There is a significant risk to the person's health, safety or welfare or to the safety of any other person.

  (What is a significant risk is a question of judgement for the health and social care professionals. The tribunal will test this assessment during an appeal or on an application for a compulsory treatment order.)

- Treatment is available which should prevent the patient's condition from deteriorating or relieve its symptoms or effects[23].

- Compulsory admission is necessary, because the person will not agree to admission and/or treatment; and

- The person's ability to make decisions about the provision of medical treatment is significantly impaired because of a mental disorder[24].

  (This means that a person with a diagnosis of mental illness or other mental disorder cannot be subject to compulsory measures unless the disorder has in some way distorted his ability to take decisions about treatment for the disorder. A person who fully understands the issues involved and takes an informed and balanced decision to refuse treatment cannot be subject to compulsory measures.)

The Mental Welfare Commission can advise in complex cases.

ORDERS AGAINST AN ABUSER

10.8 Where an adult wishes to protect himself from an abuser, he may apply to the court for various remedies.

Interdict

10.9 An interdict is a court order that can be used to prohibit an abuser from entry to the home or another place. It may include a power of arrest[25], which means that a police officer can arrest the person subject to

---

[23] The test for emergency and short-term detention is slightly different. See ss36(4) and 44(4).
[24] See, for example, MH(CT)(S)A 2003, s44(4).
[25] Protection from Abuse (Scotland) Act 2001, s1.

the interdict without warrant if there are reasonable grounds for believing that the person is in breach of the interdict and there is a risk of further breaches[26].

It is generally necessary to use a solicitor to seek an interdict.

Family orders

10.10   These orders prohibit abusive conduct from a spouse or civil partner and prevent the abuser from entering the family home or the neighbourhood[27]. They may include a power of arrest[28].

The court can grant an exclusion order if this appears necessary to protect against conduct likely to damage the physical or mental health of the applicant or any child in the house[29].

The local authority can also apply for a similar order to protect a child against harm[30].

Legal help would normally be necessary, although Citizens' Advice Bureaux and Women's Aid can give general advice.

Non-harassment order

10.11   Scots law offers particular protection to people who are victims of harassment, which can be a particular issue for people with disabilities[31].

'Harassment ' means behaviour causing alarm or distress. This need not include physical violence. A person who has been harassed may

[26]   PFA(S)A 2001, s4(1).

[27]   Matrimonial Homes (Family Protection) (Scotland) Act 1981, s14. Civil Partnership Act 2004, s113. For more detail see *Family law in Scotland,* Joe Thomson, Bloomsbury Professional (2006), chapter 5, para 13. A very readable and accessible book for lawyers and non-lawyers.

[28]   MH(FP)(S)A 1981, s15.

[29]   MH(FP)(S)A 1981, s4(2), CPA 2004, s104.

[30]   Children (Scotland) Act 1995, s76. Thomson (above), chapter 14, para 6.

[31]   See Disability Rights Commission/Capability Scotland (2004) *Hate Crime against Disabled People in Scotland: A survey report.* This research found that one in five disabled Scots had experienced harassment because of their disability. See also Berzins, K. et al (2003) *Prevalence and experience of harassment of people with mental health problems living in the community.* British Journal of Psychiatry, 183, 12, 526–533.

apply for a court order requiring the harassment to stop[32]. The court will not make an order unless there is evidence of at least two acts of harassment.

Instead of an interdict, the court may make a 'non-harassment order'. Breach of the order is a criminal offence carrying a prison sentence of up to five years. The criminal courts can also make a non-harassment order where a person is convicted of a crime involving harassment. This can offer some protection for the victim in the future[33].

BANNING ORDER

10.12 There may be circumstances where excluding the person causing risk to an adult is preferable to moving the adult[34]. The Adult Support and Protection Act gives the sheriff power to ban a person from a specified place for up to six months. This may offer protection for the adult and provide an opportunity to consider his needs for future care and protection.

Making the application

10.13 The application is made to the sheriff court for the area where the premises are situated or where the person to be excluded lives[35]. The adult at risk may apply for an order, as may the local authority and anyone entitled to occupy the premises involved[36].

The local authority must apply for an order if it is satisfied that the grounds for making an order apply. It need not apply if someone else is likely to apply for an order or is taking proceedings to eject or ban the person concerned (whether under the Adult Support and Protection Act or other legislation)[37].

[32] Protection from Harassment Act 1997, s8.
[33] PFHA 1997, s11.
[34] See Scottish Law Commission *Report on Vulnerable Adults* (1997), recommendation 12.
[35] Civil Jurisdiction and Judgments 1982, sched 8.
[36] Adult Support and Protection (Scotland) Act 2007, s22.
[37] ASP(S)A 2007, s22(2).

Local authority's duties and adult's rights

10.14 The local authority must consider the principles of the Adult Support and Protection Act. These are explained further in chapter 4. It must also consider whether the adult would be helped by the involvement of independent advocacy.

The local authority cannot apply for an order if it considers the adult will refuse to consent to the order, *unless* it considers the adult is subject to undue pressure. If there is an attorney, guardian or intervener with relevant powers, the local authority should seek that person's views.

Wherever practicable, the local authority should keep the adult at risk fully informed at every stage of the process[38].

It may be appropriate for the sheriff to appoint a safeguarder for the adult. See chapter 13.

Criteria for order

10.15 The sheriff can grant a banning order if satisfied that:

- A person is an adult at risk (see chapter 2);

- The adult at risk is being, or is likely to be, seriously harmed by another person;

- The adult 's well-being or property would be better safeguarded by banning the other person from the premises in question than it would be by moving the adult at risk; and

- Either the adult at risk is entitled or permitted to occupy the premises, or neither the adult at risk nor the person to be banned is entitled, or permitted to occupy the premises[39]. (In other words, no order can be made if the adult has no entitlement or permission to occupy and the person to be banned does.)

Perpetrator aged under 16

10.16 An adult or a child can be made subject to a banning order. Where the subject is a child, the local authority should consider whether there is

---

[38] Adult Support and Protection Act Code of Practice, para 11.11.
[39] ASP(S)A 2007, s20.

a case for referral to the Children's Reporter. If the case is urgent, the local authority should refer the case to the Children's Reporter at the same time as it applies for the order[40].

Impact of order

10.17 A banning order bans the person subject to the order from being in specified premises for a certain period[41]. Premises could include the adult's home and other places such as day services, as well as public places, such as a leisure centre or club[42]. The ban may even extend to a neighbourhood and can authorise the person's ejection from the premises or the neighbourhood[43].

The order can impose additional conditions. These may include an order that the banned person should not remove any items from the premises. The sheriff will decide which conditions are appropriate and whether or not any further steps are necessary to make sure the order operates effectively.

Instead of a total ban, the court may allow the banned person to attend during certain times or under certain other conditions for supervised visits. In fixing such conditions, the sheriff must take into account any representations made by the person applying for the order, the adult at risk, anyone with an interest in the adult's well-being or property, and the person to be banned[44]. The sheriff may waive the need for such representations in certain circumstances[45].

The sheriff may attach a power of arrest to the order[46].The police can then arrest the person if he breaches the order. The power of arrest becomes effective when the order is served on the person being banned. It continues for the duration of the order.

A banning order will specify how long it will last. The maximum period is six months, but it can be for a shorter period[47].

---

[40] Adult Support and Protection Act Code of Practice, chapter 11, para 15.
[41] ASP(S)A 2007, s19(1).
[42] Adult Support and Protection Act Code of Practice, chapter 11, para 25.
[43] ASP(S)A 2007, s19(2).
[44] ASP(S)A 2007, s19(4).
[45] ASP(S)A 2007, s41(2). See chapter 13.
[46] ASP(S)A 2007, s25.
[47] ASP(S)A 2007, s19.

Where a banning order excludes a spouse from the family home, this does not affect any occupancy rights the adult at risk may have as a non-entitled spouse[48].

Temporary orders

10.18 In an emergency, a person can apply for a temporary banning order[49]. See chapter 8 for further information.

Within six months of the application for the banning order, the sheriff must decide whether to grant a full order[50]. The temporary order expires when the sheriff decides whether to grant a full banning order or six months from the making of the order, whichever is the earlier. The sheriff may insert an earlier expiry date[51].

Notifications

10.19 If the person applying is not the adult at risk, the applicant must give notice of the order to the adult and any other person whom the sheriff decides should be notified[52].

The applicant must also notify the police if a banning order or temporary order includes a power of arrest[53].

Failure to notify the relevant parties does not affect the order's validity[54].

Appeals

10.20 A person made subject to a banning order (or a temporary order) may appeal. If the sheriff refuses to grant an order, the applicant may

---

[48] Under section 1(1) of the Matrimonial Homes (Family Protection) (Scotland) Act 1981. ASP(S)A 2007, s23.

[49] ASP(S)A 2007, s22(3).

[50] Act of Sederunt (Summary Applications, Statutory Applications and Appeals etc. Rules) 1999 SI 1999 No 929, as amended by SSI 2008 No. 335, para 3.35.3.

[51] ASP(S)A 2007, s21(5).

[52] ASP(S)A 2007, s26. Act of Sederunt (Summary Applications, Statutory Applications and Appeals etc. Rules) 1999 SI 1999 No. 929 (as amended by SSI 2008 No. 335), para 3.35.5.

[53] ASP(S)A 2007, s27. See SSI 2008 No. 335.

[54] ASP(S)A 2007, s26(4).

appeal[55]. The appeal is to the sheriff principal, and from there to the Court of Session. The sheriff principal may cancel an order, but does not have any explicit powers to vary it and the order continues to have effect until the outcome of any appeal is known[56].

An appeal must be submitted within 14 days of the granting of a banning order and seven days of the granting of a temporary order[57]. Appeals against temporary orders require the sheriff's permission, or the sheriff principal's for an appeal to the Court of Session[58].

Variation or recall of order

10.21   The sheriff can vary or cancel an order or a temporary order[59]. For example, it might be varied by attaching a power of arrest[60]. The subject of the order, the person who applied for the order, the adult at risk or anyone with an interest in the adult's well-being or property can apply for a variation or cancellation.

A banning order cannot be varied to extend beyond six months from the date on which the order was granted, and a temporary order cannot be extended beyond its due date for expiry.

Notice of recall or variation of an order must be given to the relevant parties and the police, if relevant, as above[61].

Breach of order

Order without power of arrest

10.22   Failure to comply with the terms of a banning order or temporary order is contempt of court[62] and court proceedings for breach of an order may be appropriate. Either the person who applied for the order or the adult at risk may start proceedings. It will be necessary to seek

---

[55]   ASP(S)A 2007, s51.
[56]   ASP(S)A 2007, s51(4).
[57]   SI 1999 No. 929 (as amended by SSI 2008 No. 335), para 3.35.8.
[58]   ASP(S)A 2007, s51.
[59]   ASP(S)A 2007, s24.
[60]   Adult Support and Protection Act Code of Practice, chapter 11, para 35.
[61]   ASP(S)A 2007, ss26, 27.
[62]   *Criminal Law*, G Gordon (Third Edition), W Green (2001), chapter 50, para 09.

confirmation that the procurator fiscal is not initiating proceedings over the breach[63].

If the person breaching the order has committed a criminal offence, such as assault, the procurator fiscal may commence separate criminal proceedings.

There is no obligation on the adult at risk to report any breach of an order, but he may wish to do so and seek help from the local authority.

Order containing power of arrest

10.23   A police officer can arrest a person subject to an order containing a power of arrest if:

- there are reasonable grounds for suspecting the person is in breach of the order or has breached the order in the past; and

- there is a risk he will do so in the future unless arrested[64].

The police officer does not need a warrant, so can act quickly if there are grounds for concern.

The police officer must take the person arrested to a police station as quickly as reasonably practicable and advise him why he is being arrested[65]. The police should ensure that the person detained receives information about his rights, including his right to notify a solicitor, and one other person, about the arrest.

The solicitor should be advised of the date and time of the court hearing and the person arrested is entitled to a private interview with a solicitor before the hearing[66]. The officer in charge at the police station must keep appropriate records of the person's arrest and detention[67]. If the person arrested may have a mental disorder, the police should involve an appropriate adult. (See para 13.25.)

If the person being detained is a child, the officer must, if practicable, immediately notify his parent(s), or any other person(s) with parental responsibilities and rights[68]. They have a right of reasonable access to the child[69].

---

[63]   Adult Support and Protection Act Code of Practice, chapter 11, paras 50–60.
[64]   ASP(S)A 2007, s28.
[65]   ASP(S)A 2007, s28(2).
[66]   ASP(S)A 2007, s30.
[67]   ASP(S)A 2007, s31.
[68]   ASP(S)A 2007, s30(2).
[69]   ASP(S)A 2007, s30(3).

Returning banned person to court

10.24 The person arrested will be kept in custody until he is charged with an offence or brought before the sheriff[70]. The police must issue a report to the procurator fiscal as soon possible[71].

The person must go before the sheriff court on the next court day practicable, unless the procurator fiscal has decided not to bring criminal charges in respect of the facts leading to his arrest[72]. A non-court day can be used if the sheriff is dealing with criminal cases on that day.

The procurator fiscal may ask the sheriff to extend the detention[73]. The detained person will be able to make representations to the sheriff.

If the sheriff is satisfied that the person appears to be in breach of the order and that there is a substantial risk of a further breach, he may order that the person continues to stay in police custody for up to two days more. (Non-court days do not count towards the two days)[74]. If the sheriff does not extend the detention, the person must be released from custody (unless he is also in custody for another offence).

Expiry of order

10.25 Where an adult is still at risk when a banning order expires, it may be appropriate to apply for a new order.

ANTISOCIAL BEHAVIOUR ORDERS

10.26 A local authority may be able to protect an adult at risk by seeking an antisocial behaviour order against an individual[75].

'Antisocial behaviour' is speech or conduct that causes or is likely to cause alarm or distress[76]. There must have been at least two incidents of

---

[70]   ASP(S)A 2007, s29.
[71]   ASP(S)A 2007, s29(2).
[72]   ASP(S)A 2007, s32.
[73]   ASP(S)A 2007, s33.
[74]   ASP(S)A 2007, s34.
[75]   Under the Antisocial Behaviour etc. (Scotland) Act 2004. For more information, see Scottish Executive *Guidance on Antisocial Behaviour Orders* (2004).
[76]   The 'likely to cause' ground means that the victim does not have to give evidence; someone else may explain the behaviour on his behalf.

antisocial behaviour. Orders cannot be used to deal with alarm or distress caused by a person in the same household, so are not available in cases of domestic abuse[77].

A local authority (or a registered social landlord) may apply for an antisocial behaviour order[78] in respect of an adult or a young person over the age of 12[79]. If a young person is involved, the sheriff must ask a children's hearing to advise whether the order is necessary[80]. The sheriff may also make a parenting order[81].

The local authority must consult with the police before it applies for an order[82] and a police officer may arrest someone without a warrant if he reasonably believes the person is in breach of an order[83].

A criminal court may make an antisocial behaviour order at the same time as it sentences a person convicted of an offence[84]. A victim might want to discuss this with the police or procurator fiscal service.

An antisocial behaviour order may be for a fixed term or an indefinite period[85]. The sheriff can make interim orders where appropriate[86]. These can be useful if there is immediate risk.

Applying for an antisocial behaviour order is a civil, not a criminal, matter. This means that the sheriff has to be satisfied on a balance of probabilities and not on the higher criminal law test of beyond reasonable doubt[87]. It also means that the rules of evidence are less strict. For example, if the adult at risk is not prepared to give evidence, local authority staff could give evidence of what he has said to them. The 'hearsay' rule (see chapter 13) does not allow this in criminal cases.

[77]   Antisocial Behaviour etc. (Scotland) Act 2004, s143.
[78]   AB(S)A 2004, s4.
[79]   AB(S)A 2004, s4.
[80]   AB(S)A 2004, s4(4).
[81]   AB(S)A 2004, s13.
[82]   AB(S)A 2004, s4(11).
[83]   AB(S)A 2004, s11.
[84]   Criminal Procedure (Scotland) Act 1995, s234AA.
[85]   AB(S)A 2004, s4(5).
[86]   AB(S)A 2004, s7.
[87]   Although the House of Lords has held that, in England and Wales, the court should be satisfied beyond reasonable doubt that the person has carried out antisocial acts. *Clingham v. Royal Borough of Kensington and Chelsea; R v. Crown Court at Manchester Ex p McCann and Others* [2002] UKHL 39.

Although the proceedings granting the antisocial behaviour order are civil proceedings, breach of an order is a criminal offence. An adult found to be in breach of an order can be fined or imprisoned for up to five years[88]. The court cannot detain a child or young person[89].

There may be circumstances where an order is appropriate even where someone is unable or unwilling to proceed against the person putting him at risk. An antisocial behaviour order does not need the adult's consent[90]. One advantage for the adult is that the local authority conducts the court case and the victim need not have the stress of court proceedings.

PRINCIPLES AND PRACTICE

Antisocial behaviour orders appear to be a useful way of tackling abuse against vulnerable people, and those involved in adult protection legislation may wish to explore this possibility in some cases. Although the adult protection principles do not specifically apply to antisocial behaviour order legislation, health and social care professionals will want to try to keep the adult at risk involved and will wish to seek less restrictive measures to deal with the problems if possible.

For example, in some cases of antisocial behaviour, mediation may be appropriate, and some people (particularly young people) have signed an 'acceptable behaviour contract' as an alternative to an antisocial behaviour order[91].

BAIL CONDITIONS

10.27 Where an alleged abuser has been brought before the criminal courts, the victim can ask the judge or sheriff to set bail conditions to ensure that the accused person does not make contact with the victim or approach his house. This can be a useful protection against further harm and it appears, anecdotally, that judges are prepared to do this in appropriate cases.

---

[88] AB(S)A 2004, s9.
[89] AB(S)A 2004, s10.
[90] AB(S)A 2004, s4(11).
[91] See *Use of Antisocial Behaviour Orders in Scotland*, Scottish Executive Social Research (2005), summary para 6.

CONCLUSION

10.28   The law offers a number of measures to protect adults at risk. Which, if any, is appropriate will depend on a number of factors, including the nature of the risks the adult faces, his ability and willingness to protect his own interests and the views of the adult and those close to him. The law envisages that action may have to be taken even where the person at risk resists. This is a difficult judgement for professionals to make and consideration of the adult protection principles can help decision-making.

Chapter 11

COOPERATION AND CONFIDENTIALITY

11.1 Specific public bodies are under various duties to cooperate with each other in adult protection cases. This can involve decisions to disclose information with, or without, the adult's consent. This chapter looks at the source and extent of these duties as well as some of the surrounding issues. The role of other relevant parties such as private care providers, charities, advocacy organisations, friends and family is also examined. Finally, there is a basic introduction to the rules governing data protection and freedom of information.

The duty to hand over information to the police is explored in chapter 14.

IMPACT OF ADULT SUPPORT AND PROTECTION ACT

Duty to cooperate

11.2 The Adult Support and Protection Act places a general duty on specific public bodies and office holders to cooperate with any local authority making enquiries under the legislation, as well as each other[1].

'Public bodies' currently include all local authorities, the Mental Welfare Commission, the Care Commission, the Public Guardian, the chief constables of police forces and health boards[2]. 'Office holders' are not defined and the code of practice does not give guidance about who would be included. However, the term presumably covers elected officials, board members and senior staff, for example heads of service in local authorities.

---

[1] Adult Support and Protection (Scotland) Act 2007, s5.
[2] ASP(S)A 2007, ss5(1) and (2). Further information about the roles and responsibilities of these organisations can be found in chapter 3.

The Scottish Ministers can make an order to include other public bodies in this list but at the time of writing, no such order had been made[3]. Where the term 'public bodies' is used in relation to the Adult Support and Protection Act it refers to those bodies listed above.

The general duty to cooperate will certainly involve sharing information and working together on specific cases. Many of the practical issues about how best to facilitate cooperation are likely to be dealt with by adult protection committees[4].

Legal duty to share information

11.3 Many bodies and individuals holding personal information about an adult who may be at risk will be under a general duty to keep that information confidential. Examples would be banks and building societies, the police, voluntary and independent care providers, social workers and health professionals[5]. Normally, both the common law and relevant professional codes of conduct require that personal information can only be shared with the consent of the adult to whom it relates[6]. Different issues arise in relation to sharing information about children[7].

However the law (and most professional codes of conduct) recognises that where a disclosure is deemed to be in the public interest[8], or is required by law or a court[9], information can be shared without consent.

---

[3]   ASP(S)A 2007, s5(1)(g).

[4]   For example, the National Practice Forum reported on issues around information sharing in March 2009. For more information, see www.national practiceforum.org.

[5]   For more detail, consult a specialist work. See, for example, *The Law of Professional-Client Confidentiality*, Rosemary Pattenden OUP (2003). For medical confidentiality, see *Law and Medical Ethics*, J K Mason, G T Laurie OUP (2006), chapter 8. There is also a considerable amount of very helpful information on the websites of the General Medical Council and British Medical Association.

[6]   *A-G v. Guardian Newspapers Ltd (No. 2)* [1990] AC 109.

[7]   See Alison Cleland, *Child Abuse, Child Protection and the Law* W Green (2008) for further details.

[8]   *Attorney-General v. Guardian Newspapers Ltd (No. 2)* [1990] 1 AC 109.

[9]   *W v. Edgell* [1990] Ch 359 at para 419.

Human rights law requires that any such disclosure will only be in the public interest if it is proportionate to the harm it will prevent[10].

The Adult Support and Protection Act requires a public body, and its office holders, to advise the relevant local authority where it knows or believes that someone in the local authority's area is an adult at risk and that action needs to be taken, either under the Adult Support and Protection Act or under other legislation, to protect her from harm[11]. This involves giving all the facts and circumstances of the case to the local authority.

Disclosure can, if necessary, be made under this Act without the consent of the adult, as this is 'required by law'. See the discussion below for some of the human rights implications of these provisions.

This strict legal duty applies to all employees and officers of the relevant public bodies and overrides any general duty of confidentiality. Those professions that have a strong emphasis on confidentiality, for example health professionals working for health boards, will need to understand the impact of these rules. The position of other health professionals, and in particular of general practitioners, is discussed below.

The precise extent of this duty has not been tested, but it is likely to extend to providing any information to the local authority that might indicate an adult is at risk and/or assist an ongoing investigation.

General practitioners

11.4 The legal duties to report cases of harm or abuse and to cooperate apply to (among other people) all employees and officers of health boards. This raises an issue about the position of general practitioners, who are not employed by health boards and so, as the legislation stands, are not under a strict legal duty to cooperate or disclose information.

Patients are still, therefore, entitled to assume consultations with their GP will be confidential[12]. This confidentiality survives even after the patient has died[13]. The writers understand that revised guidance from the

---

[10]   See chapter 12 for the impact of Article 8 of the European Convention of Human Rights.
[11]   ASP(S)A 2007, s5(3).
[12]   See *A-G v. Guardian Newspapers (No. 2)* 1990 1 AC 109.
[13]   Access to Health Records Act 1990, s4(3) and *AB v. CD* (1851) 14 D 177.

General Medical Council will advise GPs that they should abide by a competent patient's refusal to consent to information being disclosed, even if this leaves her at risk of continuing harm. A GP can only override a refusal where another person is at risk of serious harm and disclosure of information could prevent that harm.

This could lead to potential inconsistencies. If an adult at risk presents at an accident and emergency department with injuries indicative of abuse, the treating doctor is under a duty to report this to the relevant social work department, regardless of the patient's wishes. However, if the same patient goes to her GP, with the same injuries, and refuses to allow the information to be passed on, the GP cannot make a disclosure unless others are at risk.

If this gives rise to problems in practice, Scottish Ministers could use their powers to extend the definition of public bodies so that GPs are explicitly covered[14]. However, careful consideration would need to be given as to whether or not this is an appropriate way to proceed. A situation where people are reluctant to speak to GPs or seek medical attention, because they do not want this to be reported to the local authority, is clearly undesirable. In some cases, an open, trusting and confidential relationship with the GP may increase the prospects of a desirable outcome, as over time the patient might agree to accept help or to attend counselling.

There is provision in the GP contract to allow health boards to require doctors to provide them with specific patient information. This could be used to obtain information about a specific case in exceptional circumstances[15].

The right to examine records

11.5   In order for the local authority to decide whether action is needed to protect an adult from harm, the Adult Support and Protection Act gives a council officer[16] the power to require any person holding health,

---

[14]   Under the ASP(S)A 2007, s5(1)(g).
[15]   The National Health Service (General Medical Services Contracts) (Scotland) Regulations 2004, SSI 2004 No. 115, Schedule 5, Part 5, para 70.
[16]   The role of a council officer is explained in chapter 3.

financial or other records relating to the adult, to grant access to the records, by handing them over, or providing copies[17].

Such records could include those held by voluntary organisations, by health or social care providers, or by banks or building societies, as well as records, such as bank books, held by private individuals.

The holder of information will often be under a duty of confidentiality, so it is important she knows how to verify that the person making the request is properly authorised. This must be made clear at local level, given the possibility of criminal sanctions if the holder of information refuses a proper request[18].

Moreover, although the legislation imposes a clear duty on the holders of records to hand over relevant information, the code of practice states that the person holding the records must consider the adult's right to confidentiality in relation to her personal healthcare information (including medical details, treatment options, and wishes) before information is supplied. In particular, the relevant requirements of the regulatory body must be followed[19].

Human rights concerns mean that similar constraints apply to anyone who is asked to hand over confidential information. The law requires respect for the adult's human rights, and in particular her rights under Article 8 of the Convention[20]. The person holding the information must be satisfied that any such request is lawful and complies with the requirements of the Adult Support and Protection Act. In addition, she needs to be satisfied that the request is legitimate, that is, it is for one of the aims set out in Article 8, and that in all the circumstances of the case the request appears to be a necessary and proportionate measure[21].

Anyone concerned that a request from a council officer for confidential information is not justified may need to discuss this with the local authority and may need to seek further legal and professional advice. The Information Commissioner (see below) may also be able to advise.

---

[17] ASP(S)A 2007, s10.
[18] ASP(S)A 2007, s49.
[19] Adult Support and Protection Act Code of Practice, para 8.8.
[20] See chapter 12.
[21] See *Z v. Finland* Application No. 9/1996/627/811.

PRINCIPLES AND PRACTICE

The provisions of s10 of the Adult Support and Protection Act make clear inroads into the confidential relationship between those believed to be adults at risk and third parties. The code of practice advises that, in accordance with the principles in the Act, the adult's consent should be obtained prior to the information being disclosed. If it is not possible to obtain such consent, the adult should, if possible, be told that the information is to be shared[22].

Although the code does not state this, there may be situations where the need to access information is so urgent that it might not be possible to seek the prior consent of the adult. If the benefit to the adult could outweigh the requirement to seek his prior consent, this could be justified under the Act's principles.

The code of practice recognises the anxiety an adult might have about third parties having access to information given in confidence. It stresses that information should only be shared with those who need to know and only in so far as it is relevant to the particular concerns identified. The amount of information shared should be proportionate to addressing that concern[23].

MENTAL HEALTH (CARE AND TREATMENT) ACT AND CONFIDENTIALITY

Inquiries by local authorities

11.6 The Mental Health (Care and Treatment) Act gives local authorities powers to request the assistance of certain public bodies in their inquiries[24]. The public bodies are the Mental Welfare Commission, the Public Guardian, the Care Commission, and health boards. The public body must comply with such a request, provided it is compatible with, and does not unduly prejudice, the discharge of the public body's functions. As with the Adult Support and Protection Act duties, this could mean that confidential information is passed to the local authority.

[22] Adult Support and Protection Act Code of Practice, para 8.4.
[23] Adult Support and Protection Act Code of Practice, para 8.8.
[24] Mental Health (Care and Treatment) (Scotland) Act 2003, s34.

Disclosure of information

11.7 A patient is generally entitled to expect that her medical information will not be disclosed without her consent. This applies equally to individuals being treated under the Mental Health (Care and Treatment) Act. As previously stated, disclosures can only be made without consent where this is required by law or in the public interest.

In some circumstances, it may be important to provide information to an agency or a family member to allow proper care to be provided[25]. For example, when a patient is discharged, it might be important the carer knows the possible side effects of medication and other risk factors. This is particularly important in situations where the patient is unable to manage these matters herself.

If consent to the provision of information is not forthcoming from a competent adult, the carer has no legal entitlement to receive it. However, if this affects the carer's ability to care, the options for the patient's care might need to be reconsidered. The Mental Welfare Commission has produced useful guidance on carers and confidentiality[26].

ADULTS WITH INCAPACITY ACT IMPLICATIONS

11.8 The Public Guardian, Mental Welfare Commission and local authorities are obliged to cooperate with each other and provide information and assistance necessary to facilitate an investigation where an adult may be at risk[27]. Again, this is likely to involve sharing confidential information.

Health and social care professionals owe a duty of confidentiality even where someone lacks capacity. In such circumstances, it is only appropriate for them to pass on information where there are good reasons to do so. For example, where someone needs to be given medication or treatment by a third party, appropriate instruction may be necessary. The

---

[25] The general principles recognise the importance of providing information to the carer that he or she might need. See MH(CT)(S)A 2003, s1(5).

[26] *Carers and Confidentiality: Developing effective relationships between practitioners and carers (2006).* This is available from the MWC website www.mwcscot. org.uk.

[27] Adults with Incapacity (Scotland) Act 2000, s12(2).

general principles of the Act also require those carrying out functions under it to take into account the views of relevant others[28].

In some cases, a guardian or attorney may have the power to view records and consent to, or refuse medical treatment and social care options. In such circumstances, it is appropriate to disclose information to the guardian or attorney and reasonable efforts must be made to consult her about treatment.

THE INDEPENDENT AND VOLUNTARY SECTOR

11.9 Increasingly, services and support are paid for by the local authority but are actually provided by third parties. In addition, some individuals receive other types of service such as independent advocacy. This raises issues about the responsibilities of these third party individuals and organisations in adult protection.

The Adult Support and Protection Act does not place the independent or voluntary sector under any strict legal duty to report harm or abuse. However, the code of practice says they should discuss and share any information they have about adults at risk with the appropriate statutory agencies[29].

Despite the absence of such a legal duty, most voluntary or independent organisations will now be under an obligation to advise the local authority where there is risk to a person who could be regarded as an adult at risk. This may arise in various ways:

- Service level agreements and contracts commissioning services will often specify that the provider must report all suspected incidences of harm or abuse to the local authority. This creates a contractual obligation. The code of practice advises local authorities to review contracts to make sure they are consistent with the Adult Support and Protection Act and contain an appropriate obligation[30].

- Services and projects registered with the Care Commission are required to have appropriate adult protection policies. Such policies will generally contain a requirement that harm or abuse is reported to the local authority, the police, where appropriate, and the Care

---

[28] AWI(S)A 2000, s1(4).
[29] Adult Support and Protection Act Code of Practice, para 2.13.
[30] Adult Support and Protection Act Code of Practice, para 2.11.

Commission. Where the local authority which arranged the service is different from the area in which the service is provided, the home authority should also be advised.

- A service or project will be under a general duty of care to both the adult and other service users. This duty could extend to taking steps to ensure that the body with ultimate responsibility for investigating such abuse, the local authority, is informed.

- Projects and services will normally be expected to follow their own policies and make sure staff are properly trained. There should be robust procedures in place and staff should know how and when to report concerns.

PRINCIPLES AND PRACTICE

Many staff and volunteers develop a good working relationship with the individuals they support. While this should be supported, it does have the potential to create difficulties about roles and responsibilities.

It is important for staff and volunteers to be clear about the nature, limits and extent of the relationship. Those they support can view them as friends and there have been situations where a client has made a disclosure of abuse but clearly stated she does not want the information to be passed on.

Training and guidance about how to handle these situations is important. In some cases, the person providing the service may need to give the client clear advice that she cannot undertake to keep information private and that she may, indeed, be under a legal duty to pass it on.

PARENTS, INFORMAL CARERS, FAMILY AND FRIENDS

11.10   Those involved in the adult's life in a more informal way, such as parents, family, friends, neighbours and other informal carers, also have a role in adult protection.

In general, the legislation does not place any legal responsibility on such individuals to report harm or abuse – although, of course, if they do report abuse, this should be investigated. However, anyone with a duty of care to the adult may be obliged to report harm or abuse to the appropriate authority. This could include family members and carers, including unpaid carers, as well as those with a formal role in the adult's life, for example, an attorney or guardian, and possibly a person who is the adult's named person. In all cases people should have close regard to the relevant codes of practice[31] and apply the general principles. This will clearly need to be balanced with other principles, including the adult's right to have her views taken into account. In cases of difficulty, advice can be sought on a no names basis from the local authority or the Mental Welfare Commission.

DATA PROTECTION

11.11 The Data Protection Act 1998 sets out the law on holding and sharing personal information and gives individuals rights in relation to information held about them. The provisions were drafted to comply with Article 8 of the European Convention on Human Rights[32].

The Data Protection Act sets out eight principles that must be applied by anyone who processes personal information[33]. These principles aim to ensure that personal information is:

- Fairly and lawfully processed;

- Processed for limited purposes;

- Adequate, relevant and not excessive;

- Accurate and up to date

- Not kept for longer than necessary;

- Processed in line with rights;

- Secure; and

- Not transferred to other countries without adequate protection.

In addition, an individual has the right to find out what personal information is held about her. If an individual feels that information is being withheld, she can contact the Information Commissioner's Office for help[34]. Public authorities are under a duty to provide information in a

[31]   The codes can be found at the www.publicguardian-scotland.gov.uk.
[32]   The right to respect for private and family life. Chapter 12 covers human rights issues in more detail.
[33]   Data Protection Act 1998, Schedule 1, Part 1.
[34]   www.ico.gov.uk.

permanent form within 40 days of a request and can make a charge for the provision of information[35].

The Secretary of State can order exemptions in respect of information that is processed for the purposes of carrying out social work in relation to an individual[36].

Where a public body, local authority or other organisation is under a specific legal duty to share information, the sharing of that information is considered a lawful purpose. However, it is also important to bear in mind that public authorities are bound by the European Convention. Even when an authority acts under a statutory duty to share information, it must comply with the Convention. Of particular relevance is the right to respect for family and private life[37]. See discussion at para **11.5** above.

The Information Commissioner's Office can give further advice and information, as well as supplying a framework code of practice[38].

FREEDOM OF INFORMATION

11.12 The Freedom of Information (Scotland) Act 2002 gives everyone the right to ask a public authority for information held by it, and to request a copy. This Act does not cover personal information protected by the Data Protection Act, as there must be a balance between the need for transparency in decision-making and the privacy of individuals.

The Freedom of Information Act could be used to obtain information such as adult protection policies or the number of guardianship applications made. It was not intended to be used to obtain information about an individual case, or information that would identify an individual.

More information can be obtained from the Scottish Information Commissioner, who is responsible for enforcing and promoting the Freedom of Information Act in Scotland[39].

---

[35] £10 at the time of writing.
[36] Data Protection Act 1998, s30.
[37] Article 8, European Convention on Human Rights.
[38] Framework code of good practice for sharing personal information.
[39] See www.itspublicknowledge.info for further information.

CONCLUSION

11.13 Information indicating an adult is at risk of harm or abuse cannot always be treated as confidential. In some instances, there is a positive duty to report concerns about an adult at risk. For example, certain public bodies are under a duty to cooperate and must report certain matters. They may also be under a contractual obligation imposed in an agreement to provide services.

There is also an obligation to provide information following a particular request from an authorised council officer.

Much of the detail about how information sharing will operate in practice is likely to be worked out at local level with the involvement of adult protection committees.

It is clearly vital to the protection and support of adults that appropriate information is provided to relevant authorities. In some cases, a lack of information sharing has contributed to continuing harm or abuse. Different agencies often hold pieces of information that do not seem significant in isolation, but when added together indicate further investigation is necessary.

However, it is also essential to respect the rights of individuals to have control over personal information about them as far as this is possible and that any systems are secure and procedures proportionate to the risks. These issues are also highlighted in chapter 15.

Chapter 12

ADULT PROTECTION AND HUMAN RIGHTS

12.1 Over the last ten years, human rights have risen in prominence in the United Kingdom, largely because of legislative developments allowing individuals to use certain human rights arguments in domestic courts.

Adult protection cases can involve judgements about significant aspects of an individual's life. These might require decisions about where a person lives, whom he lives with, the medical treatment he receives, the contact he has with family and whether or not the decisions he makes are in his best interests. Many of these decisions have the potential to impact on human rights. Therefore, individuals working in adult protection need to have a basic understanding of the relevance of human rights to their work.

Some human rights are considered so fundamental that a breach is never justified, in any circumstances. An example of such an absolute right is the right not to be subjected to torture or inhuman or degrading treatment or punishment[1].

However, most human rights can be limited in specific circumstances, where this is proportionate, justified and necessary to protect others, or the interests of the wider community. Generally, any such restriction or interference must:

- Be lawful;

- Be intended to pursue a legitimate purpose;

- Be necessary in a democratic society; and

- Not be discriminatory.

[1] European Convention on Human Rights, Article 3.

When examining human rights there is often a need to balance rights against each other. For example, the right to freedom of thought and expression does not allow an individual to infringe the rights of other people by inciting racial hatred[2]. In adult protection, there is often a need to weigh an individual's rights to make his own decisions about his life, with the duty to offer adequate protection to individuals experiencing harm and abuse. It can be difficult to decide when, and how, to intervene in another person's life, and consideration of human rights principles may help inform this process.

The aim of this chapter is to introduce human rights in Scotland and highlight some current issues. Other comprehensive texts are available, providing detailed information and analysis[3].

HUMAN RIGHTS IN SCOTLAND

12.2 Human rights are a set of basic rights and freedoms that belong to everyone in the world, regardless of any provisions of domestic law. These have been recognised in one form or another in many civilisations, but became more prominent and obtained strong international support after World War II.

In 1948, the United Nations adopted the Universal Declaration of Human Rights[4]. This set out fundamental rights and freedoms, based on widely accepted core principles such as dignity, equality and respect. These principles formed the basis of the European Convention of Human Rights in 1950[5].

The Human Rights Act 1998

12.3 In 1998 the UK Parliament passed the Human Rights Act. Until then, an individual in the United Kingdom had to complain to the European Court of Human Rights in Strasbourg to pursue a claim that his rights had been breached. The Human Rights Act incorporated human

---

[2]   Public Order Act 1986, s17.

[3]   See *A Guide to Human Rights Law in Scotland*, 2nd edition Hon. Lord Reed and Jim L Murdoch, Bloomsbury Professional (2008).

[4]   For the full text, see www.un.org.

[5]   For the full text, see www.echr.coe.int.

rights into UK domestic law and the courts can now hear arguments about, and make decisions on the basis of, the Convention.

The Human Rights Act also means that legislation passed by the UK Parliament and Scottish Parliament must be compatible with, and interpreted in a way that complies with, the Convention. Domestic courts and tribunals must take account of the decisions of the European court.

Importantly, bodies carrying out functions of a public nature are under a duty not to contravene human rights[6]. This means that in adult protection cases those employed by such bodies must always respect human rights when exercising their statutory functions or using legal powers.

The Scotland Act 1998

12.4   The Scotland Act 1998 makes specific reference to the Convention. The effect is that any bill passing through the Scottish Parliament cannot include any provisions incompatible with Convention rights[7].

Every bill is scrutinised to make sure it complies with human rights and will contain a statement to this effect. If a court or tribunal finds a piece of legislation is not compliant, it can declare that part of the law unauthorised or *ultra vires*[8], with the result that it has no legal effect[9]. This power is only applicable to legislation passed by the Scottish Parliament and cannot be used in respect of UK legislation, although the latter can be declared as being incompatible with the Convention.

The duty to comply with the Convention goes beyond testing legislation at the point that it is passed by the Scottish Parliament. Even if the legislation itself is, in principle, compatible with human rights, there is a requirement that public authorities (explained below) must not use or apply the law in a way that infringes human rights[10]. This is one of the reasons it is important for those working in adult protection to have a basic knowledge of human rights.

---

[6]   Human Rights Act, s4.
[7]   Scotland Act 1998, s29.
[8]   A legal concept meaning literally 'beyond powers'.
[9]   Subordinate legislation and policy are also covered along with primary legislation.
[10]   SA 1998, s57(2).

Public authorities

12.5   The duty to respect and not do anything to infringe human rights falls on 'public authorities'. In the context of human rights, this term has a wider definition than under adult protection legislation because 'public authorities' are defined by function rather than by reference to a closed list.

In this chapter, the term 'public authorities' refers mainly to local authorities, health boards, the courts, the police and prosecution services. In addition, care homes providing support under section 12 or 13A of the Social Work (Scotland) Act 1968 are now included in the definition of public authorities[11].

In general, private or voluntary sector service providers are not considered public authorities for the purposes of human rights cases[12]. However, this position might be tested further as local authorities increasingly purchase services from other sectors, rather than providing them directly. It is also possible that future legislation could deem other providers to be public authorities in the context of human rights.

HUMAN RIGHTS ISSUES IN ADULT PROTECTION

Protection of those at risk

12.6   Article 2 of the Convention says that the law shall protect everyone's right to life. Only in very exceptional cases can this right be breached (for example, if someone acts reasonably in self-defence). As well as the duty on the state not to take life unlawfully, the courts have interpreted this Article as imposing a positive duty on the state to preserve the lives of its citizens.

The courts have said that, if the authorities know or ought to know of a real and immediate risk to the life or safety of an identified individual, they should take such measures as they can to avoid that risk[13]. For

---

[11]   Health & Social Care Act 2008, s145.

[12]   See *R v. Leonard Cheshire Foundation (a charity)* [2002] 2 All ER 936. This is the case even when a voluntary or independent organisation is providing a service normally provided by a local authority and *YL (by her litigation friend the Official Solicitor) v. Birmingham City Council and others* [2007] UKHL 27.

[13]   *Osman v. the United Kingdom* [1998] ECHR 101, para 116.

example, in a case where a vulnerable person died in prison, the European Court of Human Rights said that the UK government had breached his right to life because the prison authorities did not offer him suitable treatment for his mental health needs[14].

Similarly, Article 3 of the Convention says that no one shall be subjected to torture or inhuman or degrading treatment or punishment. Article 4 says that no one shall be held in slavery or servitude. Again, these articles impose positive obligations on the state to act to protect its citizens from the risk of such treatment[15]. If the authorities know that someone is at risk, they may have to take action. This has clear relevance in adult protection.

Right to liberty

12.7   Under Article 5, everyone has the right to 'liberty and security of person'. This right can only be restricted in specific circumstances laid down by the Convention, including where an individual has been arrested for committing a crime or lawfully convicted by a competent court. If a deprivation of liberty of any individual does not fall within the terms of Article 5, it is unlawful and he may have a right to compensation[16].

The Convention permits detention for the prevention of the spreading of infectious diseases, of persons of unsound mind and of 'alcoholics or drug addicts, or vagrants'[17]. Although the first is now theoretically possible in Scotland[18], and the Mental Health (Care and Treatment) Act permits detention of people with mental disorders, Scottish law does not envisage detention of people with certain lifestyles, unless they have committed a criminal offence.

Article 5 permits the lawful deprivation of liberty of persons of unsound mind to protect the public, or the individual subject to detention, or both[19]. This allows detention under the Mental Health (Care

---

[14]   *Keenan v. UK* [2001] 33 EHRR 913.

[15]   *X and Y v. The Netherlands* [1985] ECHR 4, *E and others v. the United Kingdom* [2002] ECHR 769, para 100 (protection against sexual abuse).

[16]   European Convention on Human Rights, Article 5(5).

[17]   European Convention on Human Rights, Article 5(1)(e).

[18]   Under the Public Health (Scotland) Act 2008.

[19]   See *A v. The Scottish Ministers* 2001 S.C. 1 for a discussion on preventative detention and Article 5(1)(e).

and Treatment) Act or other legislation where this is justified and necessary[20]. Detention must always be in the most appropriate place or environment[21].

In *Winterwerp v Netherlands*[22] the court said that there were three conditions that must be met before detention of an individual with a mental disorder could be considered justified. These are:

• The presence of a genuine mental disorder;

• The nature of the mental disorder at that particular time must justify detention; and

• The disorder must continue to justify ongoing detention.

There is a significant body of case law about human rights and detention under mental health legislation[23].

Some adult protection cases will involve consideration of whether or not an individual is deprived of his liberty. These might happen where someone is being moved into a residential home, locked in a bedroom at night to prevent wandering or receiving medication to sedate him. In other cases, he might appear free to leave a particular living environment, but, in fact, compulsory measures would be used to detain him should he attempt to do so[24].

A range of factors must be considered to decide if the circumstances amount to a deprivation of liberty. These include the existence of review procedures and safeguards, the benefit to the individual, the person's capacity to make decisions and whether or not the least restrictive option has been used[25].

---

[20]   Under Part 6 of the Adults with Incapacity (Scotland) Act 2000.
[21]   *Aerts v. Belgium* [1998] ECtHR 64.
[22]   [1979] ECtHR 4.
[23]   For a full discussion see *Mental Health, Incapacity and the Law in Scotland*, Hilary Patrick, Bloomsbury Professional (2006).
[24]   *Guzzardi v. Italy* 1980 ECHR 5, page 92. Some studies show this is relatively common – see *Shunned: Discrimination against people with mental illness* Oxford University Press by Professor Graham Thornicroft (Institute of Psychiatry).
[25]   For a full discussion on deprivation of liberty see the Mental Welfare Commission paper: *Autonomy, Benefit and Protection* (2008).

In the *Bournewood case*[26], (where a man with a learning disability which meant he was unable to consent to hospital admission, was admitted under the English law of 'necessity'), the court considered matters such as the patient's choice, the extent of free movement, his personal autonomy and contact with the outside world. It was held that he was, as a matter of fact, deprived of his liberty and was in no sense free to leave. A key factor in the decision was evidence that care professionals had *'complete and effective control over his care and movements'*.

Where it appears a deprivation of liberty has taken place, it will be necessary to consider whether this is lawful, justified and proportionate.

Controls over person's life

12.8 While deprivation of liberty safeguards will primarily need to be borne in mind when a change in an adult's care regime is being proposed, it may be that incremental changes in an adult's care or treatment, perhaps as his condition deteriorates, will mean that arrangements which were not at the outset a deprivation of liberty, become one.

For example, if a person begins to be restrained on a regular basis from leaving the place where he is living, it may be difficult to suggest he is not being deprived of his liberty. Restraint might be physical restraint, technology or the use of medication[27].

Similarly, a person who lives in accommodation providing 24-hour care and supervision, who cannot leave the accommodation without an escort, may be deprived of his liberty, particularly if he is not happy with these restrictions. (See the case of Ms A, highlighted in a Mental Welfare Commission investigation report[28].)

Moving to residential care

12.9 The Adult Support and Protection Act amended the Social Work (Scotland) Act 1968 to state explicitly that local authorities have the power to move an adult into residential accommodation where necessary to

---

[26] *R. v. Bournewood Community and Mental Health Trust, ex parte L* [1998] 1 All ER 634, *HL v. UK* [2004] ECtHR 471.

[27] See *Rights, risks and limits to freedom*, Mental Welfare Commission good practice guidance (2006).

[28] *Justice Denied*, Mental Welfare Commission (2008), paras 3.8ff.

Fig 12.1 An example of the decision making process when considering moving an adult to residential care

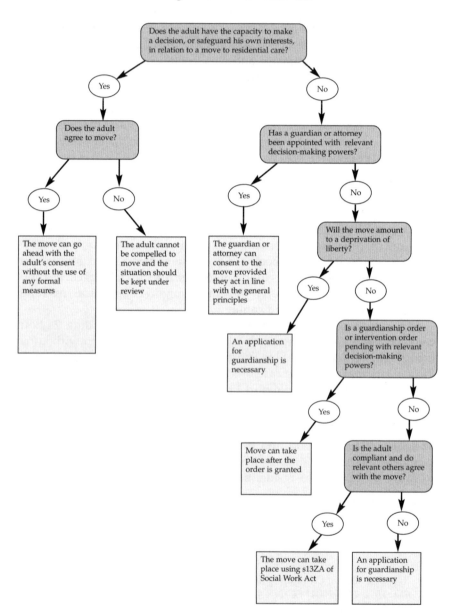

provide him with appropriate community care services[29]. The Scottish Government has issued guidance to local authorities on how to interpret the new provision[30].

The amendment followed concerns that some local authorities were unsure about the extent of their statutory powers. This led to a situation where some routinely applied for guardianship or intervention orders in every situation where an individual lacked capacity and needed to move to residential accommodation. This caused delays that meant that individuals remained in NHS hospitals for much longer than necessary.

Before using this power, the local authority must take into account the general principles of the Adults with Incapacity Act[31]. In addition, the power cannot be used where:

- A guardian or welfare attorney with powers relating to the proposed steps has already been appointed;

- An intervention order relating to the proposed steps has been granted; or

- An application has been made (but not yet decided) for an intervention order or guardianship order with powers relating to the proposed steps[32].

The local authority must still act in line with human rights. This means it should consider if any intervention amounts to a deprivation of liberty. If so, the Social Work Act cannot be used and consideration should instead be given to applying for a guardianship order.

The need for formal authority to move an individual to a care home has been considered by the sheriff court in the cases of *Muldoon*[33] and *RM and JM v. The Adult Mrs A*[34]. These decisions provide some authority for the view that a guardianship order is necessary whenever an adult who lacks capacity is living in residential care.

---

[29]   Social Work (Scotland) Act 1968, as amended by Adult Support and Protection (Scotland) Act 2007, s13ZA.

[30]   CCD5/2007, Guidance for local authorities: provision of community care services to adults with incapacity.

[31]   SW(S)A 1968, s13ZA(3). See chapter 3 for information about the general principles.

[32]   SW(S)A 1968, s13ZA(4).

[33]   2005 SCLR 613.

[34]   2009 WL 873899.

However, these cases are clearly not in line with the Scottish Government's interpretation and so there remains an element of uncertainty about how the court will view individual cases. It is likely the law will continue to develop over coming years and the circumstances in which a deprivation of liberty has taken place will be clearer.

In the meantime, local authorities must consider the issue of deprivation of liberty carefully when it arises in adult protection cases. Where there may be a deprivation of liberty and the adult cannot consent to the move, and no less restrictive alternative is available, it may be appropriate to apply for a guardianship order.

Assessment and removal orders

12.10   The Adult Support and Protection Act provides for formal court orders authorising the moving of an adult for the purposes of assessment or protection. It is intended these will be used as a last resort and only in exceptional circumstances without the adult's consent[35]. These orders do not carry any right of detention[36] and so, in some cases, they may have limited practical and legal use.

For example, a removal order allows the local authority to move an adult to a specified place. However, it is possible to envisage a situation where an adult attempts to get out of the vehicle transporting him. Locking the vehicle doors so that he is unable to leave appears to be authorised by the legislation, but there may be an argument that such action would amount to an unlawful deprivation of liberty. This is because detaining an adult for his protection or to investigate harm against him is unlikely to fall within any of the categories that permit deprivation of liberty under Article 5 (unless the person has a mental disorder, in which case it may be possible to detain him under the Mental Health (Care and Treatment) Act).

In practice, formal orders will need careful consideration where an adult is likely to be non-cooperative. However, they may still be useful in some situations, such as where it is believed that the adult can be persuaded to cooperate if he is removed from a harmful situation.

---

[35]   Adult Support and Protection Act Code of Practice, paras 9.38, 10.10 and 10.13.

[36]   See chapter 6.

Respect for private and family life

12.11   Under Article 8 of the Convention, individuals have the right to conduct their life privately and, importantly, without interference from the state, provided the rights of other people are also respected. Article 8 states that:

- Everyone has the right to respect for private and family life, home and correspondence; and

- There shall be no interference by a public authority with the exercise of this right except such as is in accordance with the law and is necessary in a democratic society in the interests of national security, public safety or the economic well-being of the country, for the prevention of disorder or crime, for the protection of health or morals, or for the protection of the rights and freedoms of others.

The terms 'family life' and 'private life' are not defined in the Convention but have been given wide meanings[37]. They include lifestyle choices, as well as the right to develop personal relationships. The right also means information about an individual should only be shared without consent, in limited circumstances[38]. (For confidentiality and human rights, see chapter 11.)

Article 8 means that individuals should be able to enter or leave their homes as they wish and have control over who else is allowed into their home. Public authorities can only interfere with the rights protected by Article 8 where they can show that their action is lawful, necessary and proportionate to protect national security, public safety, the economy, health or morals, disorder or crime or the rights and freedoms of other people. This would allow the police to enter premises where they have a warrant authorising entry or where this is justified in all the circumstances to prevent a crime[39].

Many of the possible interventions by public authorities in adult protection cases could involve interfering with the rights safeguarded by Article 8. This means a public authority should be mindful of Article 8

---

[37]   For example, '*Respect for family life must also comprise to a certain degree the right to establish and develop relationships with other human beings*' Niemietz *v. Germany* (1993) 16 EHRR 07.

[38]   *MS v. Sweden* (1997) 45 BMLR 133.

[39]   For example, see *Moffat v. McFadyen* 1999 GWD 22-1038.

and able to justify its actions as lawful, necessary and proportionate. This will particularly be the case where formal action is taken without the adult's consent.

Undue pressure and human rights

12.12   Under the Adult Support and Protection Act, it is possible for an order to be granted, or action to be taken, without the adult's consent where he has been unduly pressured[40]. This concept of undue pressure raises interesting issues in the context of human rights.

Existing legal concepts allow an individual's actions to be set aside if he has been unduly influenced or pressured. For example, disappointed beneficiaries sometimes challenge wills where they believe a relative was pressurised unfairly to leave money or property to a particular individual. As the deceased is clearly unable to give evidence about his wishes, undue influence must be established by looking at other circumstances.

In addition, contracts can sometimes be declared invalid where one party has been threatened or deliberately misled[41]. Such a claim is normally made when the individual is incapable of understanding the contract or can provide other evidence that he was pressured to sign.

However, the concept of undue pressure under the Adult Support and Protection Act goes further, in that it allows an order to be granted on the application of a third party, even where an adult is capable of making his own decisions and does not agree he has been unduly pressured.

While it is understandable that the state may wish, and indeed have a duty under human rights law, to protect someone whom it feels is being unduly pressurised to resist help, such decisions raise serious human rights issues. It is suggested that if an order was granted in such circumstances, the adult might be able to argue that overriding his wishes would infringe his rights to respect for private life, as well as (depending on how the order is exercised) potentially constituting an unlawful deprivation of liberty under Article 5. If the local authority wishes to take action in such a situation, legal advice may be necessary.

---

[40]   The concept of undue pressure is explored further in chapter 6.
[41]   For example see *Bank of Scotland v. Bennett* 1997 3 FCR 193.

Involuntary treatment and human rights

12.13   Medical treatment can take place against the patient's wishes in exceptional circumstances. However, it must be tailored to an individual's specific needs at a particular time[42].

This was discussed in *Herczegfalvy v. Austria*[43] where it was held that an incapacitated patient could be legally subjected to non-consensual treatment to preserve his physical and mental health. In such cases, Article 3 continues to provide protection from any treatment that could be considered as torture or inhumane or degrading treatment or punishment[44].

THE UN CONVENTION ON THE RIGHTS OF PERSONS WITH DISABILITIES

12.14   Although the rights contained in the original UN declaration apply to everyone, the reality is that some groups have continued to encounter physical, social and economic barriers. This has meant it is still difficult for everyone to enjoy the rights and fully participate in society. As a result, there has been a move towards additional conventions designed to bring benefits to specific groups. An example is the UN Convention on the Rights of the Child introduced in 1989[45].

On 30 March 2007, the UK was among 82 countries to sign a UN Convention on the Rights of Persons with Disabilities[46]. Although the UK

---

[42]   See Council of Europe Recommendations regarding the Rights of Persons with Mental Disorder 2003, especially articles 18 and 19 and *Progress of efforts to ensure the full recognition and enjoyment of the human rights of persons with disabilities:* Report of the Secretary-General, A/58/181 (24 July 2003), paras 45 and 46.

[43]   [1992] ECtHR 58.

[44]   For further discussion on what constitutes inhumane treatment, see *Kudla v. Poland* [2000] ECHR 510 and *Tyrer v. UK* (1978). 2 EHRR 1. For the courts' ability to question medical treatment in England and Wales, see *R (on the application of Wilkinson) v. Broadmoor Special Hospital Authority* [2001] EWCA Civ 1545, which has not been followed to date in Scotland (*M, Petitioner* 2002 SCLR 1001).

[45]   Adopted and opened for signature, ratification and accession by the UN General Assembly resolution 44/25 of 20 November 1989.

[46]   See www.un.org for the full text of the Convention.

Parliament ratified the Convention on 8 June 2009, international treaties can only be relied on in the UK if made effective by an Act of Parliament[47]. This means that while the Convention can be referred to in cases, it will not, in itself, dictate the decisions of the courts. However, the UK is bound, under international law, to comply with its obligations under the Convention and so the standards can be considered influential, if not legally enforceable at national level. The European Court of Human Rights will also interpret the European Convention on Human Rights in the light of the UN Convention[48].

The purpose of this UN Convention was to provide an international standard for the human rights of people with disabilities. This was in recognition that people with disabilities still face additional barriers and are less likely to get jobs, be able to access services and benefit fully from education and health services.

Public bodies must act in a way that respects, and does not unjustifiably infringe, the rights contained in the Convention.

Article 1 defines people with disabilities as those who have long-term physical, mental, intellectual or sensory impairments that may hinder their full and effective participation in society on an equal basis with others. This covers a range of adults, including those with learning disabilities, mental health difficulties and degenerative conditions such as dementia. The UN Convention also recognises that disability is an evolving concept[49].

The UN Convention does not create any new rights or additional entitlements, but rather expresses existing rights in a way considered relevant to people with disabilities. For example, Article 12 expands on the support people with disabilities need to have access to justice and Article 14 emphasises that any deprivation of liberty should be on an equal basis with the general population. There are also provisions designed to develop the right to live independently and expanding the definition of respect for privacy, home and family life[50].

Under Article 12, persons with disabilities have the right to equal recognition before the law and access to justice. This requires appropriate

---

[47]   The ECHR was ratified in 1951. It was not incorporated into UK law until the Human Rights Act 1998.

[48]   *Glor v. Switzerland*, Application No. 13444/04, judgment 30 April 2009.

[49]   UN Convention on the Rights of Persons with Disabilities, Preamble (e).

[50]   UN Convention on the Rights of Persons with Disabilities, Articles 19, 22 and 23.

measures to be put in place to allow an individual to use his legal rights. This could include the provision of advocacy, information and use of the Vulnerable Witnesses (Scotland) Act 2004[51].

The right to live independently and be included in the community is provided for by article 19.

CONCLUSION

12.15 Human rights have already had a significant impact in Scotland and those involved in adult protection must be very aware of the need to balance their duty to investigate and protect adults at risk with the need to respect the autonomy of the person.

In any circumstance where an intervention will interfere with a human right, the public authority must make sure that this is lawful, necessary, justified and proportionate. Even where a public authority has been given a legislative power to take action, it must still respect human rights when deciding whether and how to exercise these powers.

---

[51] See chapter 13.

Chapter 13

THE COURTS AND THE LEGAL SYSTEM

13.1   This chapter looks at the legal system supporting adult protection practice. It considers the role of the sheriff court and the mental health tribunal. The impact of rules of evidence and the support available for witnesses, including vulnerable witnesses, is also examined. The chapter also looks at instructing a solicitor and legal aid.

There are circumstances where issues relating to an adult at risk may have to come before a court or tribunal. The sheriff court deals with both civil and criminal cases, and hears applications under the Adults with Incapacity Act and the Adult Support and Protection Act. District courts can deal with Adult Support and Protection Act emergencies. District courts are summary criminal courts administered by the local authority. Justice of the Peace courts are gradually replacing them[1].

A person subject to a short-term order under the Mental Health (Care and Treatment) Act has a right of appeal to a mental health tribunal. Long-term orders under the Mental Health (Care and Treatment) Act require the prior approval of the tribunal.

This section looks in outline at some of the features of the courts and the tribunals[2]. Their specific powers are dealt with elsewhere in the text.

SHERIFF COURT

13.2   The sheriff court deals with a wide variety of cases, including family matters and some criminal matters. Glasgow has a specialist domestic abuse court, which may become involved with some adult protection cases[3]. There is useful information about the sheriff courts on

---

[1]   Under the Criminal Proceedings etc (Reform) (Scotland) Act 2007.
[2]   For more detail, see *Mental Health, Incapacity and the Law in Scotland*, Hilary Patrick, Bloomsbury Professional (2006), chapters 3 and 24.
[3]   See *Support services for domestic abuse*, Scottish Government press release, 23/06/2008.

the Witnesses in Scotland website, including information for people with communication or other additional support needs[4]. What follows is a brief description of some special rules for the Adults with Incapacity Act and Adult Support and Protection Act cases.

Adults with Incapacity Act

13.3 The sheriff has wide powers and considerable discretion in dealing with applications under the Adults with Incapacity Act. Some sheriffs hear cases in open court, but rules allow the hearing to take place in private, at a hospital or another place if appropriate[5].

Respect for privacy

13.4 The Mental Welfare Commission has expressed concern about hearings taking place in open court, to which the public can have access[6]. It believes that generally hearings should be in private to protect the adult's privacy. Anyone concerned can formally ask the sheriff to hear a case in private.

There now appears to be a practice of reporting such cases with the names of those involved anonymised. Unfortunately this was not always the case, with the result that details of clients' private affairs were available on the Scottish courts website. There is an argument that this was a breach of adults' rights to privacy under the European Convention on Human Rights[7].

Notice to adult

13.5 Despite the possible incapacity of the adult, the rules impose a clear legal duty to give the adult notice of the proceedings. The sheriff can dispense with notice only if two medical certificates, including one from a Mental Health (Care and Treatment) Act approved doctor, confirm that giving notice would be likely to pose a serious risk to the health of the

---

[4]   See www.witnessesinscotland.com.
[5]   Act of Sederunt (Summary Applications, Statutory Applications and Appeals etc. rules) 1999 SI No. 1999/929 (as amended), para 3.16.3.
[6]   Annual report (2002–3), para 3.3.
[7]   Article 8 of the Convention.

adult[8]. The sheriff will need to be satisfied that this is the case before dispensing with notice[9].

Protecting adult's interests

13.6 Where someone is unable to instruct a solicitor, the court may appoint a curator *ad litem*. This will usually be a solicitor with experience in mental health law issues. The curator interviews all the relevant people and reports to the court.

In addition, or as an alternative, the sheriff may consider whether it is necessary to appoint a safeguarder for the adult[10]. The safeguarder protects the interests of the adult, and, in particular, tries to establish the adult's views. In some circumstances the sheriff may even appoint two safeguarders, one to protect the adult's interests and the other to advise the sheriff of the adult's views[11]. The legal aid position of safeguarders is discussed below.

Appeals

13.7 There is a right to appeal most decisions of the sheriff to the sheriff principal and, with his[12] leave, to the Court of Session[13]. Certain complex medical decisions go straight to the Court of Session, which can also appoint a safeguarder.

Adult Support and Protection Act cases

13.8 Adult protection cases, like Adults with Incapacity Act cases, raise difficult ethical issues. The courts may have to balance an adult's dignity and privacy with the need to protect a vulnerable person against abuse. The court procedure, with its strict rules of evidence and adversarial procedure may not be best adapted to this task.

---

[8]   SI 1999/929, para 3.16.5.
[9]   See comments of the sheriff in *Application in respect of Mrs L C*, Glasgow Sheriff Court AW 38/05.
[10]   Adults with Incapacity (Scotland) Act 2000, s3(4).
[11]   AWI(S)A 2000, s3(5).
[12]   There are currently no female sheriffs principal.
[13]   AWI(S)A 2000, s2(3).

It is interesting to look at how the courts deal with child protection cases, which raise similar issues. The courts have said that they regard such cases as unique in the legal system. Their primary concern is the welfare of the child or young person who is the subject of the proceedings[14].

Scottish judges in child protection cases have said that, although the courts must respect the basic rules of evidence, they should not allow rigid rules of evidence to interfere with the court's duty to protect the interests of the child[15]. Human rights law reinforces this approach[16].

It is too soon to see what approach the courts will take in adult protection cases. The courts need to be satisfied as to risk, but where an adult is unable to protect her own interests, it may be appropriate for the sheriff to take a more inquisitorial approach as she considers whether the grounds for an order apply.

Procedure

13.9 The procedural rules for adult protection cases largely follow those in the Adults with Incapacity Act, though there are differences. The procedure is by way of summary application[17], which involves submitting a writ to the court. A solicitor will normally be involved.

The person applying for an order must generally give notice to the person to whom the application relates and to the adult at risk. In some instances, this will be the same person. Those receiving notice of the application must have a chance to make representations to the sheriff, either in person or through a solicitor. A friend, relative or other representative (such as an independent advocate) may accompany the adult to the hearing[18].

---

[14] *McGregor v. D* 1997 SC 330.

[15] *W v. Kennedy* 1988 SCLR 236. But see *McMichael v. UK* (1995) 20 EHRR 205. See *Walker and Walker The Law of Evidence in Scotland* (Third Edition), Margaret Ross and James Chalmers, Bloomsbury Professional (2009), para 28.3.

[16] *X and Y v. Netherlands* (Application no. 8978/80) (1985).

[17] Under the Act of Sederunt (Summary Applications, Statutory Applications and Appeals etc. Rules) 1999, SI 1999 No. 929 (as amended by SSI 2008 No. 335, 2008 No. 375). The form of writ is set out in the rules.

[18] Adult Support and Protection (Scotland) Act 2007, s41.

Protecting adult's interests

13.10 If the local authority, or anyone else, has concerns that an adult does not understand the process, they should inform the court[19]. Where the adult is unable to instruct a solicitor the sheriff may appoint a curator *ad litem*.

The sheriff may also appoint a safeguarder[20]. The code of practice suggests that the sheriff might ask a safeguarder to consider the question of whether the adult consents to the order[21] (and, presumably, also whether the adult is able to consent and/or whether there is undue pressure on the adult).

Dispensing with protections

13.11 The sheriff may dispense with any of the above protections if she thinks this will protect the adult from serious harm or that to do so would not prejudice any of the parties[22]. Unlike the Adults with Incapacity Act, there is no requirement to seek medical certificates before dispensing with notice, but the sheriff must respect human rights law. This guarantees both the adult, and anyone allegedly putting her at risk, the right to a fair hearing[23].

The sheriff may also dispense with hearing the parties in relation to a removal order or banning order (or the variation of such an order) on the same grounds[24].

The code of practice suggests that if a local authority, or any other person, considers that it will prejudice the adult's welfare for the adult to attend a hearing, the sheriff should be asked to dispense with notice to the adult[25].

It would probably be more accurate to say that if there is concern about notifying the adult or about the adult (or any other person) attending, the

---

[19]   Adult Support and Protection Act Code of Practice, para 11.38.
[20]   ASP(S)A 2007, s41(6).
[21]   See for example, para 11.39.
[22]   ASP(S)A 2007, s41(2).
[23]   Article 6. See comments of Adrian Ward, in *Adult Incapacity* W Green (2003), para 5.9.
[24]   ASP(S)A, s41(2).
[25]   Adult Support and Protection Act Code of Practice, chapter 9, para 37, chapter 11, para 45.

person concerned should notify the sheriff. It might be prejudicial to the adult's welfare for her to attend, but entirely appropriate for her to appoint a solicitor to represent her. Failing to give notice would mean that this opportunity was lost.

Protecting vulnerable adult

13.12 If an individual suspected of harming the adult wishes to attend court, the code of practice recommends that the local authority advise the sheriff. The court can consider whether a witness may need special protective measures under the vulnerable witness provisions[26]. (See below.)

If the sheriff considers it appropriate, the hearing may be held in private[27]. Where the risk to the adult is of self-harm, the importance of protecting her right to privacy might suggest a hearing in private. In other cases, the sheriff may have to weigh up the adult's right to privacy against the right of an alleged abuser to a fair and open hearing.

More details of the court procedure are set out in the court rules[28].

Appeals

13.13 There is no appeal against the granting of an assessment or removal order, but there is a right to appeal against the making, or the refusal of the sheriff to make, a banning order[29].

MENTAL HEALTH TRIBUNALS

13.14 The Mental Health Tribunal for Scotland was set up under the Mental Health (Care and Treatment) Act[30] and deals with appeals and applications under that Act[31]. A legally qualified convener chairs each tribunal. She sits with a medical member (usually a consultant

---

[26]   Chapter 11, paras 40 and 45.
[27]   Act of Sederunt (Summary Applications, Statutory Applications and Appeals etc. Rules) 1999 SI 1999/929, rule 3.35.9.
[28]   SI 1999/929 above, as amended by SSIs 2008 No. 335, 2008 No. 375.
[29]   ASP(S)A 2007, s51.
[30]   Mental Health (Care and Treatment) (Scotland) Act 2003, s21.
[31]   For more details, see Part 4 of *Mental Health, Incapacity and the Law in Scotland*, Hilary Patrick, Bloomsbury Professional (2006).

psychiatrist) and a general member with specific experience of providing or using mental health services (including experience gained as a user of services and/or as a carer).

Tribunals are held in various locations throughout the country, including both hospital and community settings. The proceedings are less formal than a court setting, but still relatively formal, in view of the importance of the matters under discussion. Hearings take place in private[32].

All parties receive notice of the hearing, together with the papers for the hearing. This has caused problems in practice, where confidential details have been sent to people whom the patient would not wish to have such information[33]. The tribunal can withhold information from any party, including the patient, if the tribunal is satisfied that disclosure could cause serious harm to the patient or any other person[34].

The patient and her named person are entitled to attend the hearing, and the patient should be encouraged to do so. The patient's primary carer, and any welfare guardian or attorney, are also entitled to make representations to the tribunal[35]. As in Adults with Incapacity Act cases, the tribunal can appoint a curator *ad litem* if the person is unable to instruct a solicitor. If a party is unable to attend, the Convenor or other members of the tribunal should offer her a chance to meet to explain why she cannot attend and whether she wishes to proceed[36].

As well as a legal representative, the patient can have an independent advocate for support at the hearing[37].

There is a right of appeal against a tribunal's decision only where a party alleges that the tribunal has made a legal mistake or that there were irregularities in the hearing[38].

---

[32] Mental Health Tribunal for Scotland (Practice and Procedure) (No. 2) Tribunal Rules 2005 SSI 2005/519 ('the Tribunal Rules), rule 66(1).

[33] See the consultation document prepared by the McManus Committee as part of the limited review of the Mental Health (Care and Treatment) Act (2008).

[34] Tribunal rules, rule 47(1).

[35] MH(CT)(S)A 2003, s64(3).

[36] Tribunal rules, rule 70(3).

[37] Tribunal rules, rule 66(6).

[38] MH(CT)(S)A 2003, s324(2).

RULES OF EVIDENCE

13.15 What follows is a brief introduction to some of the rules of evidence that might be relevant in an adult protection case, in particular where there are questions about the adequacy of evidence. For more detailed information, a specialist work on the rules of evidence should be consulted[39].

The burden of proof

13.16 Most people know that in the criminal courts, the case for the prosecution must prove the accused person's guilt 'beyond reasonable doubt', whilst in a civil case, the court has to be satisfied on the lesser standard of the 'balance of probabilities'.

Most adult protection cases involve civil proceedings. When a court or a mental health tribunal deals with an application under the Adults with Incapacity Act, the Adult Support and Protection Act or the Mental Health (Care and Treatment) Act it must satisfy itself that the case meets the civil standards of proof. On the other hand, the prosecution of an alleged abuser requires the court to be satisfied according to the criminal standard.

Hearsay

13.17 Hearsay is evidence from one witness of what another person has said. Generally, this has limited value as a form of evidence, and the court will require the person who made the original statement to give evidence. The civil courts will admit hearsay evidence[40], but the criminal courts do not generally allow it.

There are some circumstances where even the criminal courts may admit hearsay evidence.

Prior statements

13.18 The court can allow hearsay evidence of a prior statement made by a witness if it is satisfied that when the witness made the statement she

---

[39] Walker and Walker (above).
[40] Civil Evidence (Scotland) Act 1988, s2(1).

would have been a competent witness but that by the time of the trial, she is unfit or unable to give evidence because of physical or mental infirmity[41]. This could be useful where an adult gives a credible account of what happens, but later becomes unable to give evidence, perhaps because of a progressive or fluctuating illness.

Only a voluntary or spontaneous statement made by the witness is allowed under this rule. A statement made to lawyers for the defence or prosecution to help them establish whether there is a legal case to answer (known as a 'precognition') is not allowed, unless it has been made under oath[42]. A precognition is a note of what a witness is expected (or hoped) to say in court, so any statement taken with court action in mind is likely to be viewed as a precognition[43].

A statement made to the police at an early stage of their investigations would not generally amount to a precognition and could, therefore, be relied on in court. An interview with social workers might or might not amount to a precognition, depending on the circumstances. For example, in one child protection case, a semi-structured interview with social workers which allowed children at risk to speak spontaneously about what had happened was not treated as a precognition, and was thus admitted to court[44].

This rule may be useful in some situations. However, it would not have resolved the situation reported by the Mental Welfare Commission in *Justice Denied*[45], where a witness gave an account of alleged abuse to some of her care workers. Because the prosecution received information that

---

[41]   Criminal Procedure (Scotland) Act 1995, s259.

[42]   CP(S)A 1995, s262(1). See discussion at Walker and Walker (above) at para 8.7.2.

[43]   See *Kerr v. HM Advocate* 1958 JC 14, at 20 per the Lord Justice-Clerk (Thomson) *'In considering the circumstances the stage which the proceedings have reached is bound to be of importance, though not necessarily decisive. As long as we are in the stage of preliminary investigations, statements made to the police .... will not readily be regarded as being in the nature of precognitions. But, once the police have begun to build up a case against certain people who have been .... charged with some criminal offence, we have passed beyond the exploratory stage of preliminary investigations and have got into the stage of preparation for the leading of evidence.... But it is all so much a question of degree...'*

[44]   *F v. Kennedy (No. 2)* 1992 SCLR 750.

[45]   Mental Welfare Commission (2008).

she was not a credible or reliable witness, the court could not admit the evidence from the care workers. The law requires that the witness appears to be a credible or reliable witness at the time she made the statement.

Moreover, even where the court does allow a prior statement under the hearsay rule, it is possible that the court might say that the inability of the accused person to cross-examine the witness will prejudice the accused person's right to a fair trial[46].

PRINCIPLES AND PRACTICE: ENSURING ACCESS TO JUSTICE

The prior statements rule could be useful where a person has fluctuating health or her condition is deteriorating. Care workers and others need to know how to protect the evidence if a client reveals details of conduct that could amount to a crime.

The care worker should attempt to record any such statement as accurately as possible and date and sign this.

Statement as evidence of facts

13.19   Where a statement is evidence of something which happened at the same time as the offence, it may be allowed. In one case it was alleged that a woman with a mental impairment had been abused. Her mother was able to give evidence about her cries just after the alleged incident[47]. These were regarded not as hearsay but as proof that the alleged assault had happened.

Vulnerable witnesses

13.20   Where an adult is regarded as a vulnerable witness (see below) prior statements she has made may be accepted by the courts. This is an important exception to the hearsay rules.

---

[46]   *N v. HM Advocate* 2003 JC 140.
[47]   *Murray* (1866) 5 Irv 232. But *Cinci v. HM Advocate* 2004 JC 103 suggests that it is unlikely that such statements could be included unless they were made at the time of the alleged assault.

Corroboration

13.21 In criminal cases every essential fact in the case requires proof from two different sources, for example oral evidence from two separate witnesses or oral evidence from one witness and one piece of physical or circumstantial evidence. This rule does not apply in civil cases[48], even in proceedings for breach of interdict, where the evidence of only one person will be sufficient[49].

The rule on corroboration can make it hard to prove a case where someone alleges abuse, as often the only witnesses will be the victim and the alleged abuser. In the absence of any physical or circumstantial evidence, the evidence of the alleged victim will not, on its own, be sufficient.

In some cases of rape or sexual assault (see chapter 14) an alleged victim may lack capacity and be unable to give evidence. If there is corroborated evidence of sexual activity and of her incapacity to consent, the fact that the witness cannot give evidence herself should not preclude the case proceeding.

The corroboration rule can sometimes operate in a slightly different way where someone has allegedly abused more than one person. In these circumstances, the evidence of one witness to a crime can corroborate the evidence of another witness, if the allegations involve the same accused person and the crimes charged are very similar, with very similar features[50]. This might be the situation where an abuser targets a particular type of victim, such as women with learning disabilities or residents in a care home, and subjects them to a particular type of abuse. There has to be some time relationship between the various incidents[51] but each case depends on its facts.

---

[48] Civil Evidence (Scotland) Act 1988, s8(3).
[49] *Byrne v. Ross* 1993 SLT 307.
[50] Under the so-called Moorov doctrine. *Moorov v. HM Advocate* 1930 JC 86. Moorov was charged with a series of indecent assaults, all in similar circumstances. For more detail, see Walker and Walker, paras 5.10.1 to 5.10.3.
[51] See Walker and Walker at 5.10.3.

Competence of witnesses

13.22   In Scotland, there used to be a 'competence test' for witnesses[52]. This involved assessing both a potential witness's ability to be able to recall and explain the events she has seen, and her ability to understand the duty on witnesses to tell the truth.

The then Scottish Executive argued that some children and some adults with learning disabilities might be able to give a perfectly coherent account of what had happened but be unable to answer abstract questions as part of a 'test' of their ability to tell the truth. Some people might find hypothetical questions difficult. For example, if a sheriff asked *'What would you say if I told you my (blue) tie was red?'* the witness might be unable to answer. This may not detract from her ability to explain various events in her life. A competence test might mean that her evidence could not come before the court, with the potential effect that a prosecution would fall[53].

With this in mind, the Vulnerable Witnesses Act has modified the competence test. The court can no longer ask preliminary questions of a witness to ascertain whether the witness understands the difference between the truth and a lie and the duty to give truthful evidence[54]. This new rule applies for both criminal and civil cases.

The effect of abolishing the competence test should allow many more witnesses to give evidence. The court (or the jury) can then decide how credible and reliable their evidence is. However, despite the abolition of the formal competency test, it may be necessary, at some stage during the proceedings, for the court to assess the competency of the witness. For instance, where a witness is not able to give a coherent account of the events in question[55] it may still be necessary to hear arguments (and perhaps expert evidence[56]) in court as to whether she is able to give

---

[52]   See Walker and Walker (above) at para 13.2.1.
[53]   *Vital voices, helping vulnerable witnesses give evidence* Scottish Executive (2003), para 4.
[54]   Vulnerable Witnesses (Scotland) Act 2004, s24.
[55]   *HMA v. Skene Black* (1887) 1 White 365.
[56]   *HMA v. Stott* (1894) 1 Adam 386 where a patient in a psychiatric hospital was able to give a coherent account of what happened but the court heard expert evidence that he suffered from gross delusions which may have affected his evidence. The court advised the jury that it could not rely on his evidence.

evidence. Some academics have argued that the law is unclear as to when this might happen during the court procedure in Scotland[57].

In England and Wales the law is somewhat clearer. A person who is not able to understand the questions put to her in court or give coherent answers is not a competent witness[58]. There is no such statutory provision in Scotland.

Reliability and credibility of witnesses

13.23 Even where a witness is competent, there will be questions (as in any case) about whether the witness's evidence appears to be credible and reliable and thus what weight her evidence will have. If it becomes clear that a witness is unable to describe or remember the events in question (and special measures for vulnerable witnesses cannot help with this), there may be issues about her credibility or reliability.

Credibility is a question of whether the witness is telling the truth. Reliability is a question of whether the evidence can be relied upon.

A witness can be cross-examined to attempt to establish whether she is credible and reliable[59]. This could involve questions involving her learning disability or mental health challenges. Special measures for vulnerable witnesses may lessen the anxiety for a witness in such a situation, but considerable stress could still be caused to a witness whose abilities or mental weaknesses may be examined and brought into the public arena. A witness will need to be made aware that this may happen.

The courts will not generally accept expert evidence about the credibility or reliability of a witness, because this is a matter for the judge and/or jury to assess. However where a witness has a mental illness which could affect the quality of her evidence, the courts might accept psychiatric evidence about the nature of the illness and its implications on a witness's evidence[60]. The courts have considered expert opinion suggesting that the evidence given by a witness is likely to be impaired by a mental disorder such as personality disorder[61].

---

[57] See discussion in Walker and Walker, paras 13.2.4 to 13.2.8.
[58] Youth Justice and Criminal Evidence Act 1999, s53(3).
[59] *King v. King* (1841) 4 D 124.
[60] *HM Advocate v. Grimmond* 2002 SLT 508.
[61] *McBrearty v. HM Advocate* 2004 SLT 917.

The law now allows expert psychological or psychiatric evidence relating to any behaviour or statement of an alleged victim made after the alleged incident. However this is only allowed if it is necessary to remove any adverse effect on a witness's credibility or reliability which the behaviour or statement may otherwise have caused[62]. For example, it might be assumed that a victim of an assault would be tearful and go immediately to the police, while in fact some victims initially act in the opposite way.

There is also now some protection to victims of certain sexual offences. The accused person cannot personally cross-examine prosecution witnesses[63]. Additionally in all cases involving vulnerable witnesses the court may bar cross-examination by the accused person[64].

SUPPORT FOR WITNESSES

Ensuring courts are accessible

13.24 The law recognises the need to make courts and court procedures accessible to witnesses and accused people who have disabilities. The Scottish Court Service must make reasonable adjustments to its premises, its policies and its procedures to make them accessible to people with disabilities[65]. This extends to both physical and mental impairments. In addition, the Court Service is subject to the more general Disability Equality Duty, which requires it to avoid unlawful disability discrimination, promote equality of opportunity and encourage the participation of disabled people in public life[66].

The Judicial Studies Committee (the body responsible for training judges and sheriffs) has produced an Equal Treatment bench book, which gives some guidance to the court[67]. We understand that the book is currently being revised to consider the needs of witnesses with learning disabilities. The Scottish Court Service has published a disability equality scheme, and the Crown Office and Court Service have produced a joint

---

[62] CP(S)A 1995, s275C inserted by Vulnerable Witnesses (Scotland) Act 2004.
[63] CP(S)A 1995, s288C.
[64] CP(S)A 1995, s288F.
[65] Disability Discrimination Act 1995, s21.
[66] DDA 1995 (as amended by the Disability Discrimination Act 2005), s49A.
[67] Available on the Judicial Studies Committee's website.

statement on how they intend to support crown witnesses (witnesses for the prosecution). The statement particularly mentions the need to respond to witnesses with special needs and vulnerable witnesses.

Following the Mental Welfare Commission's *Justice denied* report, the Scottish Government published an action plan for meeting the needs of witnesses with learning disabilities[68]. One area in which further training is required is in communication skills for those involved in the legal process. *Justice denied* highlights some important resources[69]. Table **13.1** gives some guidelines.

Table 13.1 – Communicating with a witness with special needs[70]
Each person is an individual, but some general guidelines may help communication with people with special needs: • Speak clearly. • Use plain English. Avoid legal or other jargon. • Use open-ended questions wherever possible. Break questions down. Avoid having more than one idea or point in each question. • Avoid 'leading' questions. If someone does not understand a question, she may give the answer that she thinks the other person wants or expects. • If possible, speak to the person directly rather than using someone as an intermediary. • Avoid offering a choice of answer. The way a questioner presents information and choices can influence a person with special needs. • Give the person time to understand the question. Reassure the person that *'I don't understand'*, *'I don't know'* or *'I don't remember'* are acceptable answers. • People with special needs do not always have their views listened to. Other people present may influence them, even if they have a different view themselves. • It may be necessary to ask a question in different ways before finding a form of words the person understands. Contradictory answers may mean the person does not understand the way the other person has explained something, not that she cannot understand the idea at all.

[68] *Adults with learning disabilities in the criminal justice system: their rights and our responsibilities* (2009).
[69] Chapter 3, para 2.c.10.
[70] Adapted from *Special Measures for Vulnerable Adults and Child Witnesses* guidance pack from the Scottish Government (2006).

- Allow the person time to think. Do not interrupt or pre-empt what someone wants to say by finishing her sentences or suggesting words. People with special needs may need longer to think about a question and find the right words to express themselves.
- If there is doubt as to the level of a witness's understanding, consider arranging a second meeting to see whether the person is giving consistent evidence.

There are various ways of improving communication and support for vulnerable witnesses in the criminal justice system.

Appropriate adults

13.25 The police may believe that a person whom they are interviewing has a mental disorder.

Scottish Government guidance says that whenever the police interview someone who may have a mental disorder, an 'appropriate adult' must be present to assist with the interview[71]. This applies to people with mental illness, learning disability, acquired brain damage or dementia. An appropriate adult should be present whenever the police are interviewing an alleged victim, a witness or someone under suspicion of having committed a crime.

An appropriate adult is someone who has received special training, who understands the mental disability from which the person suffers and who will help the person understand the police interview process. A relative, friend or carer does not qualify as an appropriate adult, although she may be present at an interview in addition to the appropriate adult if the police allow this.

The appropriate adult should support the person, assist communication, make sure the person understands police questions, and ensure that a person under suspicion understands her rights. The appropriate adult cannot advise a witness not to answer questions or give legal advice[72].

---

[71] *Interviewing people who are mentally disordered: Appropriate Adult schemes* Scottish Office June 1998. See also Scottish Executive circular NHS HDL (2006) 56.

[72] For more detail, see *Mental Health, Incapacity and the Law in Scotland*, Hilary Patrick, Bloomsbury Professional (2006) chapter 44, paras 03–9.

An appropriate adult should be present to support a person with a mental disorder who is an alleged victim of crime, a witness to a crime or suspected of, or charged with, an offence. An appropriate adult should always attend when the police interview a patient in a psychiatric hospital[73].

Unfortunately, research carried out for the Scottish Government suggests that the scheme is still not fully understood and appropriate adults are not available for everyone who requires them[74].

Victim Information and Advice

13.26   The Victim Information and Advice Service is part of the Crown Office and Procurator Fiscal Service. It can help inform victims of serious crime and vulnerable witnesses about the courts and the court process before any proceedings commence. Staff will explain the process, arrange court visits, and give advice about other agencies offering help. They also keep victims and witnesses informed about the progress of the case as it affects them.

The work of this unit can help reassure people and encourage them to engage in the criminal justice process. Anyone wishing to access the service should contact the Procurator Fiscal.

The service is only funded to deal with criminal cases and so will not be able to offer support in civil cases under adult protection legislation.

Victim Support Scotland

13.27   Any victim of a crime or witness to a crime may contact Victim Support Scotland for support. Victim Support Scotland is a voluntary organisation that helps people affected by crime. Its volunteers provide emotional support, practical help and information to victims, witnesses and others affected by crime.

Services are locally based, both in the community and through court based witness services. It can also help with criminal injuries compensation claims (see chapter 14).

---

[73]   Scottish Executive circular NHS HDL (2006) 56 above.

[74]   *An Evaluation of Appropriate Adult Schemes in Scotland* Dr Lindsay Thomson, Viki Galt, Dr Rajan Darjee, Scottish Executive Social Research 78/2004.

Counselling

13.28 Counselling a victim of abuse can sometimes raise legal difficulties for a subsequent criminal prosecution. The counsellor must ensure that she does not inadvertently influence the person's recollection of the events. This could 'contaminate' the witness's evidence and ultimately mean the court will not accept what the person says.

Government guidance recognises the importance of counselling and support to a person who has suffered abuse, but stresses that there must be no suggestion that a counsellor has 'coached' a witness about the evidence she is to give to the court[75]. The guidance suggests that counsellors should avoid any discussions surrounding the material facts of the event in question, because this may be open to challenge during the trial or hearing[76].

The code gives further advice to counsellors. It states, for example, that where a witness who has made a prior statement discloses new evidence, the counsellor should inform relevant agencies, such as the police[77]. This advice appears to undermine the confidential relationship between counsellor and client and counsellors may need to take their own legal advice. The guidance recognises that maintaining trust is crucial in the provision of therapy, but says therapists and witnesses must understand the prosecution's duty to disclose relevant material to the defence[78].

Similar issues arise in child abuse cases. An expert committee in England and Wales recommended that one way to reduce the tensions in this relationship and to provide necessary therapy to a victim at an early stage would be to organise the taking of evidence on Commission (see below) soon after the alleged incidents. This evidence would be videotaped and made available to the court. This would end the alleged victim's involvement in the proceedings at an earlier stage and would mean that therapy could take place without concerns about contamination of evidence or the need to disclose confidential discussions to the defence[79].

---

[75] *Code of practice to facilitate the provision of therapeutic support to adult witnesses in court proceedings*, included in the Special Measures for vulnerable adults and child witnesses guidance pack from the Scottish Government (2006).

[76] Para 24.

[77] Para 29.

[78] See para 43.

[79] *Report of the Advisory Group on Video Evidence* (by the Pigot Committee) Home Office (1989).

SPECIAL MEASURES FOR VULNERABLE WITNESSES

13.29   A witness or victim of abuse may have a mental illness or a learning disability or may be too intimidated to give evidence in court. The Vulnerable Witnesses (Scotland) Act 2004 allows the court to authorise special measures to reduce the stress of court proceedings. Special measures can be used in both the criminal and the civil courts[80].

The court must decide whether there is a significant risk that either a mental disorder or fear or distress about giving evidence at the trial will affect the quality of the person's evidence to the court, whether the person should give evidence using special measures and, if so, which measures would be appropriate[81]. The final decision is with the court and there is no right of appeal[82].

A person who believes she is a vulnerable witness should tell the person calling her to give evidence. If that person fails to bring the matter to the attention of the court, the witness can raise the matter with the court.

Any of the following special measures may be authorised:

- Giving evidence using a live television link[83].

- Taking of evidence by a Commissioner[84] instead of the witness attending court.

- Submitting a prior written statement instead of giving evidence in chief[85]. (This is only available in criminal cases and the witness will still be cross-examined.)

---

[80]   For more detailed information, see *Mental Health, Incapacity and the Law in Scotland*, Hilary Patrick, Bloomsbury Professional (2006). References below are to the criminal court provisions. For civil provisions, see the Part 2 of the Vulnerable Witnesses (Scotland) Act 2004.

[81]   CP(S)A 1995, as amended by Vulnerable Witnesses (Scotland) Act 2004, ss271(1), 271C(8).

[82]   CP(S)A 1995, s271C(7), VW(S)A 2004 s12(6).

[83]   Vulnerable Witnesses (Scotland) Act 2004, s20.

[84]   See Act of Adjournal (Criminal Procedure Rules Amendment No. 6) (Vulnerable Witnesses (Scotland) Act 2004) (Evidence on Commission) 2005 SSI 2005 No. 574.

[85]   CP(S)A 1995, s271H. Evidence in chief is the evidence the witness gives to the person who asked her to attend court. This might be a procurator fiscal, advocate depute, the person's own solicitor or the solicitor of another party to the proceedings who asked the witness to attend court.

- Using a screen so the witness will not see the accused (although the accused will be able to see her)[86].

- Having a supporter in court[87].

Evidence on Commission

13.30 The Commissioner taking the evidence will be a High Court judge, for High Court cases, or a sheriff, for all other proceedings[88].

In some ways the procedure is similar to giving evidence in court. The witness will be required to give evidence and will be cross-examined by the lawyers for the accused person. However it may be easier to adapt the proceedings to the needs of the witness and to make them less formal than court proceedings. The Commissioner can come to the witness's home if necessary.

The accused person has the right to see and hear the taking of evidence on Commission, but she cannot be present in the room where the witness is giving evidence[89].

If there are questions about the competency of a witness, there might be advantages in resolving this at the Commission stage, rather than at a subsequent trial.

Evidence on Commission has not been widely used, but there are some examples of its use for vulnerable witnesses[90].

Supporters

13.31 A supporter can be available in court during the trial to provide reassurance to the witness. A supporter should be able to advise the court if a witness is becoming unduly distressed or is in need of a break. The judge or sheriff is responsible for maintaining proper order and can take what action is necessary.

The supporter cannot communicate with the witness in any way, so is not allowed to touch or speak to the witness during evidence. Instead, the

---

[86] Vulnerable Witnesses (Scotland) Act 2004, s21.

[87] VW(S)A 2004, s22.

[88] CP(S)A 1995, (as amended by the Criminal Proceedings etc. (Reform) (Scotland) Act 2007) s271I(8).

[89] CP(S)A 1995, s271I(3).

[90] See *Turning up the volume: the Vulnerable Witnesses (Scotland) Act 2004* (2008). Available from www.scotland.gov.uk.

supporter is intended to provide moral support by being present with her in court.

Ideally, the witness herself will be able to choose who acts as a supporter. However, in some cases a family member or friend might not be able to act in this role, for example where the preferred supporter is also a witness in the case. The judge has the final say in who can be a supporter in an individual case.

Prior statements

13.32   As explained above, the criminal courts do not generally admit evidence of a prior statement a person has made, because they regard this as hearsay. The best evidence rules require that, with some exceptions, the courts require a witness to attend court and give evidence in person. See para **13.17** above.

The Vulnerable Witnesses Act modifies this rule. The criminal court can admit a prior statement made by a vulnerable witness. This could be important in a situation where a witness has made statements that support the prosecution case, but may have difficulty in remembering crucial events or be unwilling, or unable, to give evidence of traumatic events at a later stage. At least some of the evidence can be recorded and submitted to the court in advance of the trial.

A prior statement could be a formal statement on oath[91] or it could be introduced to the court in other ways. For example, a police officer's notebook may contain the statement the witness made to the officer. It may be possible to record or transcribe an interview with, for example, a social worker or a support worker and lead this in evidence[92].

The court will decide whether the statement is admissible, that is, whether it would be fair to allow it to be relied on in evidence. It appears that the court does not have to establish whether the witness is a competent witness before receiving the statement[93].

If a prior statement adequately covers the facts of the case, it may form the main evidence of that witness, thus possibly sparing the witness considerable anxiety and stress about giving evidence and preserving evidence that might otherwise be lost.

---

[91]   Under the CP(S)A 1995, s291.
[92]   Provided it did not breach the prohibition on 'precognitions'.
[93]   See Walker and Walker, para 13.3.6.

If all parties agree the witness's statement, the court can accept the statement in evidence. However, the use of a prior statement may not remove the need for the witness to attend court (whether in person or via video link). The court may require the person to attend court to give the defence an opportunity to cross-examine her. It should not be necessary for the court to ask the witness to repeat all the evidence set out in her prior statement[94] and there is no requirement that the witness must 'adopt' the statement in court[95].

In practice, prior statements have not been widely used to replace vulnerable witnesses' attendance at court. Research carried out on behalf of the Scottish Government uncovered only one example of a prior statement replacing evidence given by the witness herself[96].

Intermediaries

13.33 An intermediary is a person who can help communication between a vulnerable witness and the court. Such a person could help where a witness has communication needs, perhaps because of a learning disability or mental illness[97]. Intermediaries are not included in the special measures available under the Vulnerable Witnesses Act, but the Act contains powers to introduce them. The Scottish Government consulted on the use of intermediaries in January 2008, but does not currently appear to be taking this forward.

SOLICITORS AND LEGAL AID

13.34 In many adult protection cases the adult at risk or the person to whom the application relates should seek legal advice. In some cases non-means-tested legal aid will be available.

The Law Society has a list of local solicitors for each area. The list includes details of the work they will take on, but is not a guarantee of expertise. A few solicitors have expert accreditation from the Law Society in mental health or incapacity work, which means their expertise has

---

[94] *W v. Kennedy* 1988 SCLR 236.
[95] CP(S)A 1995, s271M.
[96] See *Turning up the volume* (above).
[97] See research in England and Wales, *The Go-Between: evaluation of intermediary pathfinder projects* Plotnikoff and Wolfson (2007).

been independently verified. Social workers and independent advocacy projects should also be able to advise about finding a solicitor.

Civil legal aid is now available, regardless of the adult or applicant's means, for applications for welfare guardianship and for joint financial and welfare guardianship[98]. However the applicant will have to satisfy the Scottish Legal Aid Board that she has a case that merits a decision by the courts. Similarly, legal aid without means testing is now available to everyone who is the subject of an application under the Mental Health (Care and Treatment) Act and to their named person, if any (under the Assistance by Means of Representation (ABWOR) scheme)[99].

At the time of writing, it is not clear whether legal aid without a means test will be available for applications under the Adult Support and Protection Act. Current rules require the resources of the adult to be taken into account. To obtain a grant of civil legal aid for representation in court, the applicant will have to satisfy the Scottish Legal Aid Board that she has a good case and that she meets the financial eligibility requirements.

Legal aid is not available for safeguarders appointed under the Adults with Incapacity Act or the Adult Support and Protection Act. Although the court often appoints solicitors to the role, the Scottish Legal Aid Board does not see them as providing legal services to the client. Generally, therefore, the court requires the applicant (which is often a local authority) to meet the cost of any safeguarders appointed.

The Scottish Legal Aid Board has raised other technical issues about the working of legal aid in adult protection cases[100]. At the time of writing these remain unresolved.

Legal aid is available to an accused person, regardless of her means, in all criminal cases.

CONCLUSION

13.35 Over the past few years, the legal system has begun to make efforts to accommodate witnesses with additional support or

[98] The Civil Legal Aid (Scotland) Amendment (No. 2) Regulations 2006 SSI 2006/325.
[99] Advice and Assistance (Assistance by Way of Representation) (Scotland) Regulations 2003, SSI 2003/179, (as amended by SSI 2005/482), reg 9.
[100] In its submission to the Scottish Parliament Health Committee during its consideration of the Adult Support and Protection (Scotland) Bill.

communication needs. Reforms in both the law and working practices have improved access to the courts. The disability discrimination and vulnerable witnesses legislation have underlined the need for all legal professionals to make reasonable adjustments to their practice and procedures. This is also a requirement of human rights law.

Those working with an adult at risk should expect any legal process to be appropriate to the adult's needs and should be prepared to ask questions if this is not the case.

Chapter 14

THE CRIMINAL JUSTICE SYSTEM

14.1 This chapter looks at the role of the police and prosecution services and considers some of the offences relevant to adult protection law. There is also a brief introduction to criminal injuries compensation.

IMPORTANCE OF INVOLVING POLICE

14.2 A crucial feature of effective adult protection is the role of the police where a crime may have been committed. It is essential that the police are involved, not just to protect any evidence and improve the likelihood of a successful prosecution, but to benefit from their expertise in how to conduct the investigation[1].

In the past there has been concern that health and social care professionals did not always recognise assaults on victims with impairments as crimes[2]. In addition, care staff may be unclear about whether to report a possible crime to the police if the adult does not wish this[3]. Local adult protection committees must develop good practice protocols. In particular, staff will need to consider an alleged victim's capacity to safeguard his own welfare interests and to take decisions about involving the police.

Anyone may report concerns about an adult at risk to the police. This can be in addition to, or instead of, informing the local authority. The police can be informed whether or not the adult consents, although, in practice, if the adult does not agree to the police's involvement it may be difficult for them to carry out inquiries.

A specialist police officer from a domestic abuse unit of the police may investigate risk to an adult from a member of his household. All but one of the eight police forces in Scotland have designated domestic abuse

---

[1] Adult Support and Protection Act Code of Practice, chapter 4, para 11.
[2] See discussion in *Justice denied* (Mental Welfare Commission (2008), para 3.2.a ff.
[3] *Justice Denied* (above) at chapter 4, para 1.2.

officers[4]. They could have a particular role in adult protection cases and some forces have put into place effective systems to share good practice.

ANSWERING POLICE INQUIRIES

14.3 When the police are making inquiries in adult protection cases, service providers are not always sure of their duty to answer police questions. If a service provider is asked to hand over confidential information to the police without a warrant, he may need to seek legal advice.

While a person suspected of a crime must give the police his name and address if requested[5], it is not otherwise an offence to refuse to answer questions or to hand over information, unless the police have a warrant (see chapter 6)[6].

Normally, the police must obtain a warrant to search or enter premises but they can search without a warrant in urgent situations[7]. A person may agree to the police searching even if they have no warrant, but if the person being searched is suspected of a crime, the police must caution him that he is not obliged to allow the search[8] .

It is an offence to assault, resist, obstruct or hinder a police officer in the course of his duty[9]. This relates to physically or verbally impeding an officer[10].

Attempting to pervert the course of justice is a crime, and giving wrong information to the police could amount to this[11]. It is also an offence to attempt to persuade another person to give false information to the police[12] or to destroy, or attempt to destroy, evidence[13].

---

[4]   *Thematic inspection of domestic abuse,* Her Majesty's Inspectorate of Constabulary in Scotland (2008).

[5]   Criminal Procedure (Scotland) Act 1995, s13.

[6]   *The Criminal Law of Scotland,* Gerald Gordon (Third Edition) W Green, (2001), para 47.39.

[7]   *Criminal procedure* Renton and Brown W Green Part II.

[8]   *Davidson v. Brown* 1990 JC 324.

[9]   Police (Scotland) Act 1967, s41.

[10]   *Curlett v. McKechnie* 1938 JC 176, *Walsh v. McFadyen* 2002 JC 93.

[11]   *Kerr v. Hill* 1936 JC 71.

[12]   *Dalton v. HM Advocate* 1951 JC 76.

[13]   Gordon, para 48.36.

It is an offence under the adult protection legislation to refuse to hand over records to an authorised council officer or to obstruct anyone acting pursuant to an adult protection order or warrant[14].

DECISION TO PROSECUTE

14.4 The police report the results of their investigations to the Crown Office and the Procurator Fiscal service, the public prosecutor in Scotland which takes decisions about prosecution. This depends on the quality of the evidence, and its reliability and sufficiency, as well as whether it is in the public interest to prosecute. The Crown Office prosecution code explains the type of considerations prosecutors take into account, including the seriousness of the crime, its effect on the victim, any mitigating circumstances and the effect of any possible prosecution on the alleged victim[15].

In cases that could lead to a jury trial, a procurator fiscal interviews witnesses and reviews the evidence. He then reports to the Crown Office, where an Advocate Depute, (sometimes referred to as Crown Counsel), will review the case. Advocate Deputes are senior lawyers employed in the Crown Office. They generally conduct prosecutions in the High Court and make the decision whether to prosecute sheriff and jury cases (although sheriff court cases are conducted by depute procurators fiscal).

Even where the decision is taken not to prosecute there are alternatives to prosecution, such as a fine, a warning or diversion from prosecution into a support or treatment programme.

Victims often find it difficult to accept that the prosecution service will not divulge the reasons for its decision not to prosecute, but there could be good reasons for this, such as protecting confidential information or preserving evidence for a future prosecution[16].

SOME RELEVANT CRIMINAL OFFENCES

14.5 Abuse of an adult at risk could involve physical assaults, a property crime such as theft or fraud, sexual assaults including rape, and

---

[14] Adult Support and Protection (Scotland) Act 2007, s49.
[15] The Code is available on the Crown Office Procurator Fiscal Service's website.
[16] See Crown Office prosecution code (above).

harassment or breach of the peace. This section looks at some of these offences in outline and considers special offences created under the adult protection legislation[17].

PRINCIPLES AND PRACTICE: ACCESS TO JUSTICE

The authors suggest that in all adult protection cases involving harm or abuse caused by a third party, staff should formally consider whether or not a crime may have been committed and the police should be involved. Classifying conduct as 'abuse', or an 'adult protection matter', rather than a potential crime means that crimes against some vulnerable victims, such as people with learning disabilities, are underreported, despite an increased risk of sexual assault.

Research shows historically low levels of prosecutions for such crimes. This can lead to predators deliberately targeting vulnerable victims[18].

Assault

14.6 Any deliberate attack or attempted attack on another person is an assault, whether there is injury resulting or not. Threatening gestures can also amount to assault[19]. Making serious threats to life or limb or to damage a person's property or reputation is also a crime. Other threats may constitute a breach of the peace.

Breach of the peace

14.7 Any conduct that is likely to place a member of the public in a state of fear and alarm could constitute a breach of the peace. This could include, for example, threats or taunts, swearing, name-calling or

---

[17]   For more detailed information, a criminal law textbook should be consulted. For lawyers the classic work is *Criminal law*, Gerald Gordon (Third Edition) W Green (2001).

[18]   The research evidence is discussed in *Justice Denied* (above), paras 3.2.1 to 3.2.9.

[19]   Gordon, *Criminal law* paras 29.01, 02.

throwing missiles[20]. Many disabled people have experience of such conduct.

This can be a crime even if the victim is not actually alarmed, provided a reasonable person would think that the perpetrator's intention was to create fear or alarm.

While breach of the peace was originally a public order offence, it may now be relevant even where the behaviour takes place in private[21].

Fraud and theft

14.8   Misusing a person's benefit money, or taking money from a person who is not able to understand, may constitute fraud or theft[22]. Theft is the dishonest taking of the goods of another. Theft can be aggravated by violence or intimidation and in such cases is robbery.

A person who misuses property he originally received legally, for example as an appointee, may be guilty of the crimes of breach of trust or embezzlement. Misleading a person into handing over property or money, or into otherwise acting to his disadvantage, could constitute fraud. Threatening a person in order to force him to hand over money, or to comply with any other demand, is extortion or assault and robbery.

Neglect and ill treatment

14.9   Where a person has a duty of care to another and neglects that person, he may be guilty of a common law crime if the person suffers injury or death. The crime would be culpably and recklessly causing injury or culpably and recklessly causing danger to others[23]. In some cases, where the behaviour has brought about death, the crime will be culpable homicide or even murder[24]. Such conduct could also amount to the crime of 'cruel and unnatural treatment'[25].

Anyone exercising personal welfare powers under the Adults with Incapacity Act who ill-treats or wilfully neglects the adult with incapacity

---

[20]   For discussion of the cases, see *Smith v. Donnelly* 2001 SLT 1007.
[21]   *Young v. Heatly* 1959 JC 66.
[22]   Gordon, chapters 14–18.
[23]   Gordon, para 29.57.
[24]   Gordon, para 25.07.
[25]   Gordon, para 29.49.

commits an offence[26]. This could apply to a welfare guardian, a welfare attorney, someone acting under an intervention order, or someone with welfare powers delegated to him. A financial guardian who fails to make proper provision for an adult would not commit a crime under this provision, but a complaint to the Public Guardian might be in order.

Similarly it is an offence for a provider of care services (paid or unpaid) or a hospital employee, manager or contractor to ill-treat or wilfully neglect anyone with a mental disorder[27].

Wilful neglect will normally be intentional or deliberate[28]. The intention can be inferred from the circumstances. In an English case, a parent was charged with wilful neglect. He had failed to look after a child through ignorance and was found not guilty[29], but the Scottish courts have not accepted ignorance as a defence[30].

Sexual offences

Rape and sexual assault

14.10 A non-consensual sexual act with a person with mental illness, learning disability or personality disorder is a statutory criminal offence, quite apart from any crime that it may comprise at common law or under any other statute[31]. Such an act is an offence if the mentally disordered person does not consent to the act or is incapable of consenting[32]. Apparent consent is not a true consent if the accused person placed the victim in a state of such fear, or subjected him to threats, intimidation, deceit or persuasion, that the consent was ineffective[33].

The Scottish Parliament passed a new Sexual Offences Act in 2009, which largely implements the recommendations of the Scottish Law Commission in its report on rape and other sexual offences in 2007[34].

[26] Adults with Incapacity (Scotland) Act 2000, s83.
[27] Mental Health (Care and Treatment) (Scotland) Act 2003, s315.
[28] *H v. Lees, D v. Orr* 1994 SLT 908.
[29] *R v. Shepherd and anor* [1981] AC (HL) 394.
[30] See discussion in *Child Abuse, Child Protection and the Law*, Alison Cleland W Green (2008) para 4.019.
[31] MH(CT)(S)A 2003, s311.
[32] MH(CT)(S)A 2003, s311(1).
[33] MH(CT)(S)A 2003, s311(3).
[34] Scottish Law Commission 209.

The Act introduces a new offence of rape, based on sexual intercourse without the free consent of the victim. A person does not give consent if he is incapable of consenting because of the effects of alcohol or other substances, if consent is obtained through threats or because the person is unlawfully detained, or where there is deception[35]. A person with mental disorder cannot consent if he is unable to understand the proposed conduct, make a decision or communicate that decision[36].

The new law will apply to rape, sexual assault and other crimes. It will replace the Mental Health (Care and Treatment) Act offence. The Act is likely to come into effect in 2010.

Abuse of trust

14.11   If a person who provides certain care or personal services to a client with a mental illness, learning disability or personality disorder engages in sexual conduct with that client, this is presumed to be exploitative, whether or not the client appears to consent.

Such conduct will be an offence regardless of consent if the person provides care services to a mentally disordered client in hospital or the community[37]. Spouses and partners who are carers are excluded[38].

It is a defence to prove that, at the time of the sexual act, the person charged did not know (and could not reasonably have been expected to know) that the client had a mental disorder[39].

The Sexual Offences Act will replace these provisions with a new crime of sexual abuse of trust of a mentally disordered person. The new offence largely replicates the Mental Health (Care and Treatment) Act offence[40].

Offences under adult protection legislation

14.12   There are various offences under the Mental Health (Care and Treatment) Act, including helping a person abscond[41], making false statements[42] and obstruction[43].

---

[35]   Sexual Offences (Scotland) Act 2009, s10.
[36]   SO(S)A 2009, s13.
[37]   MH(CT)(S)A 2003, s313.
[38]   MH(CT)(S)A 2003, s313(3).
[39]   MH(CT)(S)A 2003, s313(3)(a)(i).
[40]   SO(S)A 2009, s35.
[41]   MH(CT)(S)A 2003, s316.
[42]   MH(CT)(S)A 2003, s318.
[43]   MH(CT)(S)A 2003, s317.

It is an offence to prevent or obstruct an authorised person from carrying out his duties under the Adult Support and Protection Act, without reasonable excuse[44] or to allow an authorised person access to records under section 10 of the Act. The adult at risk cannot become liable for prosecution under this provision. See chapter 11 for discussion of this provision.

CRIMINAL INJURIES COMPENSATION

14.13   A person injured because of a crime may be entitled to criminal injuries compensation. Full details of the scheme are available from the Criminal Injuries Compensation Authority[45]. Physical and mental injuries are covered. In some cases mental injury on its own is covered.

A person can apply for criminal injuries compensation even where there has been no prosecution or conviction, as applications are decided on the civil standard of proof. Some solicitors and law centres will assist with applications.

CONCLUSION

14.14   Where an adult suffers harm because of the criminal conduct of others, it is important that those supporting him involve the police and prosecution services. The police have a crucial role in effective adult protection and their contribution to the adult protection committees offers the possibility of a more coordinated response.

The authors have argued that wherever a person is subjected to harm or abuse the local authority should formally consider and record whether a crime may have been committed, and, if so, should involve the police. Concerns about whether an alleged victim will be a reliable witness should not mean that local authority workers act as gatekeepers and deprive police and prosecution services of the opportunity to consider the case.

---

[44]   ASP(S)A 2007, s49.
[45]   *www.cica.gov.uk.*

Chapter 15

THE FUTURE OF ADULT PROTECTION

15.1 The last two decades have seen significant changes to the way community care and support services are provided. Individuals are more likely to be supported in the community, receive a personalised service and participate in decisions. Community-based treatment for mental disorder is common, and initiatives such as direct payments have the potential to allow people much more flexibility, freedom and choice in terms of the services they receive.

Although many of these developments are welcome, the changing landscape of adult protection creates both challenges and opportunities. This chapter introduces some current issues.

PARTNERSHIP WORKING

15.2 The Adult Support and Protection Act requires every local authority to have an adult protection committee[1], although some smaller local authorities are likely to establish joint committees. The roles and responsibilities of these committees are explored in detail in chapter 3.

At the time of writing the committees were still being established, so there was little information about how they will operate in practice. However, it is clear that the systems for cooperation and sharing information will be key to making sure the legislation delivers improvements in adult protection.

In 2004, a Mental Welfare Commission inquiry highlighted the lack of information sharing and co-ordination within and between key agencies, including social work, health, education, housing and the police[2]. The

---

[1] Adult Support and Protection (Scotland) Act 2007, s42.
[2] *Investigations into Scottish Borders Council and NHS Borders Services for People with Learning Disabilities: Joint Statement from the Mental Welfare Commission and the Social Work Services Inspectorate* (2004).

Commission's investigation concluded that several agencies had been aware of different aspects of the case and, had all this information been properly shared, the outcome might have been more satisfactory.

Establishing appropriate information-sharing mechanisms that are secure and proportionate will be crucial. Many cases will involve dealing with personal and sensitive information about individuals who will want to be assured their details are only available to those with proper authorisation.

Finally, organisations providing services, such as supported living and residential care, will need to develop clear policies about disclosing information. Some of the issues around information sharing are covered in chapter 11.

CROSS BORDER ISSUES

Allocation between local authorities

15.3 Adult protection cases can involve issues about which authority is responsible for investigation and this may depend on which legislation is relevant:

- Under the Adult Support and Protection Act and Mental Health (Care and Treatment) Act, the local authority responsible for the area in which the adult is physically situated has the responsibility for investigating abuse and taking any necessary action[3].

- The Adults with Incapacity Act is worded differently. This places a duty on both the local authority in which the adult resides and the area in which the adult currently is present to investigate. However, the local authority for the area in which the adult normally resides remains responsible for taking necessary action[4].

- If there is a need for community care services, the local authority where the adult is physically situated at that time is responsible for

---

[3]   ASP(S)A 2007, s53(1) and the Mental Health (Care and Treatment) Act 2003, s33(1).
[4]   Adults with Incapacity (Scotland) Act 2000, s10(d) and s87(1).

carrying out a community care assessment and providing services. However, it may be able to recover the costs of providing any service from the authority where the adult is normally resident[5]. This also applies where the adult is in another area on a temporary basis, such as on holiday.

Adults outwith Scotland

15.4 The situation can also arise when before, or during, an investigation into harm and abuse, the adult moves to another country. This might be a planned move or an attempt to prevent further investigations. In such circumstances, it might be important that local authorities share information with their counterparts in other jurisdictions to prevent further abuse.

The UK has ratified the Hague Convention on the International Protection of Adults[6]. This allocates the responsibility for adults who are unable to protect their own interests. The objectives of the Convention are to:

- Determine which country can take measures to protect adults and their property.

- Set out which country's laws should be used.

- Provide for the recognition and enforcement of measures of adult protection. This will include measures under Scottish adult protection legislation, which should be recognised in other participating countries; and

- Establish cooperation between countries signed up to the Convention[7].

There is also provision for action in cases of urgency[8].

Finally, it may be possible to use the Adult Support and Protection Act to involve the police where it appears an adult has moved to obstruct an investigation[9].

---

[5]   Social Work (Scotland) Act 1968, s86(1).
[6]   In respect of Scotland. For full text and details of signatories, see www.hcch.net.
[7]   Convention on the International Protection of Adults, Article 1.
[8]   Convention on the International Protection of Adults, Article 10.
[9]   ASP(S)A 2007, s49(1).

SELF DIRECTED SUPPORT

15.5 Direct payments were introduced in 1996 and represented the first formal opportunity for service users to be in control of the services they received[10]. The scheme means that while local authorities continue to be under a duty to carry out an assessment of an individual's needs, the individual becomes entitled to receive a sum of money rather than having the local authority arrange services. The service user can then use these funds to purchase her care.

Since direct payments were first introduced, the concept has evolved, and many now consider that everyone should be entitled to a personalised service, with as much control over their care as they want. This is reflected in a general move towards a system of social care where an individual is allocated her own personal budget, based on the cost of the services the local authority thinks she needs. The service user can then use those funds to purchase the type of care and support she wants to enhance her life.

In some cases, the service user will become an employer and manage the money independently. In other cases, she will choose services, with finances continuing to be dealt with by the local authority. For example, instead of being allocated a week at a respite facility, the person would be allocated a sum of money and could choose to arrange a holiday with a carer instead. The precise arrangements will depend on how each local authority decides to operate the system.

This approach clearly gives significant opportunities for service users to receive much more flexible services, and recognises that people themselves are often best placed to decide the type of support they need.

However, increased flexibility presents challenges for adult protection. Local authorities may have less control over the services an individual receives, particularly where care is purchased from a self-employed person. In many cases, this will be appropriate and the individual will receive good quality support, but it could also mean there are fewer formal safeguards.

These developments stress the importance of adult protection committees working with a wide range of bodies to achieve appropriate adult protection procedures. The committees bring together the key

---

[10]   Community Care (Direct Payments) Act 1996 (amending the Social Work (Scotland) Act 1968).

public bodies traditionally responsible for delivering and monitoring services. However, society has moved away from local authority service provision and increasingly individuals purchase care from private companies, charities and individuals. This trend is likely to continue, with local authorities directly providing a much lower percentage of social care. This means that those represented on the committee are only some of those involved in dealing with abuse and harm.

The private and voluntary sector can, of course, be invited to sit on committees. However, those attending will only ever represent a proportion of providers and will have little control over the procedures other organisations have in place. Further thought may need to be given to how information from all those involved in the provision of care can be appropriately shared. Committees may also need to think about their role in relation to self-directed support.

PROTECTING VULNERABLE GROUPS

15.6 The Protection of Vulnerable Groups (Scotland) Act 2007 was introduced following the Bichard Inquiry Report in 2004[11]. It introduces a new membership scheme to improve the current disclosure arrangements for people who work or volunteer with children and 'protected adults'[12]. The term 'protected adults' refers to people over the age of 16 who receive certain care or welfare services. Those who carry out the type of work listed in the legislation will have to become members of the new scheme[13]. Over time, it is estimated that between 700 000 and 800 000 people working or volunteering with vulnerable groups in Scotland will be part of the scheme[14].

The scheme will be managed and delivered by Disclosure Scotland[15]. Regular updating means any new information about a potential risk an individual poses should be acted on promptly. For example, if a person is convicted of a relevant crime, such as sexual assault, or is dismissed

---

[11] For the full report, see www.police.homeoffice.gov.uk.
[12] Protection of Vulnerable Groups (Scotland) Act 2007, s94.
[13] Regulated work is defined by POVG(S)A 2007, sch 3.
[14] Figures from Scottish Government website – www.scotland.gov.uk.
[15] An executive agency of the Scottish Government, which provides potential employers and voluntary organisations with criminal history information on individuals applying for posts. See www.disclosurescotland.co.uk.

following allegations of abuse, this should be reported to Disclosure Scotland. This new information will be included on that person's records and a decision will be made about what to do next. This could include deciding the individual should be banned from working with specific groups. The new scheme has also been designed to avoid the need for multiple disclosure checks.

Lists of people banned from working with children and protected adults will also be established. Although these will be two separate lists, it is expected that most people banned from working with one group will appear on both.

The scheme is due to come into effect in 2010. Retrospective checking of the current workforce will be phased in. Much of the detail about how the scheme will operate is being dealt with by regulations. Up-to-date information can be found on the Scottish Government's website[16].

'HATE CRIMES'

15.7 The Scottish Parliament passed the Offences (Aggravation by Prejudice) (Scotland) Act on 3 June 2009[17]. It does not create any new offences but instead extends the current law on 'statutory aggravation' where there is evidence a crime was motivated by malice or ill will based on an actual, or perceived, characteristic of the victim.

This new provision allows the court to increase the punishment for an offence if it is satisfied, on the balance of probabilities, that the crime was motivated by hate. In Scotland, this is currently possible if the hatred is as a result of the victim's actual or perceived race or religion. This Act extends the provisions to include sexual orientation, transgender identity or disability.

Significantly, the Act also means that 'hate crimes' must be recorded at all levels of the criminal justice system, from the initial report of the crime until sentencing. This is important in the field of adult protection, particularly where an individual is targeted because she has a disability.

It is generally understood that people with disabilities have an increased risk of being victims of crime, particularly harassment and assault. (See para **10.11** above.) Recording reports and progress of cases

---

[16]   www.scotland.gov.uk

[17]   This was introduced by Patrick Harvie MSP as a private members bill on 19 May 2008 and was often referred to as the 'Hate Crimes Bill'.

will, over time, build up a much better picture of the extent of such crimes and the outcomes.

REVIEW OF SCRUTINY BOARDS

15.8   In June 2006, Professor Lorne Crerar was commissioned by The Scottish Ministers to look at the current system for the regulation, audit and inspection of public services in Scotland. The Crerar report was published in 2007[18] and on 28 May 2009 the Public Services Reform (Scotland) Bill was introduced to the Scottish Parliament. This has the intention of simplifying the system of public scrutiny in Scotland and is part of a government commitment to reduce the number of public and scrutiny bodies by 25% by 2011.

Throughout this book, reference is made to statutory organisations affected by the review, including the Care Commission and Mental Welfare Commission.

At the time of writing, the Bill was at an early stage and so may be subject to significant amendment. However, the proposal is to establish:

- A new body called 'Social Care and Social Work Improvement Scotland'. This will be a non-department public body, with the responsibility for the improvement and scrutiny of local authority social work services and registered care services.

- A new body called 'Healthcare Improvement Scotland'. This will be a health body with responsibility for the improvement and scrutiny of all registered independent healthcare services and the NHS in Scotland.

The Bill seeks to abolish the existing Care Commission, NHS Quality Improvement Scotland and the Social Work Inspection Agency. The new organisations will take over the functions of these existing bodies.

The Scottish Government originally proposed that the Mental Welfare Commission should be absorbed into one of the new bodies. Many stakeholders were concerned at the potential loss of independence of the Commission, as well as the potential compromise of its safeguarding role under mental health and incapacity legislation. At the time of writing a separate consultation on the Commission's future had been issued.

---

[18]   www.scotland.gov.uk.

YOUNG PEOPLE AND ADULT PROTECTION

15.9 As discussed in chapter 2, adult protection legislation applies to people over the age of 16[19]. However, the local authority may be under additional responsibilities in respect of those aged 16 to 18 in terms of the Children (Scotland) Act 1995[20]. The topic of child protection is outside the scope of this book and there are other, valuable and comprehensive texts available[21]. However, where any individual involved is under the age of 16, adult protection staff will need to liaise with child protection services.

The Adult Support and Protection Act code of practice[22] recognises the possibility of crossover between child and adult protection. There are generally two classes of overlap:

- Where a family has both children and adults at risk. Information that starts as a child protection investigation could trigger an adult protection investigation and vice versa; and

- An individual aged 16 to 18 might be classed as both a child and an adult.

The code highlights the need for proper transitional arrangements between services, as well as cooperation between adult protection and child protection committees.

CONCLUSION

15.10 Over the last decade, there have been major changes in the legal framework relevant to adult protection. These changes have generally been welcomed and represent a move towards a more flexible, modern and person-centred approach. However, changes in the ways community care services are delivered, and the number of individuals, organisations and companies now involved, creates challenges in regulation, information sharing and making sure appropriate safeguards are in place.

---

[19] Although some of the provisions of the MH(CT)(S)A 2003 apply to medical treatment of children for a mental disorder.

[20] The definition of child in this legislation extends to those up to the age of 18 in some circumstances. Children (Scotland) Act 1995, ss15 and 93.

[21] See Alison Cleland, *Child Abuse, Child Protection and The Law* W Green (2008).

[22] Adult Support and Protection Act Code of Practice, para 8.5.

It is vital that systems are kept under review and that sufficient resources are allocated for training and awareness-raising about the nature of harm and abuse, the duties of local authorities and the complex ethical challenges facing adult protection practitioners. We hope that this book has made a contribution to these resources.

INDEX

[all references are to paragraph number]

Abolition of slavery
human rights, and, 12.6
Abuse and harm
categories
domestic abuse, 5.13
eating disorders, 5.12
financial abuse, 5.14
neglect by third party, 5.9
physical abuse, 5.7
self-harm, 5.11
self-neglect, 5.10
sexual abuse, 5.8
definitions
AWI(S)A 2000, in, 5.5
ASP(S)A 2007, in, 5.3
MH(CT)(S)A 2003, in, 5.4
domestic abuse, 5.13
eating disorders, 5.12
financial abuse, 5.14
neglect by third party, 5.9
physical abuse, 5.7
recognition of
concerns raised following
behaviour changes, 5.21
disclosure by adult, 5.19
disclosure by third party, 5.20
medical care and treatment, 5.22
self-harm, 5.11
self-neglect, 5.10
setting
at home, 5.16
in community, 5.17
sexual abuse, 5.8
Abuse of trust
criminal justice system, and, 14.11
Access to facilities
Mental Welfare Commission, and,
7.11

Access to funds
financial support and advice, and,
9.16
Access to records
local authorities, and
ASP(S)A 2007, under, 6.8
MH(CT)(S)A 2003, under, 6.39–
6.40
Mental Welfare Commission, and,
7.10
Accessibility of courts
witness support, and, 13.24
Adult protection
meaning, 1.2
risk, and, 1.4
Adult protection committees
generally, 2.8
persons involved in adult
protection cases, and
generally, 3.4
membership, 3.5
statutory basis, 2.8
Adult protection law
balancing risk and protection,
1.4
development, 1.1–1.6
framework
And see **Legal framework**
generally, 2.1–2.40
principles
AWI(S)A 2000, in, 4.3
ASP(S)A 2007, in, 4.5
background, 4.2
human rights, and, 4.6
indemnity, 4.8
legal impact, 4.7
MH(CT)(S)A 2003, in, 4.4
promotion, 4.9

Adult protection law – *contd*
  scope of legislation, 1.3
  wider context, 1.5
Adult protection offences 14.12
**Adult Support and Protection
  (Scotland) Act 2007**
  access to records, 6.8
  adult protection committees, 2.8
  'adults at risk', 2.3
  assessment orders
    appeals, 6.14
    applications, 6.11
    consent of adult, 6.27
    grounds, 6.10
    impact, 6.13
    limits to powers, 6.12
  banning orders
    consent of adult, 6.27
    generally, 6.26
  cooperation
    examination of records, 11.5
    general duty, 11.2
    general practitioners, 11.4
    scope of provisions, 2.6
    sharing of information, 11.3
  harm and abuse, 5.3
  information requirements
    adults, relatives and carers, of,
      2.10
    advice agencies, of, 2.11
    service providers, of, 2.11
  investigations
    allocation of inquiries, 6.3
    generally, 6.2
  investigations, 2.5
  medical examinations, 6.7
  new orders, 2.7
  people covered, 2.3
  powers and duties of local
    authorities
    access to records, 6.8
    assessment orders, 6.9–6.14
    banning orders, 6.26–6.29
    investigations, 6.2–6.3
    medical examinations, 6.7

**Adult Support and Protection
  (Scotland) Act 2007** – *contd*
  powers and duties of local
    authorities – *contd*
    removal orders, 6.15–6.25
    visits, 6.4–6.6
  principles, 4.5
  removal orders
    appeals, 6.25
    applications, 6.16
    consent of adult, 6.27
    contact conditions, 6.22
    detention, and, 6.20
    emergency applications, 6.17
    expiry, 6.21
    grounds, 6.18
    impact, 6.19
    protection of property, and, 6.24
    recall, 6.23
    variation, 6.23
  scope
    adult protection committees,
      2.8
    cooperation, 2.6
    generally, 2.4
    investigations, 2.5
    new orders, 2.7
  use, 2.9
  visits
    generally, 6.4
    interviews, 6.6
    warrants, 6.5
  warrants for visits, 6.5
Adults
  information requirements, and
    AWI(S)A 2000, under, 2.33
    ASP(S)A 2007, under, 2.10
    MH(CT)(S)A 2003, under, 2.21
'Adults at risk'
  definition, 2.3
**Adults with Incapacity (Scotland)
  Act 2000**
  attorneys, 2.27
  bank accounts, 2.28
  cooperation, and, 11.8

Adults with Incapacity (Scotland) Act 2000 – *contd*
emergencies
  generally 8.7
  interim guardianship, 8.8
generally, 2.23
guardianship orders, 2.31
harm and abuse, 5.5
'incapacity', 2.24
information requirements
  adults, relatives and carers, of, 2.33
  advice agencies, of, 2.34
  service providers, of, 2.34
intervention orders, 2.31
investigations
  generally, 6.31
making medical decisions, 2.30
managing bank accounts, 2.28
managing residents' finances, 2.29
medical decisions, 2.30
medical examinations, 6.33
medical treatment, 6.33
people covered, 2.24
powers and duties of local
    authorities
  emergencies, in, 6.32
  investigations, 6.31
  medical examinations, 6.33
  medical treatment, 6.33
principles, 4.3
relevance to adult protection, 2.32
residents' finances, 2.29
scope
  attorneys, 2.27
  generally, 2.25
  guardianship orders, 2.31
  intervention orders, 2.31
  investigations, 2.26
  making medical decisions, 2.30
  managing bank accounts, 2.28
  managing residents' finances, 2.29
Advance directives
support for adults, and, 9.21

Advance statements
scope of MH(CT)(S)A 2003, and, 2.19
support for adults, and, 9.22
Advice agencies
information requirements, and
  AWI(S)A 2000, under, 2.34
  ASP(S)A 2007, under 2.11
  MH(CT)(S)A 2003, under, 2.22
Answering police inquiries
criminal justice system, and, 14.3
Antisocial behaviour orders
emergencies, and, 8.13
generally, 10.26
Appeals
assessment orders, and, 6.14
removal orders, and
  ASP(S)A 2007, under, 6.25
  MH(CT)(S)A 2003, under, 6.44
sheriff court
  AWI(S)A 2000, under, 13.7
  ASP(S)A 2007, under, 13.13
Appointment of attorney
support for adults, and, 9.24–9.25
Appointment of named person
support for adults, and, 9.26
Appropriate adults
witness support, and, 13.25
Assault
criminal justice system, and, 14.6
Assessment orders
appeals, 6.14
applications, 6.11
consent of adult, 6.27
grounds, 6.10
impact, 6.13
limits to powers, 6.12
Attorneys
appointment, 9.24–9.25
persons involved in adult
    protection cases, and, 3.13
scope of AWI(S)A 2000, and, 2.27
Bail conditions
generally, 10.27

Bank accounts
scope of AWI(S)A 2000, and, 2.28
Banning orders
adult's rights, 10.14
appeals, 10.20
applications, 10.13
breach, 10.22–10.24
consent of adult, 6.27
criteria, 10.15
emergencies, and, 8.5
expiry, 10.25
generally, 6.26
impact, 10.17
local authorities' duties, 10.14
notifications, 10.19
perpetrator aged under 16, 10.16
recall, 10.21
temporary measures, 10.18
variation, 10.21
Behaviour changes
harm and abuse, and, 5.21
Breach of the peace
criminal justice system, and,
14.7
Burden of proof
rules of evidence, and, 13.16
Care Commission
contacting, 7.6
enforcement, 7.5
future of, 15.8
inspections, 7.4
investigation of risk, 7.3
persons involved in adult
protection cases, and, 3.8
powers and duties
enforcement, 7.5
inspections, 7.4
investigation of risk, 7.3
Care providers
generally, 3.11
Carers
information requirements, and
AWI(S)A 2000, under, 2.33
ASP(S)A 2007, under, 2.10
MH(CT)(S)A 2003, under, 2.21

Carers' assessments
community care services, and, 9.8
**Chronically Sick and Disabled
Persons Act 1970**
community care services, and, 9.9
generally, 2.38
Codes of practice
generally, 2.35
Community care assessments
community care services, and, 9.7
Community care services
carers' assessments, 9.8
community care assessments, 9.7
free personal and nursing care, 9.11
MH(CT)(S)A 2003, under, 9.10
provision of suitable housing, 9.12
services under Chronically Sick
and Disabled Persons Act, 9.9
Criminal injuries compensation
criminal justice system, and, 14.13
Competence of witnesses
rules of evidence, and, 13.22
Confidentiality
data protection, 11.11
freedom of information, 11.12
Cooperation
AWI(S)A 2000, and, 11.8
ASP(S)A 2007, and
examination of records, 11.5
general duty, 11.2
general practitioners, 11.4
scope of provisions, 2.6
sharing of information, 11.3
data protection, 11.11
disclosure of information, 11.7
examination of records, 11.5
family and friends, 11.10
freedom of information, 11.12
independent sector, 11.9
informal carers, 11.10
inquiries by local authorities, 11.6
MH(CT)(S)A 2003, and
disclosure of information, 11.7
inquiries by local authorities, 11.6
scope of provisions, 2.16

Cooperation – *contd*
  parents, 11.10
  sharing of information, 11.3
  voluntary sector, 11.9
Coordinated working
  generally, 15.2
Corroboration
  rules of evidence, and, 13.21
Council officers
  generally, 3.3
Counselling
  support for adults, and, 9.27
  witness support, and, 13.28
Court measures of protection
  abusers, against
    family orders, 10.10
    interdicts, 10.9
    non-harassment orders, 10.11
  anti-social behaviour orders, 10.26
  bail conditions, 10.27
  banning orders
    adult's rights, 10.14
    appeals, 10.20
    applications, 10.13
    breach, 10.22–10.24
    criteria, 10.15
    expiry, 10.25
    impact, 10.17
    local authorities' duties, 10.14
    notifications, 10.19
    perpetrator aged under 16, 10.16
    recall, 10.21
    temporary measures, 10.18
    variation, 10.21
  family orders, 10.10
  guardianship orders
    complaints about guardian, 10.5
    generally, 10.3
    misappropriation of funds, 10.6
  interdicts, 10.9
  intervention orders
    complaints about intervener,
      10.5
    generally, 10.4
    misappropriation of funds, 10.6

Court measures of protection – *contd*
  MH(CT)(S)A 2003, under, 10.7
  misappropriation of funds, 10.6
  non-harassment orders, 10.11
Court system
  See also **Criminal justice system**
  accessibility of courts, 13.24
  appropriate adults, 13.25
  burden of proof, 13.16
  competence of witnesses, 13.22
  corroboration, 13.21
  counselling, 13.28
  credibility of witnesses, 13.23
  district courts, 13.1
  evidence
    burden of proof, 13.16
    commission, on, 13.30
    competence of witnesses, 13.22
    corroboration, 13.21
    credibility of witnesses, 13.23
    generally, 13.15
    hearsay, 13.17–13.20
    reliability of witnesses, 13.23
  evidence on Commission, 13.30
  hearsay
    generally, 13.17
    prior statements, 13.18
    statements as evidence of facts,
      13.19
    vulnerable witnesses, 13.20
  legal aid, 13.34
  mental health tribunals, 13.14
  prior statements
    generally, 13.18
    special measures for vulnerable
      witnesses, 13.32
  reliability of witnesses, 13.23
  representation, 13.34
  sheriff court
    AWI(S)A 2000, under, 13.3–13.7
    ASP(S)A 2007, under, 13.8–13.13
  sheriff court (AWI(S)A 2000)
    appeals, 13.7
    generally, 13.3
    notice to adult, 13.5

Court system – *contd*
  sheriff court (AWI(S)A 2000) –
      contd
    protecting adult's interests, 13.6
    respect for privacy, 13.4
  sheriff court (ASP(S)A 2007)
    appeals, 13.13
    dispensing with protections,
        13.11
    generally, 13.8
    procedure, 13.9
    protecting adult's interests, 13.10
    protecting vulnerable adult,
        13.12
  special measures for vulnerable
      witnesses
    evidence on Commission, 13.30
    generally, 13.29
    intermediaries, 13.33
    prior statements, 13.32
    supporters, 13.31
  solicitor representation, 13.34
  statements as evidence of facts,
      13.19
  support for witnesses
    accessibility of courts, 13.24
    appropriate adults, 13.25
    counselling, 13.28
  Victim Information and Advice
      Service, 13.26
  Victim Support Scotland, 13.27
  vulnerable witnesses
    hearsay, 13.20
    special measures, 13.29–13.33
  witnesses
    competence, 13.22
    credibility, 13.23
    reliability, 13.23
    special measures, 13.29–13.33
    support for, 13.24–13.28
    vulnerable, 13.20
Credibility of witnesses
  rules of evidence, and, 13.23
Crerar report (2007)
  generally, 15.8

Criminal investigations
  emergencies, and, 8.12
Criminal justice system
  abuse of trust, 14.11
  adult protection offences, 14.12
  answering police inquiries, 14.3
  assault, 14.6
  breach of the peace, 14.7
  criminal injuries compensation,
      14.13
  decision to prosecute, 14.4
  fraud, 14.8
  neglect and ill treatment, 14.9
  police role
    answering police inquiries, 14.3
    importance of involvement, 14.2
  rape, 14.10
  relevant offences, 14.5–14.12
  sexual assault, 14.10
  sexual offences
    abuse of trust, 14.11
    rape, 14.10
    sexual assault, 14.10
  theft, 14.8
Cross border issues
  adults outside Scotland, 15.4
  allocation between local
      authorities, 15.3
**Crown Office Procurator Fiscal
    Service**
  generally, 3.18
Data protection
  confidentiality, and, 11.11
Decision to prosecute
  criminal justice system, and, 14.4
Detention
  emergencies, and, 8.11
  scope of MH(CT)(S)A 2003, and,
      2.17
Direct payments
  generally, 15.5
Disclosure of information
  cooperation, and, 11.7
Domestic abuse
  harm and abuse, and, 5.13

Eating disorders
harm and abuse, and, 5.12
Emergencies
AWI(S)A 2000, under
generally, 8.7
interim guardianship, 8.8
anti-social behaviour orders, 8.13
ASP(S)A 2007, under
applications to JP, 8.3
involvement of adult, 8.4
temporary banning orders, 8.5
use of measures, 8.6
banning orders, 8.5
criminal investigations, 8.12
detention, 8.11
interim guardianship, 8.8
local authorities' powers and
duties, and
generally, 6.32
removal orders, 6.17
medical treatment, 8.14
MH(CT)(S)A 2003, under
detention, 8.11
removal to place of safety, 8.10
removal orders
applications to JP, 8.3
generally, 8.2
involvement of adult, 8.4
use of measures, 8.6
removal to place of safety, 8.10
temporary banning orders, 8.5
urgent medical treatment, 8.14
warrants for entry
applications to JP, 8.3
involvement of adult, 8.4
use of measures, 8.6
Enforcement
Care Commission, and, 7.5
Office of the Public Guardian, and,
7.16
Evidence
burden of proof, 13.16
commission, on, 13.30
competence of witnesses, 13.22
corroboration, 13.21

Evidence – *contd*
credibility of witnesses, 13.23
generally, 13.15
hearsay
generally, 13.17
prior statements, 13.18
statements as evidence of facts,
13.19
vulnerable witnesses, 13.20
reliability of witnesses, 13.23
Examination of records
cooperation, and, 11.5
Family orders
generally, 10.10
Financial abuse
harm and abuse, and, 5.14
Financial support and advice
access to funds, 9.16
appointees, 9.14–9.15
investigation of withdrawer, 9.17
management of funds in
residential homes, 9.18–9.19
Formal inquiries
Mental Welfare Commission, and,
7.8
Fraud
criminal justice system, and, 14.8
Free personal and nursing care
community care services, and, 9.11
Freedom of information
confidentiality, and, 11.12
Guardians
generally, 3.13
Guardianship orders
complaints about guardian, 10.5
emergencies, and, 8.8
generally, 10.3
misappropriation of funds, 10.6
scope of AWI(S)A 2000, and, 2.31
Harm and abuse
categories
domestic abuse, 5.13
eating disorders, 5.12
financial abuse, 5.14
neglect by third party, 5.9

Harm and abuse – *contd*
  categories – *contd*
    physical abuse, 5.7
    self-harm, 5.11
    self-neglect, 5.10
    sexual abuse, 5.8
  definitions
    AWI(S)A 2000, in, 5.5
    ASP(S)A 2007, in, 5.3
    MH(CT)(S)A 2003, in, 5.4
  domestic abuse, 5.13
  eating disorders, 5.12
  financial abuse, 5.14
  neglect by third party, 5.9
  physical abuse, 5.7
  recognition of
    concerns raised following
      behaviour changes, 5.21
    disclosure by adult, 5.19
    disclosure by third party, 5.20
    medical care and treatment, 5.22
  self-harm, 5.11
  self-neglect, 5.10
  setting
    at home, 5.16
    in community, 5.17
  sexual abuse, 5.8
'Hate' crimes
  generally, 15.7
Health care providers
  generally, 3.6
Healthcare Improvement Scotland
  generally, 15.8
Hearsay
  generally, 13.17
  prior statements, 13.18
  statements as evidence of facts,
    13.19
  vulnerable witnesses, 13.20
Housing (Scotland) Act 1987
  generally, 2.39
Human rights
  abolition of slavery, 12.6
  adult protection, in
    involuntary treatment, 12.13

Human rights – *contd*
  adult protection, in – *contd*
    prohibition of inhuman or
      degrading treatment or
      punishment, 12.6
    prohibition of torture, 12.6
    right to liberty, 12.7–12.10
    right to life, 12.6
    right to respect for private and
      family life, 12.11
    undue pressure, and, 12.12
  Human Rights Act 1998, 12.3
  inhuman or degrading treatment
    or punishment, 12.6
  involuntary treatment, 12.13
  principles, and, 4.6
  private and family life, 12.11
  prohibition of inhuman or
    degrading treatment or
    punishment, 12.6
  prohibition of torture, 12.6
  public authorities, 12.5
  right to liberty, 12.7–12.10
  right to life, 12.6
  right to respect for private and
    family life, 12.11
  Scotland, in
    Human Rights Act 1998, 12.3
    public authorities, 12.5
    Scotland Act 1998, 12.4
  slavery, 12.6
  torture, 12.6
  UN Convention on the Rights of
    Disabled People, 12.14
  undue pressure, and, 12.12
'Incapacity'
  scope of AWI(S)A 2000, and, 2.24
Indemnity
  principles, and, 4.8
Independent advocates
  ASP(S)A 2007, under 9.4
  generally, 9.2
  legal right to advocacy, 9.3
  MH(CT)(S)A 2003, under, 9.3
  principles, and, 9.5

Informal carers
cooperation, and, 11.10
Information requirements
AWI(S)A 2000, and
adults, relatives and carers, of,
2.33
advice agencies, of, 2.34
service providers, of, 2.34
ASP(S)A 2007, and
adults, relatives and carers, of,
2.10
advice agencies, of, 2.11
service providers, of, 2.11
MH(CT)(S)A 2003, and
adults, relatives and carers, of,
2.21
advice agencies, of, 2.22
service providers, of, 2.22
**Inhuman or degrading treatment or
punishment**
human rights, and, 12.6
Inquiries by local authorities
cooperation, and, 11.6
Inspections
Care Commission, and, 7.4
Interdicts
generally, 10.9
Interim guardianship
emergencies, and, 8.8
Intervention orders
complaints about intervener, 10.5
generally, 10.4
misappropriation of funds, 10.6
persons involved in adult
protection cases, and, 3.13
scope of AWI(S)A 2000, and, 2.31
Interviews
Mental Welfare Commission, and,
7.10
Investigations
AWI(S)A 2000, under
generally, 6.31
ASP(S)A 2007, under
allocation of inquiries, 6.3
generally, 6.2

Investigations – *contd*
Care Commission, and, 7.4
financial support and advice, and,
9.17
Mental Welfare Commission, and,
7.7
MH(CT)(S)A 2003, under
cooperation with local authority,
6.36
generally, 6.35
warrants for entry, 6.37
Office of the Public Guardian, and
duty, 7.14
power, 7.15
professional regulators, and, 7.25
Involuntary treatment
human rights, and, 12.13
Legal aid
legal system, and, 13.34
Legal framework
Adult Support and Protection
(Scotland) Act 2007
adult protection committees, 2.8
'adults at risk', 2.3
cooperation, 2.6
information requirements, 2.10–
2.11
investigations, 2.5
new orders, 2.7
people covered, 2.3
scope, 2.4–2.8
use, 2.9
Adults with Incapacity (Scotland)
Act 2000
attorneys, 2.27
generally, 2.23
guardianship orders, 2.31
information requirements, 2.33–
2.34
intervention orders, 2.31
investigations, 2.26
making medical decisions, 2.30
managing bank accounts, 2.28
managing residents' finances,
2.29

Legal framework – *contd*
  Adults with Incapacity (Scotland)
      Act 2000 – *contd*
    people covered, 2.24
    relevance to adult protection,
        2.32
    scope, 2.25–2.31
  Chronically Sick and Disabled
      Persons Act 1970, 2.38
  codes of practice, 2.35
  Housing (Scotland) Act 1987, 2.39
  Mental Health (Care and
      Treatment) (Scotland) Act
      2003
    advance statements, 2.19
    cooperation, 2.16
    detention, 2.17
    information requirements, 2.21–
        2.22
    investigations, 2.15
    mental health tribunals, 2.18
    people covered, 2.13
    relevance to adult protection,
        2.20
    scope, 2.14–2.19
  Social Work (Scotland) 1968, 2.37
  Vulnerable Witnesses (Scotland)
      Act 2004, 2.36
Legal system
  accessibility of courts, 13.24
  appropriate adults, 13.25
  burden of proof, 13.16
  competence of witnesses, 13.22
  corroboration, 13.21
  counselling, 13.28
  credibility of witnesses, 13.23
  evidence
    burden of proof, 13.16
    commission, on, 13.30
    competence of witnesses, 13.22
    corroboration, 13.21
    credibility of witnesses, 13.23
    generally, 13.15
    hearsay, 13.17–13.20
    reliability of witnesses, 13.23

Legal system – *contd*
  evidence on commission, 13.30
  hearsay
    generally, 13.17
    prior statements, 13.18
    statements as evidence of facts,
        13.19
    vulnerable witnesses, 13.20
  legal aid, 13.34
  mental health tribunals, 13.14
  prior statements
    generally, 13.18
    special measures for vulnerable
        witnesses, 13.32
  reliability of witnesses, 13.23
  representation, 13.34
  sheriff court
    AWI(S)A 2000, under, 13.3–13.7
    ASP(S)A 2007, under, 13.8–13.13
  sheriff court (AWI(S)A 2000)
    appeals, 13.7
    generally, 13.3
    notice to adult, 13.5
    protecting adult's interests, 13.6
    respect for privacy, 13.4
  sheriff court (ASP(S)A 2007)
    appeals, 13.13
    dispensing with protections,
        13.11
    generally, 13.8
    procedure, 13.9
    protecting adult's interests,
        13.10
    protecting vulnerable adult,
        13.12
  special measures for vulnerable
      witnesses
    evidence on commission, 13.30
    generally, 13.29
    intermediaries, 13.33
    prior statements, 13.32
    supporters, 13.31
  solicitor representation, 13.34
  statements as evidence of facts,
      13.19

Legal system – *contd*
  support for witnesses
    accessibility of courts, 13.24
    appropriate adults, 13.25
    counselling, 13.28
    Victim Information and Advice
      Service, 13.26
    Victim Support Scotland,
      13.27
  Victim Information and Advice
    Service, 13.26
  Victim Support Scotland, 13.27
  vulnerable witnesses
    hearsay, 13.20
    special measures, 13.29–13.33
  witnesses
    competence, 13.22
    credibility, 13.23
    reliability, 13.23
    special measures, 13.29–13.33
    support for, 13.24–13.28
    vulnerable, 13.20
Local authorities
  access to records
    ASP(S)A 2007, under, 6.8
    MH(CT)(S)A 2003, under, 6.39–
      6.40
  assessment orders
    appeals, 6.14
    applications, 6.11
    consent of adult, 6.27
    grounds, 6.10
    impact, 6.13
    limits to powers, 6.12
  banning orders
    consent of adult, 6.27
    generally, 6.26
  choice of procedures, 6.47
  consent of adult, 6.27
  investigations under AWI(S)A
    2000, 6.31
  investigations under ASP(S)A
    2007
    allocation of inquiries, 6.3
    generally, 6.2

Local authorities – *contd*
  investigations under MH(CT)(S)A
    2003
    cooperation with local authority,
      6.36
    generally, 6.35
    warrants for entry, 6.37
  medical examinations
    AWI(S)A 2000, under, 6.33
    ASP(S)A 2007, under, 6.7
  outcome of inquiries, 6.29
  parties involved in protection case,
    and
    council officers, 3.3
    generally, 3.2
  powers and duties under AWI(S)A
    2000
    emergencies, in, 6.32
    investigations, 6.31
    medical examinations, 6.33
    medical treatment, 6.33
  powers and duties under ASP(S)A
    2007
    access to records, 6.8
    assessment orders, 6.9–6.14
    banning orders, 6.26–6.29
    investigations, 6.2–6.3
    medical examinations, 6.7
    removal orders, 6.15–6.25
    visits, 6.4–6.6
  powers and duties under
    MH(CT)(S)A 2003
    access to records, 6.39–6.40
    investigations, 6.35–6.36
    medical examinations, 6.38
    removal orders, 6.41–6.46
    warrants for entry, 6.37
  removal orders under ASP(S)A 2007
    appeals, 6.25
    applications, 6.16
    consent of adult, 6.27
    contact conditions, 6.22
    detention, and, 6.20
    emergency applications, 6.17
    expiry, 6.21

Local authorities – *contd*
removal orders under ASP(S)A
2007 – *contd*
grounds, 6.18
impact, 6.19
protection of property, and,
6.24
recall, 6.23
variation, 6.23
removal orders under MH(CT)(S)A
2003
appeals, 6.44
applications, 6.42
cancellation, 6.46
effect, 6.43
place of safety, 6.45
variation, 6.46
role, 6.1
undue pressure, 6.28
visits
generally, 6.4
interviews, 6.6
warrants, 6.5
warrants for entry, 6.37
warrants for visits, 6.5
Managing bank accounts
scope of AWI(S)A 2000, and,
2.28
Managing residents' finances
financial support and advice, and,
9.18–9.19
scope of AWI(S)A 2000, and, 2.29
Mediation
support for adults, and, 9.27
Medical care and treatment
harm and abuse, and, 5.22
Medical decisions
scope of AWI(S)A 2000, and, 2.30
Medical examinations
AWI(S)A 2000, under, 6.33
ASP(S)A 2007, under, 6.7
police, and, 7.21
Medical treatment
emergencies, and, 8.14
harm and abuse, and, 5.22

**Mental Health (Care and Treatment)
(Scotland) Act 2003**
access to records, 6.39–6.40
advance statements, 2.19
community care services, and,
9.10
cooperation, and
disclosure of information, 11.7
inquiries by local authorities,
11.6
scope of provisions, 2.16
court measures of protection, and,
10.7
detention, 2.17
emergencies
detention, 8.11
removal to place of safety, 8.10
harm and abuse, 5.4
independent advocates, and, 9.3
information requirements
adults, relatives and carers, of,
2.21
advice agencies, of, 2.22
service providers, of, 2.22
investigations
cooperation with local authority,
6.36
generally, 6.35
warrants for entry, 6.37
powers and duties of local
authorities
access to records, 6.39–6.40
investigations, 6.35–6.36
medical examinations, 6.38
removal orders, 6.41–6.46
warrants for entry, 6.37
mental health tribunals, 2.18
people covered, 2.13
principles, 4.4
relevance to adult protection, 2.20
removal orders
appeals, 6.44
applications, 6.42
cancellation, 6.46
effect, 6.43

Mental Health (Care and Treatment) (Scotland) Act 2003 – *contd*
removal orders – *contd*
place of safety, 6.45
variation, 6.46
scope
advance statements, 2.19
cooperation, 2.16
detention, 2.17
generally, 2.14
investigations, 2.15
mental health tribunals, 2.18
warrants for entry, 6.37
Mental health tribunals
legal system, and, 13.14
scope of MH(CT)(S)A 2003, and, 2.18
Mental Welfare Commission
access to facilities, 7.11
access to records, 7.10
formal inquiries, 7.8
generally, 3.10
interviews, 7.10
investigations, 7.7
overlap of role
local authorities, with, 7.12
other bodies, with, 7.13
powers and duties
access to facilities, 7.11
access to records, 7.10
formal inquiries, 7.8
interviews, 7.10
investigations, 7.7
visits, 7.9
visits, 7.9
Misappropriation of funds
court measures of protection, and, 10.6
Named person
appointments, 9.26
generally, 3.14
Nearest relative
generally, 3.14
Neglect and ill treatment
criminal justice system, and, 14.9

Neglect by third party
harm and abuse, and, 5.9
Non-harassment orders
generally, 10.11
Office of the Public Guardian
enforcement, 7.16
investigations
duty, 7.14
power, 7.15
overlap of role
Care Commission, with, 7.18
local authorities, with, 7.17
powers and duties
enforcement, 7.16
investigations, 7.14–7.15
proposals for reform, 15.8
Organisations and individuals
adult protection committees
generally, 3.4
membership, 3.5
attorneys, 3.13
Care Commission, 3.8
care providers, 3.11
council officers, 3.3
criminal justice system
Crown Office Procurator Fiscal Service, 3.18
police, 3.17
Crown Office Procurator Fiscal Service, 3.18
guardians, 3.13
health care providers, 3.6
independent advocates, 3.15
intervention orders, and, 3.13
local authorities
council officers, 3.3
generally, 3.2
Mental Welfare Commission, 3.10
named person, 3.14
nearest relative, 3.14
persons supporting an adult
attorneys, 3.13
guardians, 3.13
independent advocates, 3.15
intervention orders, and, 3.13

Organisations and individuals – *contd*
  persons supporting an adult – *contd*
    named person, 3.14
    nearest relative, 3.14
  police, 3.17
  Procurator Fiscal Service, 3.18
  protective bodies, 3.7
  Public Guardian, 3.9
Parents
  cooperation, and, 11.10
Partnership working
  generally, 15.2
Persons supporting an adult
  attorneys, 3.13
  guardians, 3.13
  independent advocates, 3.15
  intervention orders, and, 3.13
  named person, 3.14
  nearest relative, 3.14
Physical abuse
  harm and abuse, and, 5.7
Place of safety
  emergencies, and, 8.10
  removal orders, and, 6.45
Police
  criminal justice system, and
    answering police inquiries, 14.3
    importance of involvement, 14.2
  generally, 3.17
  medical examinations, 7.21
  notifications, 7.22
  powers and duties
    people at risk in public, 7.20–7.22
    people not in public place, 7.23
  role in adult protection, 7.19
Principles
  AWI(S)A 2000, in, 4.3
  ASP(S)A 2007, in, 4.5
  background, 4.2
  human rights, and, 4.6
  indemnity, 4.8
  legal impact, 4.7

Principles – *contd*
  MH(CT)(S)A 2003, in, 4.4
  promotion, 4.9
Prior statements
  generally, 13.18
  special measures for vulnerable witnesses, 13.32
Private and family life
  human rights, and, 12.11
Procurator Fiscal Service
  generally, 3.18
Professional regulators
  contacting, 7.27
  powers and duties
    investigations, 7.25
    removal from practice, 7.26
Prohibition of inhuman or degrading treatment or punishment
  human rights, and, 12.6
Prohibition of torture
  human rights, and, 12.6
Protection of vulnerable groups
  generally, 15.6
Protective bodies
  generally, 3.7
Provision of suitable housing
  community care services, and, 9.12
Public authorities
  human rights, and, 12.5
Public Guardian
  enforcement, 7.16
  generally, 3.9
  investigations
    duty, 7.14
    power, 7.15
  overlap of role
    Care Commission, with, 7.18
    local authorities, with, 7.17
  powers and duties
    enforcement, 7.16
    investigations, 7.14–7.15
Public Services Reform (Scotland) Bill
  generally, 15.8

Rape
criminal justice system, and, 14.10
Relatives
information requirements, and
AWI(S)A 2000, under, 2.33
ASP(S)A 2007, under, 2.10
MH(CT)(S)A 2003, under, 2.21
Reliability of witnesses
legal system, and, 13.23
Removal orders (ASP(S)A 2007)
appeals, 6.25
applications, 6.16
consent of adult, 6.27
contact conditions, 6.22
detention, and, 6.20
emergencies, and
applications to JP, 8.3
generally, 8.2
involvement of adult, 8.4
use of measures, 8.6
expiry, 6.21
grounds, 6.18
impact, 6.19
protection of property, and, 6.24
recall, 6.23
variation, 6.23
Removal orders (MH(CT)(S)A 2003)
appeals, 6.44
applications, 6.42
cancellation, 6.46
effect, 6.43
place of safety, 6.45
variation, 6.46
Representation
legal system, and, 13.34
Residents' finances
scope of AWI(S)A 2000, and, 2.29
Right to liberty
human rights, and, 12.7–12.10
Right to life
human rights, and, 12.6
Right to respect for private and family life
human rights, and, 12.11

Risk investigation
Care Commission, and, 7.3
Rules of evidence
burden of proof, 13.16
commission, on, 13.30
competence of witnesses, 13.22
corroboration, 13.21
credibility of witnesses, 13.23
generally, 13.15
hearsay
generally, 13.17
prior statements, 13.18
statements as evidence of facts, 13.19
vulnerable witnesses, 13.20
reliability of witnesses, 13.23
Scotland Act 1998
human rights, and, 12.4
Self directed support
generally, 15.5
Self-harm
harm and abuse, and, 5.11
Self-neglect
harm and abuse, and, 5.10
Service providers
information requirements, and
AWI(S)A 2000, under, 2.34
ASP(S)A 2007, under 2.11
MH(CT)(S)A 2003, under, 2.22
Services under Chronically Sick and Disabled Persons Act
community care services, and, 9.9
Sexual abuse
harm and abuse, and, 5.8
Sexual assault
criminal justice system, and, 14.10
Sexual offences
criminal justice system, and
abuse of trust, 14.11
rape, 14.10
sexual assault, 14.10
Sharing of information
cooperation, and, 11.3

Sheriff court
AWI(S)A 2000, under
appeals, 13.7
generally, 13.3
notice to adult, 13.5
protecting adult's interests, 13.6
respect for privacy, 13.4
ASP(S)A 2007, under
appeals, 13.13
dispensing with protections,
13.11
generally, 13.8
procedure, 13.9
protecting adult's interests,
13.10
protecting vulnerable adult,
13.12
Slavery
human rights, and, 12.6
**Social Care and Social Work
Improvement Scotland**
generally, 15.8
Social Work (Scotland) 1968
generally, 2.37
**Special measures for vulnerable
witnesses**
evidence on commission, 13.30
generally, 13.29
intermediaries, 13.33
prior statements, 13.32
supporters, 13.31
Statement as evidence of fact
hearsay, and, 13.19
Statement of wishes and feelings
support for adults, and, 9.23
Support for the adult
access to funds, 9.16
advance directives, 9.21
advance statements, 9.22
appointment of attorney, 9.24–
9.25
appointment of named person,
9.26
carers' assessments, 9.8
community care assessments, 9.7

Support for the adult – *contd*
community care services
carers' assessments, 9.8
community care assessments,
9.7
free personal and nursing care,
9.11
MH(CT)(S)A 2003, under, 9.10
provision of suitable housing,
9.12
services under Chronically Sick
and Disabled Persons Act,
9.9
counselling and mediation, 9.27
financial support and advice
access to funds, 9.16
appointees, 9.14–9.15
investigation of withdrawer,
9.17
management of funds in
residential homes, 9.18–9.19
free personal and nursing care,
9.11
future planning
advance directives, 9.21
advance statements, 9.22
appointment of attorney, 9.24–
9.25
appointment of named person,
9.26
statement of wishes and feelings,
9.23
independent advocates
ASP(S)A 2007, under 9.4
generally, 9.2
legal right to advocacy, 9.3
MH(CT)(S)A 2003, under, 9.3
principles, and, 9.5
management of funds in
residential homes, 9.18–9.19
provision of suitable housing, 9.12
services under Chronically Sick
and Disabled Persons Act, 9.9
statement of wishes and feelings,
9.23

Support for witnesses
accessibility of courts, 13.24
appropriate adults, 13.25
counselling, 13.28
Victim Information and Advice
Service, 13.26
Victim Support Scotland, 13.27
Temporary banning orders
generally, 8.5
Theft
criminal justice system, and,
14.8
Third party disclosure
harm and abuse, and, 5.20
Torture
human rights, and, 12.6
**UN Convention on the Rights of
Disabled People**
human rights, and, 12.14
Undue pressure
human rights, and, 12.12
local authorities' powers and
duties, and, 6.28
Urgent medical treatment
emergencies, and, 8.14
**Victim Information and Advice
Service**
witness support, and, 13.26
Victim Support Scotland
witness support, and, 13.27
Visits
local authorities, and
generally, 6.4
interviews, 6.6
warrants, 6.5
Mental Welfare Commission, and,
7.9

Voluntary sector
cooperation, and, 11.9
Vulnerable witnesses
hearsay, 13.20
special measures, 13.29–13.33
**Vulnerable Witnesses (Scotland) Act
2004**
generally, 2.36
Warrants for entry
emergencies, and
applications to JP, 8.3
involvement of adult, 8.4
local authorities, and, 6.37
Warrants for visits
local authorities, and, 6.5
Witnesses
competence, 13.22
credibility, 13.23
reliability, 13.23
special measures
evidence on commission, 13.30
generally, 13.29
intermediaries, 13.33
prior statements, 13.32
supporters, 13.31
support for
accessibility of courts, 13.24
appropriate adults, 13.25
counselling, 13.28
Victim Information and Advice
Service, 13.26
Victim Support Scotland, 13.27
vulnerable
hearsay, 13.20
special measures, 13.29–13.33
Young people
application of legislation, 15.9